THE YOUNG SINGERS by Luca della Robbia in the Opera
del Duomo, Florence, Italy

A GENERAL OUTLINE OF A COURSE
IN MUSIC APPRECIATION BASED ON
CULTURAL BACKGROUNDS

MUSIC
AND MAN

HOWARD D. McKINNEY, Mus. D.
PROFESSOR OF MUSIC,
RUTGERS UNIVERSITY

AMERICAN BOOK COMPANY NEW YORK CINCINNATI
CHICAGO   BOSTON   ATLANTA   DALLAS   SAN FRANCISCO

McKINNEY, MUSIC AND MAN

E. P. 1

MADE IN U. S. A.

FOREWORD

You will find a great deal about things other than music in this book. It may surprise you at first upon leafing through a volume that bears the title *Music and Man* to find so many pictures of architecture and painting, references to history, and suggestions for social and political understanding. And yet, if you stop to think about it for a moment, you will see that this is a perfectly reasonable way to treat the story of music.

This most popular of the arts did not grow up and develop all by itself, in a vacuum, so to speak, out of touch with everything else in the world. From its earliest days music has been in very close contact with the lives of the people who produced it. As it developed through the ages its qualities and beauties depended upon how these people felt, what they believed in, and their general historical and political backgrounds. This is just as true of our own time as it has been for any other period in history. And so, as we start our study with American music, we need to know something of what makes us tick as a nation, how we differ from our neighboring Americans to the south of us, and how we all inherit the general characteristics of European musical life and thought.

Only then can we realize what an important part of man's cultural heritage music is and how much it can contribute to our own lives. And in the process we will learn a lot about the art of music itself!

HOWARD D. McKINNEY

ACKNOWLEDGMENTS

The author and publisher herewith offer thanks to the following, who have kindly given permission to reproduce copyrighted material:

Coward-McCann, Inc. for the Stage Manager's Speech on pages 35–37, reprinted from *Our Town*, A Play in Three Acts, by Thornton Wilder. Copyright, 1938, by Coward-McCann, Inc.

Little, Brown & Company for the excerpt on pages 14–16 from *So This Is Jazz* by Henry O. Osgood.

The Macmillan Company for the quotation on page 200 from Erico Verissimo: *Brazilian Literature*. Copyright 1945 by The Macmillan Company and used with their permission.

New York Herald Tribune for the articles on pages 98–99 and 153–158 by Walter Terry and Paul Bowles.

Public Schools of Montclair, New Jersey and Rochester, New York for photographs of high-school students engaged in musical activities.

Random House, Inc. for the excerpt on pages 114–115 from *Really the Blues* by Mezzrow and Wolfe.

Simon and Schuster, Inc. for the verses on page 30, reprinted from *My Country* by permission of Simon and Schuster, Inc. Copyright, 1944, by Russell W. Davenport. Also for the paragraphs on pages 189–190, reprinted from *Of Men and Music* by permission of Simon and Schuster, Inc. Copyright, 1937, by Deems Taylor.

The Newspaper *PM* Inc. for the poem on page 21, *My America*, by Jeannette Jamison.

Time, the Weekly Newsmagazine, for the article on pages 63–65 by Marian Anderson, reprinted by courtesy of *Time*, copyright Time, Inc., 1946.

Dr. Karl Wecker for the photograph of the "Hollywood Bowl, Home of Symphonies under the Stars."

Yale University Press for the excerpt on pages 151–152 from *The Haitian People* by James G. Leyburn.

ART WORK BY BEN JORJ HARRIS

CONTENTS

PART ONE

CONTEMPORARY AMERICAN MUSIC

THE SONG OF THE POET, a painting by Peppino Mangravite

In strong contrast to the practical aspect of the machine is this depiction of the place of the artist in the world. What is the poet singing about?

2

CHAPTER I. *WHY STUDY MUSIC?*

Flood-tide below me! I see you face to face!
Clouds of the west — sun there half an hour
high — I see you also face to face.

Crowds of men . . . how curious you are to me!
On the ferry-boats the hundreds and hundreds
that cross, returning home, are more curious
to me than you suppose,
And you that shall cross from shore to shore
years hence are more to me, and more in my
meditations, than you might suppose.

WALT WHITMAN,[1] one of the greatest American poets, wrote these lines nearly a hundred years ago as he watched the crowds thronging home at evening across a great river ferry. It is not difficult to imagine the Good Gray Poet as he leaned against the rail of the boat and observed his fellow passengers: some quickly settling down in the nearest place available, opening their newspapers, talking with their neighbors, or thinking about what awaited them on the other side. Others, more

[1] See Sidelight 1 at the end of this chapter.

curious and imaginative, looking at the river and the sky, watching the numberless masts of the ships and the thick-stemmed pipes of steamboats, finally arrive at their destination "refreshed by the gladness of the river and the bright flow."

People have not changed very much since the poet wrote his *Crossing Brooklyn Ferry* in 1856. If you observe them to-day as they throng across the bay on a San Francisco or New York ferry, you will find the majority of them still concerned mostly in getting to their destination as quickly as possible. But there are those who, since they have to use the ferry, are interested in what happens on their journey. They take the time and energy to climb to the upper deck and watch the busy activities of the harbor as their boat steams along. Here we have neatly symbolized one of the fundamental differences in people: some of them seem chiefly occupied with attaining ends, others are principally concerned with receiving experiences.

We acknowledge these differences by describing some people as *practical*, others as *imaginative*; or by saying that there is a great difference in the same person between the practical and imaginative ways of looking at life. All about us are men so preoccupied with going places and earning money that their lives seem to consist of little else than activities for achieving these ends. The principal thing they think about is driving towards a goal, and they are not greatly concerned about enjoying themselves as they go. Others have come to realize that their journey through life need not be just a means of getting somewhere, but that they can learn to cherish certain things and to travel in such a manner as to make their journey a useful, pleasurable, and vital experience.

4

Certainly both these attitudes toward life are important and necessary. We must learn to cultivate an ability to achieve something in life, to stand firmly on our own feet. The very existence of our country has been the result of the peculiar ability of its people, from the earliest days of our history, to learn how to do things easily and quickly and well. Above all else the American spirit is a practical one, self-reliant, conscious of its ability to forge ahead through the application of knowledge to its own useful ends, always willing to work in the present for the sake of the future.

But we have also come to understand that man cannot live for this alone and that, while it is a real merit in a nation to be practical, it is a great fault to be overpractical. We of all peoples should be able to see what an overemphasis on practicability can do in the world, for it is this above all else that fostered such greed for position, wealth, and power as to bring about two great world wars within the memory of one generation. We are finding out that such an understanding of the laws of nature as practical people try to obtain does not necessarily make man any better or more useful. And no more does the ability to control these laws so as to develop the great age of science, machinery, and speed in which we live today make men more civilized.

The great fault with the world is that, in its eagerness to be practical, to acquire power and wealth, it has forgotten the need for cultivating an imaginative attitude toward life as well. This attitude has nothing whatever to do with *things*. Rather, is consists of the cherishing of such spiritual concepts as affection and sympathy, love and friendship, freedom and justice, beauty and understanding, character and conduct. We know

A POSTER OF THE PARIS
UNDERGROUND

These sprang up on the walls, during the Nazi
occupation of the city, when the hour of re-
volt arrived.

in our hearts that these are just as necessary for our existence
as such physical possessions as money, food, and clothes. Yet
we have been inclined to neglect them, since everyone else has
seemed to be so largely concerned with the acquisition of tangible possessions. But if history teaches us anything at all, it

6

teaches that of all the conquests of man, only those endure that embrace his dreams and ideals.

One of the most important human activities for encouraging the growth of spiritual and imaginative values is religion — the service and adoration of a Higher Power and the attempt to obey His commands as we understand them. Another is what we have come to call art, that activity by which man, in all the years he has lived here in the world, has somehow been able to communicate his experiences to his fellows and to transform the things he finds about him into objects of beauty that help to make the world a better place in which to live.

On definite occasions, no matter how simple our lives may be, we have realized that there are certain facts beyond the eating and the drinking, the walking and the talking that give us a sense of how great and strange and beautiful our existence is. We have felt this, perhaps, on some cold winter's night on looking into the jeweled spaces of the heavens above us; or as we wander through the vast magnificence of some great cathedral church; or upon hearing one of the symphonies of such a composer as Beethoven. The artist is simply a particular man who has been able to feel these things more strongly than most people and who is able, through such means as painting, poetry, or music, to communicate some of his feelings to us so that we can experience them too. And by transforming simple materials such as stone and wood, canvas and sound, into what we call sculpture, architecture, painting, literature, and music he makes the world a better place to live in. And he also makes his fellows better members of its society. Thus, in giving order and direction to the experiences that are more or less common to us all, such artists as

7

Beethoven, Shakespeare, and Michelangelo have made us partakers of their thoughts, their dreams, and their visions.

One of the outstanding Russian writers, Tolstoy (Sidelight 2), has said that art is a great matter and its task enormous. What he meant by this was simply that it can touch our lives at many points and has come to be an essential part of many of our activities. This love for the beautiful that we call art is something that we all possess in varying degrees; and the more we learn about art and give it a chance to develop in our lives, the greater meaning it can have for us and thus contribute to our own and our world's betterment. And what is more, the more we learn to appreciate things that are beautiful and sincere, the more we will want to avoid those that are cheap and ugly. Anyone who learns to know and like the works of good writers will not be satisfied with the cheap magazines and newspapers that flood the newsstands. If a person takes the trouble to learn to appreciate the music of Mozart and Brahms, the chances are that he will not be so enthusiastic about the music of Tin Pan Alley (Sidelight 3). And as we become familiar with good examples of architecture, buildings that have stood the test of time, we will want our houses and churches, our schools and business places to be beautiful as well as useful structures.

Of all the arts, the one that affects our lives most directly is music. This is something that we can understand, take part in, and like. It is not something that needs to be set apart and heard only on occasions when we feel like it; it is an essential part of our experience from the time when we first learn to sing or whistle a tune. We can all to some degree learn to make music as well as to understand its language — a universal

8

Photograph by Horydczak

THE GOTHIC CHOIR OF THE WASHINGTON
CATHEDRAL

9

language which does not have to be translated and which can suggest things to us that are beyond the powers of the other arts to express. Its essentials, rhythm and melody, can be understood by all people. It gives us impressions that anyone can comprehend and unites people in common bonds of friendship and understanding. It leads us into that world of fantasy and imagination that lies just beyond our consciousness (Sidelight 4). Since music does not have to deal exactly with thoughts and ideas, it can speak to us with unusual force; since it is so largely concerned with our emotions, it can affect us all very powerfully. It is thus an ideal means for transmitting the experiences of such great men as Beethoven and Bach directly to anyone who cares to listen. It has no limitations of race, creed, or color. Through it, with a little experience, we can learn to sympathize with the ideals of various kinds of people as well as the feelings and aspirations of our fellow beings in many different parts of the world.

Music is such a many-sided subject that we can approach it in many different ways. We can become interested in reading about it and will find that our libraries are full of fascinating books which give information about music and those who make it. Or we may become excited about listening to it. There are thousands of active listeners in this country, some who are enthusiastic about jazz, others who love symphonic and operatic music. Many people devote a good deal of time to learning how to make music — to obtaining the skill necessary for playing the piano or the clarinet or violin. This gives them a great deal of pleasure and often furnishes them with a new interest in life. Others realize the need for learning how to appreciate music — for trying to understand what a great thing

Courtesy of the Albright Art Gallery, Buffalo, N. Y.

THE TEMPLE OF THE MIND, a painting by Albert Pinkham
Ryder

this art has been in the development of mankind through the
centuries and how important and satisfying it can be in their
own lives.

While each of these various activities can contribute a great
deal to our understanding of the significance of music, it is the
last which is the most satisfying approach to it for most of us.

11

For it is through such an approach that we come to understand how to use music to enlarge our own experience, how it can

THE BALLOON JIB, a mezzotint by Frederick L. Owen

give us a means for understanding the present by developing our understanding of the past, and how it can lift us out of ourselves into another world above the time and place and circumstances of everyday life.

This is what we mean by *music appreciation*. And if we study music in this way we will have something that is far deeper and more adequate than mere enjoyment, something that will give us a satisfaction that is bound to become one of the greatest treasures in life. As you go along in it, you will find that this book has been written to help you gain such an appreciation, and that its study will give new pleasure and add new meanings to your life.

SIDELIGHTS

1. Born in West Hills, Long Island, New York in 1819, Walt Whitman was one of the keenest and most enthusiastic observers of the "common man," especially the American common man, that ever lived. He has come to be recognized as the greatest of our native poets as well as the medium through which the self-reliant, kindly, cynical-sentimental, average American has taken his place among national types. Listen to him as he sings in *A Song for Occupations:*

... Will you seek afar off? you surely come back at last,
In things best known to you finding the best, or as good as
the best,
In folks nearest to you finding the sweetest, strongest, lov-
ingest,
Happiness, knowledge, not in another place but this place,
not for another hour but this hour,
Man in the first you see or touch, always in friend, brother,
nighest neighbor — woman in mother, sister, wife,
The popular tastes and employments taking precedence in
poems or anywhere,
You workwomen and workmen of these states having your
own divine and strong life,
And all else giving place to men and women like you.

13

O you robust, sacred!
I cannot tell you how I love you;
All I love America for, is contained in men and women like
 you.

2. Count Leo Nikolaevich Tolstoy (1828–1910), author of what many critics say is the greatest novel ever written, *War and Peace,* was one of the few novelists who troubled to take time enough from his writing to try to find out how art and artists fit into the world around about them. He wrote a book (*What Is Art?*) which contains many ideas that are still considered valuable on this subject. In it he said: *Art is a human activity, consisting in this, that one man consciously, by means of certain external signs, hands on to others feelings he has lived through, and that other people are infected by these feelings and also experience them.* Can you illustrate this from your own experience?

3. The term Tin Pan Alley was originally used in connection with that part of Broadway in New York City in which the headquarters of the publishers of popular music are located. It has come to represent the changeable, commercial influences that have helped shape American music. The name probably came from the tinny sound of the old pianos in these offices. Here is an amusing description of Tin Pan Alley written in 1926. Probably conditions are not very different there today.

The professional department of a popular publishing house is like an extra noisy hour at the psychopathic ward in Bellevue Hospital. Extra noisy, mind you; ordinarily the professional

14

department is much louder and wilder than the hospital. It is quite an experience to visit a professional department for the first time. Don't do so much before noon. If you do, you will think you have dropped into a cemetery during a period of unusually good public health. All the artists having overworked themselves for twenty minutes the afternoon previous and twenty more in the evening have become quite restored by noon and begin to drop in, looking for new material, fearing that they may find it and have to spend a lot of energy learning it, when heaven knows why the old act shouldn't be good for another thirty years!

Then the Bellevue part begins. There is the big reception room, generally decorated in the purest à la cabaret style, sometimes in the more plutocratic houses with a fountain in the middle which used to spout genuine water back in 1893. All around are cubicles, theoretically sound proof, each with a piano of uncertain vintage and still more uncertain pitch. As the artists arrive, they are greeted by the manager, an expert in the skillful gradation of ceremonial according to the professional, social, and financial standing of the visitors, and turned over to the care of young piano players, who conduct them into a cubicle, ascertain their ideas — generally nebulous — in regard to the kind of material wanted, then, cheerfully disregarding these, proceed to fasten on them, if possible, the firm's latest publications.

If they are up to "sight reading" (with the aid of a sturdy finger on the pianist's right hand) they sing through the song themselves; if they are not inclined to so much exertion so early in the day, one of the sweet-voiced "pluggers" of the firm stops in and sings a novelty or two for them. From about

15

eleven-thirty to two P.M. *the cubicles have a noisy time of it. The shrieks of highest and hardest soprano mingle with the growls of lowest bass; male quartet contends with female baritone, a rain-barrel alto with a falsetto tenor, and through, over, above, around, and under all are the notes of steel-wire pianos smitten by earnest, cast-iron young men. It took more than this bedlam to dissuade George Gershwin (who started his professional musical career as one of these Tin Pan Alley pianists) from his love of music.*

4. No better example of the world of fantasy and imagination (with a marvelous touch of humor added) could possibly be found than that described by Lewis Carroll in his *Alice's Adventures in Wonderland* and *Through the Looking-Glass.* Written years ago by a British professor of mathematics for the purpose of amusing one of his young friends, these stories have intrigued thousands of readers, young and old, ever since. As Carroll puts it in his Introduction to *Through the Looking-Glass:*

> *A tale begun in other days,*
> *When summer suns were glowing —*
> *A simple chime, that served to time*
> *The rhythm of our rowing —*
> *Whose echoes live in memory yet,*
> *Though envious years would say, "forget."*

If you would see how closely allied are literary and musical imagery, listen to the music written by an American composer, Deems Taylor, to illustrate the following selections of Carroll's immortal tales (Columbia M-350):

16

WHY STUDY MUSIC?

1. *The Poem of the Jabberwocky*

"It seems pretty," said Alice when she had finished it, "but it's rather hard to understand! Somehow it seems to fill my head with ideas — only I don't know what they are!"

2. *Looking-Glass Insects*

A musical picture of the Diptera which so awed Alice: the Bee-elephant, the Gnat, the Rocking-horse-fly, the Snapdragon-fly, and the Bread-and-butter-fly.

QUESTIONS FOR DISCUSSION

Can you describe some differences between the *practical* and the *imaginative* way of life?

Do you know of any poetic descriptions of experiences which to most of us would seem like ordinary incidents in everyday life?

The distinction is often made between the Fine Arts (architecture, painting, literature, sculpture, and music) and the Useful Arts (such as furniture making, weaving, wood carving, etc.). Why is such a distinction possible, and is it a good one in your opinion?

What do you think the author means by the statement that music has no limitations of race, creed, or color? Do you agree?

Can you prove by history that "of all the conquests of man, only those endure that embrace his dreams?"

Do you think an understanding of the past will help our understanding and evaluation of the present? Why? Cite some examples that prove your point.

17

MUSIC TO LISTEN TO

Moussorgsky: *Prelude to Khovantchina* [2]   v   14415

Delius: *On Hearing the First Cuckoo in Spring*

                                                             v   4496

Here are two musical descriptions of experiences which to most of us would seem ordinary experiences in everyday life. The first describes a cold daybreak in winter; the second the composer's feelings on hearing the first birdcall of spring after experiencing a long, cold, dark winter. Can you learn from these two pieces anything about the people of the countries in which the music was written?

Grieg: *Peer Gynt Suite No. 1*   c   MX 180

    Morning

    Ase's Death

Sousa: *The Stars and Stripes Forever*   v   20132

Delius: *Over the Hills and Far Away*   c   M 290

Bach: *Air* from *Orchestral Suite No. 3 in*

    D Major   v   DM 339

Associate the emotions which these different pieces arouse in you with those suggested by the pictures in this chapter. In this connection we must remember that the psychologists mean by emotions any such departures from the usual calm of our existence as would produce strong feelings in us or an impulse to some kind of action. Thus we designate fear, anger, disgust, longing, grief, joy, etc., as states of emotion.

---

[2] The symbols in the list of records may be interpreted as follows:
       v   Victor   c   Columbia

Johann Strauss: *Emperor Waltz*
      (played by the Vienna
      Philharmonic Orchestra)   V   ALBUM M 805
Johann Sebastian Bach: *Jesu, Joy of Man's*
      Desiring   C   M 232
Wagner: *Ride of the Valkyries*   V   A 1135

Even the use of music can have practical as well as imaginative aspects. In other words, some of it has been written for such practical purposes as dancing and for use in the church or theater. And some of it has no excuse for being other than that of stimulating the dreams and ideals of man. Here are some examples of the practical type. Can you think of any others?

Beethoven: *Symphony in C Minor, No. 5*   V   M 640

What do you think it is that Beethoven ("a man who as artist was able to feel more strongly than most people") wanted to communicate to us through the four movements of this famous symphony?

THE GOOD SIGHTS AND SOUNDS OF THE
AMERICAN HOMELAND, an etching by Childe
Hassam

CHAPTER II. *"I HEAR AMERICA SINGING"*

My America is in the making.
It is young and strong; often it is wrong,
But it will grow. You and I will make it.
What you are, what I am, means far more
  than all our coal mines,
More than skyline silhouettes
  along the river's edge.
Your friendly words, my friendly smile,
  our work, our common hopes —
All of these go into our America.

     *   *   *

People build noble things working together.
It was our ideal long ago,
This joy in finding solutions together.
It must be again. It must be now.
My America is a land of promise.
We cannot fail; we have given our word!
—Jeannette Jamison

WE WHO live today are suddenly conscious of the importance of our country, the United States of America, in the present world. Perhaps most of us had not given much thought to the fact that we had become the earth's strongest nation before we were plunged into that terrible struggle for survival, World War II. It is evident enough now, however, that a great deal of the

Courtesy of Arvard Fairbanks,
University of Utah

FREEDOM FROM FEAR,
sculpture by Florence Peterson

hope for the world's future rests with us. It was our power and strength which, although terribly late when thrown into the struggle against tyrannies that tried to subdue the world,

22

finally turned the tide. And it is this tremendous strength, coupled with the fortunate fact that we have suffered relatively little in this war (in comparison with the other great countries), that will make the nations turn to us as leader. What we say and do, the way we think, the degree to which we accept our obligations, these are the factors that will determine the future of the world in the years immediately ahead. All the developments of recent years have tended to make us, willingly or not, the leaders of world opinion.

The story of our rapid rise and development as a nation is so familiar that we are apt to forget what a wonderful, almost magical, tale it is. It has never been better told than in Stephen Vincent Benét's little hundred-page book *America*, written in 1942, just before he died. This biography of the spirit of America describes in poetic fashion how, within a period of less than three hundred fifty years from the date of its first settlements in the wilderness of Virginia and on the rock-bound coasts of New England, this country became one of the great nations of the world. It was founded largely by immigrants — by men and women who wanted to get away from the devastations and endless strifes of Europe or who fled from the impressment of human beings for service in the armies of kings and princes constantly engaged in wars; by those who had a longing for an opportunity to find honest work for themselves and to create better chances for their children and who were eager to escape religious persecutions and to found communities in which man could worship God in his own way without the domination of church or government officials. From people such as these this country has evolved certain traits that have made it unique in the world of nations.

CONTEMPORARY AMERICAN MUSIC

We have been blessed by the natural wealth of a continent that has made us the richest country on earth. Our people have arisen from a mixture of bloods and temperaments unlike any that has ever existed in history. We believe firmly in the idea that life in general can be made better, and we are anxious to improve it in every way possible. We have not been afraid to proclaim the ideals of democracy to such an extent that they have established a relationship of man to man quite different from that found in other countries. From our earliest days we have possessed a spirit of pioneering and have never hesitated to try something new simply because it had never been tried before. Through our enormous energy and the faith that we have fostered in work and in being "practical," we have produced a machine-age civilization that has given us a higher standard of physical living than that of any other country. Blood, Frontier, Democracy, God — these are the forces which have given America her peculiar characteristics, characteristics that not only have set us apart from our European ancestors but make us different from all other peoples today.

Yet we have also to realize that there is something of a reverse side to this picture. The American character has some definite defects, many of them the inevitable result of its virtues. Because of our great success as a nation, we are apt to be somewhat intolerant of the ideas of other peoples, for we think that our own ways of doing things and our standards of life are the only ones valid for today. Because of the newness of the country and the need in the past for concentrating so largely on physical development and material progress, we are apt to become prejudiced against spiritual qualities and forget that they, too, need to be cultivated. Since our progress has

24

been partly the result of an independent attitude in life, of our willingness to try anything once, we are sometimes impatient with the past and what it has accomplished and forget that all solid achievement must rest upon what our ancestors and, in

Collection of The Whitney Museum of American Art, New York

THE DEMPSEY-FIRPO PRIZE FIGHT, 1924, a lithograph by
George Bellows

turn, upon what their predecessors have done. Since we have had such great spaces into which to develop and have been so successful in becoming the masters of a great continent, we are prone to think ourselves self-sufficient and to disregard the fact that in these days there can be no political or social isolation. Because we have been able to produce for ourselves a land flowing with milk and honey, we have somehow felt that this

25

machine age is all there is to existence and that science and invention can protect us from harm, can give us power and control and make our lives interesting and pleasant.

And, although we are all proud that we live under a form of government labeled Democracy, we are apt to forget that it is, as Louis H. Sullivan [1] has said, the essence of Democracy that the individual man be free in his body and free in his soul. So we must learn to set up something that resembles a responsible government within ourselves, learn to govern and restrain ourselves so that we can contribute the greatest good to the most people. Democracy does not mean, as so many seem to think, merely freedom to do as we like, regardless of the effect upon the world.

Even such a short summary as this, of the reasons why America and the Americans are what they are today, can give us a good idea of the national characteristics that would naturally be the basis for the art which this country creates. For it is plain enough that, like everything else a country produces, its art — music, literature, handicrafts, painting, architecture — comes directly out of the particular qualities and backgrounds of its people. Nothing so reveals a nation as its art; and if we have any peculiar ways of living and thinking, here is where they will be revealed.

What are some of these American characteristics? First of all, as any foreigner would tell you, we have a certain liveliness and hopefulness (someone has called it "bounce") that are peculiar to an optimistic people. We are bold enough to look on the bright side of things, largely because we have lived in a

[1] Louis H. Sullivan (1856–1924) was the first architect to break away from the restricting style of European architecture.

Photograph of the drawing from Brown Bros.

A FINE PLAN FOR A MODERN AMERI-
CAN BUILDING, suggesting that the architect
wants it to be beautiful as well as useful. In what
does this beauty consist?

land blessed beyond most by nature and geography. This is
what an understanding European meant when he said: *Experience does not have in America the same meaning as in
Europe. It is not a matter of wisdom from the past but of an
adventure with the future. The American needs horizons and
needs to be surrounded by friends. Then he goes forward!*

We have a real sense of humor, one that is obvious and
contagious, based on a love for fun and an impatience with

27

"stuffed shirts" and all they stand for. Americans generally understand and like humor, in contrast to a people like the Germans, who do neither. This good humor is part of the inveterate optimism that has so colored American life from the beginning.

And then we have a certain vision of the purpose of life, a vision that comes from living in a country where every man has had the opportunity of deciding his own destiny. Such idealism may be directed toward attaining material ends and, as we have said, it very often is so directed, to the detriment of spiritual development. But few of our people are content with things as they are; there is a real desire in most Americans for improvement and change, a desire that is in strong contrast to most European peoples, who have been content with things as they were (Sidelight 1).

Above all else, we are practical-minded, aware of the existence of problems and self-assured of our ability to solve them. This has given us our genius for invention and our love for gadgets and machines. It is no accident that the phonograph, electric light, automobile, and airplane are all American developments. Unfortunately we have not as yet learned to fully control our inventions; and often machines, instead of being the means for better and more effective living that they could be, have come near destroying us. Indeed, we are by no means sure that this will not actually happen.

We have a love for and understanding of the common people (Sidelight 2). We believe, as one of the greatest Americans said, that God must love the common people, for He made so many of them. This understanding comes directly from the fact that from its very beginning there have been no conscious

28

THE MACHINE, a mural in the library of Dartmouth College
by José C. Orozco

In 1934 a famous Mexican artist finished a series of wall paintings for the library of Dartmouth College, giving his interpretation of the constructive and destructive forces which have shaped the life of this continent. Here is his idea of the machine, showing the tremendous force of the industrial development that has received so much emphasis in this country. How do you interpret Orozco's meaning in this picture?

class distinctions in this country and that during the first two centuries of its existence the people everywhere worked with their hands and shared common experiences, joys, and sorrows. So there is a mass understanding here such as exists in no other country.

29

The fact that our ancestors lived in a pioneer land in which the first necessity was hustling for a living has given us a drive and energy, a spirit of enterprise, that is essentially American (Sidelight 3). Even though we no longer live in a pioneer country, this habit of hurrying and pushing so that we can get everything possible from life still persists. We are *the builders of dynamic things*, as Russell W. Davenport puts it in his poem *My Country*.

> *Boilers and bars, propellers, wheels and wings*
> *To run and fly and dive at our behest,*
> *Through which the mighty wind of freedom sings,*
> *America is not a land of rest.*

Our pioneer backgrounds are also responsible for our love for standardization, a desire for being sure that we do not differ too much from the other inhabitants of our country. No American likes to be thought provincial, from the backwoods; and so we try to think the same thoughts, wear the same clothes, and act the same way as our neighbors. This tends to equalize and standardize our thoughts and actions in an unfortunate way and threatens to destroy the very individuality and independence that are at the root of all our national greatness.

These characteristics of ours explain to a great degree why we have as yet produced no really great American art. For, again quoting Davenport,

> *We have not paused from action to beget*
> *Heroic simile and song and frieze;*
> *We have no empire of the mind as yet,*
> *Nor have we shed our light within the grave.*

This is the reason why we have, for example, produced better architecture in this country than painting, literature, or music. Our practical-mindedness and love of invention, as well as our

Courtesy of Thomas Airviews

AN AMERICAN CITY CENTER: Rockefeller
Center, New York

drive for attaining material success, have made us think that it is primarily important to develop fine houses to live in and efficient skyscrapers to do business in. In painting and literature, instead of trying to emphasize native qualities, we have been content until quite recently to imitate the styles and the

31

mannerisms of other countries. In music our national characteristics have produced that kind of strongly rhythmic, vitally buoyant, generally popular expression that is known the world over as *American*. It is this popular music of the people, in one form or another, that has received more general recognition outside our own country than any other form of art we have yet produced.

There is good reason for this. The literature of this American popular music is in real truth a literature of democracy. No other people has ever made music in just the same way. Although there has always been a music of the people in other countries, there has never before been a music of the whole people. In Europe, in the old days, the Lord of the Manor might like to watch his tenants and peasants dancing and listen to them singing. He would probably remember these dances and songs as being essentially those of his own country whenever he went abroad and heard the music of other countries. But he would never think of dancing or singing with his tenants and peasants, never dream of making up tunes with them as they hauled their boats on the rivers or brought in their harvests from the fields.[2]

In this country there have been few barriers of custom or culture to divide the people. And it is this community of thought and unity of experience that give American popular music its peculiar character and vitality. Like the popular music of no other country, ours gives, in the words of Carl Sandburg, the *feel and atmosphere, the layout and lingo of religions, of breeds of men, of customs and slogans.* Some of

---

[2] This idea is developed at some length in the Introduction to A *Treasury of American Song* by Olin Downes.

Collection of The Whitney Museum of American Art, New York

WINTER TWILIGHT, 1930, a painting by Charles Burchfield

this American popular music had its beginnings in *folk music* [3] of one kind or another. A great deal of it is out-and-out dance music. Some of it originated in the theater or was first heard in the movies. And much of it has come from the atmosphere of Tin Pan Alley.

Here is a list of its backgrounds. Of course, it is impossible and undesirable to separate these into completely watertight

[3] The term *folk music* is hardly an American one, for, as has so often been said, we have plenty of folks in this country, but no "folk." It is used technically to describe that type of music that originates among the common people of a country and thus embodies their characteristic qualities and feelings.

33

compartments; there is bound to be some overlapping. For example, it is possible to list jazz under both *The Music of the Negro* and *Broadway and Its Echoes*. And a great deal of the folk music of Stephen Foster was originally written for the use of the black-face minstrels that were so popular in the American theater before the War between the States. But in general these backgrounds suggest the principal sources out of which our popular music has come:

1. The Music of the Indian
2. The Music of the Negro
    Spirituals
    Work and Secular Songs
    Modern Developments, including Jazz
3. American Folk Music
    Southern Mountain Music
    Plantation Songs; Stephen Foster
    Cowboy Songs
    Work and Play Songs
    Patriotic Songs of America's Wars
4. The Music of the American Theater
    Black-face Minstrel Songs
    Sentimental Songs of the Nineteenth Century
    Operetta and Comic-opera Music
5. Film and Radio Music
6. Broadway and Its Echoes: The Development of Tin Pan Alley

SIDELIGHTS

1. Here is a creed which someone has made up for those of us who love this country and believe in what it stands for:

"I HEAR AMERICA SINGING"

A Creed for America

May this country never forget that its power has come from the efforts of its citizens, living in freedom and equality.

May this country hold in piety and steadfast faith those who have battled and died to give it new opportunities for service and growth.

May it reserve its contempt for those who see in it only an instrument for their own selfish interests.

May it marshal its righteous wrath against those who would divide it by racial struggles.

May it lavish its scorn upon the faint-hearted.

And may this country always give its support to those who have engaged with us against oppression and who will continue with us in the struggle for a vital, creative peace.

Notice how the same ideas are expressed (even more forcefully, perhaps) in John Latouche's *Ballad for Americans*.

2. Thornton Wilder, in the Introduction to his play *Our Town*, has described the simplicity and sincerity of life in a typical American small town. The following speech by the Stage Manager, as the play begins without stage props or scenery, could be used to describe thousands of American villages:

The name of the town is Grover's Corners, New Hampshire, just across the Massachusetts line.... The First Act shows a day in our town. The day is May 7, 1901. The time is just before dawn.

The sky is beginning to show some streaks of light over in the east there, behind our mountain.

35

The morning star always gets wonderful bright the minute before it has to go.

I'd better show you how our town lies. Up here is Main Street. Way back there is the railway station; tracks go that way. Polish Town's across the tracks and some Canuck families. Over there is the Congregational Church; across the street's the Presbyterian.

Methodist and Unitarian are over there.

Baptist is down in the holla' by the river.

Catholic Church is over beyond the tracks.

Here's the Town Hall and Post Office combined; jail's in the basement.

Bryan once made a speech from these steps here.

Along here's a row of stores. Hitching posts and horse blocks in front of them.

First automobile's going to come along in about five years — belonged to Banker Cartwright, our richest citizen ... lives in the big white house up on the hill.

Here's the grocery store and here's Mr. Morgan's drugstore. Most everybody in town manages to look into these two stores once a day.

Public school's over yonder. High School's still farther over. Quarter of nine mornings, noontimes, and three o'clock afternoons, the 'hull' town can hear the yelling and screaming from those schoolyards.

This is our doctor's house — Doc Gibbs'....

There's a garden here. Corn, peas, beans, hollyhocks, heliotrope, and a lot of burdock ...

And this is Mrs. Webb's garden.

Just like Mrs. Gibbs', only it's got a lot of sunflowers, too.

36

"I HEAR AMERICA SINGING"

Nice town, y'know what I mean?

Nobody very remarkable ever come out of it — s'far as we know.

The earliest tombstones in the cemetery up there on the mountain say 1670–1860 — they're Grovers and Cartwrights and Gibbses and Herseys — same names as are around here now.[4]

Read the whole play. You will find it most enjoyable.

3. . . . Have the elder races halted?
Do they droop and end their lessons, wearied over there beyond
    the seas?
We take up the task eternal, and the burden and the lesson,
        Pioneers! O pioneers! . . .
        All the pulses of the world,
Falling in they beat for us, with the Western movement beat,
Holding single or together, steady moving to the front, all
    for us,
        Pioneers! O pioneers! . . .

        Minstrels latent on the prairies!
(Shrouded bards of other lands, you may rest, you have done
    your work,)
Soon I hear you coming warbling, soon you rise and tramp
    amid us,
        Pioneers! O pioneers! . . .
           —Walt Whitman, 1865

[4] Reprinted from *Our Town*, A Play in Three Acts, by Thornton Wilder. Copyright, 1938, by Coward-McCann, Inc.

37

QUESTIONS FOR DISCUSSION

Can you add any other typically American characteristics to those mentioned by the author? Do you agree with all his? If not, why not?

One of the best American poets, Stephen Vincent Benét, has said *people of other lands would understand our country better if they could meet us in our own back yard, learn something of our habits and our history, hear what we have to say, and see what we stand for.* Discuss this statement in connection with the participation of the United States in World War II and the great difficulty we are finding in making peace after it. Do people abroad know and understand us better because our soldiers fought in Europe and Asia?

Which of the examples of art mentioned below seems to you to be most characteristically American? Which least? Why?

A SHORT LIST OF SOME CHARACTERISTIC EXAMPLES
OF AMERICAN ART

LITERATURE

Mark Twain: *Life on the Mississippi*
Sinclair Lewis: *Main Street*
Thomas Wolfe: *Look Homeward, Angel*
Thornton Wilder: *Our Town* (a play)
Stephen Vincent Benét: *John Brown's Body* (a poem)

SCULPTURE

Florence Peterson: *Freedom from Fear*, University of Utah

38

MURAL PAINTING

José Clemente Orozco: *The Machine*, Library, Dartmouth College

ETCHING

Childe Hassam: *The Good Sights and Sounds of the American Homeland* from *Fair Is Our Land*, Hastings House, New York

ARCHITECTURE

Thomas Airviews: *An American City Center: Rockefeller Center, New York*, Air View

LITHOGRAPH

George Bellows: *The Dempsey-Firpo Prize Fight*, The Whitney Museum of American Art, New York

PAINTING

Charles Burchfield: *Winter Twilight*, 1930, The Whitney Museum of American Art, New York

MUSIC

Edward MacDowell: *Woodland Sketches*
George Gershwin: *An American in Paris*
Roy Harris: *When Johnny Comes Marching Home*
Aaron Copland: *Appalachian Spring*
Louis Armstrong: Jazz: *Cornet Chop Suey*
Earl Robinson: *Ballad for Americans* (text by John Latouche)

SWING LOW, SWEET CHARIOT, a painting by John McCrady

Swing low, sweet chariot,
Comin' for to carry me home;
Swing low, sweet chariot,
Comin' for to carry me home;
I looked over Jordan
And what did I see,
Comin' for to carry me home?
A band of angels comin' after me,
Comin' for to carry me home.

THE MUSIC OF THE AMERICAN INDIAN

The Great Mystery called this land to be....
It was meant by the Great Mystery that the
Indians should give it to all people. But there
are two roads, the White Man's and the
Indian's. Neither has ever known the other.
— Chief Haomori.

MUSIC has been an essential part of
America's life ever since man first came
to this continent. It was a vital and integral factor in the great
civilizations developed by such ancient American peoples as
the Mayas of Central America, the Aztecs of Mexico, and the
Incas of Peru. As we will see in a later chapter, these peoples
were far different from those we are accustomed to think of as
Indians today, for they established great empires, built large
and impressive cities, held elaborate religious and civic ceremonies, and developed a complicated calendar and a system
of picture writing.

The hundreds of Indian tribes that wandered the mountains and plains of North America were the lineal descendants
of the original Mongolian settlers who came to this continent

from Asia during a period of several thousand years, long be-fore the time of the white man. That music, especially singing, was an important factor in their lives has been attested by the reports of many early European explorers and colonists. William Wood, writing of his visit to Plymouth and Massa-chusetts Bay in 1634, said of the singing of the Indians: *To hear one of these Indians unseene, a good eare might easily mistake their untaught voyce for the warbling of a well tuned instrument. Such command have they of their voices.*

Even though these original inhabitants of our continent have been under the cultural influences of the white man for nearly four centuries, they have retained and are still develop-ing a fine body of songs which reveal their artistic and spiritual strength. Thus a well-known expert, Mrs. Laura Boulton, writes of Indian music: *Through his songs and dances the Indian worships his gods. Through the power of prayer, by singing and dancing the spirits are propitiated, sickness and famine and drought are driven away, and the people blessed with plentiful food, good health, and many children. Thus the Indian has kept what many more "progressive" civilizations have lost and are striving to recover: a rich, intimate and nat-ural use of music and art in their ordinary lives.*[1]

Nevertheless, because it has been so definitely associated with tribal customs and because these customs are so far re-moved from the ordinary life of what we call progressive civi-lization, Indian music has had little effect upon later develop-ments in this country. Since Indians sing differently from white men, using different scales and a very unusual method

[1] Mrs. Boulton's *Indian Music of the Southwest* (v P 49) is the most au-thentic collection of Indian records available.

42

A RELIGIOUS DANCE, an engraving by Theodore de Bry

This interesting engraving, first published in 1590, was made by a Flemish engraver and publisher from an original water color painted by John White, the leader of the first expedition organized by Sir Walter Raleigh to come to Virginia in 1585. White came to this continent again in 1587 as governor of Raleigh's second expedition, the expedition of the famous "lost colony" of Roanoke Island. During his stay here White made over sixty fine water colors, the first authentic pictorial record of the New World. This one shows a dance of the Indians, observed by White in Virginia some time between 1585 and 1587. — From *The New World*, edited by Stefan Lorant. New York: Duell, Sloan & Pearce.

of producing tone (Sidelight 1), their music is bound to sound rather queer to our ears. We can become interested in it as a

Collection of The Museum of Modern Art, New York

GREEN CORN CEREMONY of the American Indians, a painting by Awa Tsirch

curiosity and realize that it represents the cultural and religious background of the earliest settlers of our country. But we have not absorbed it into our own music.

THE MUSIC OF THE NEGRO

Whether or not we consider Negro music as really American, it has probably made a deeper impression on American life than has any other class of songs. — John Tasker Howard in Our American Music.

There are many ways in which the music of the American Negro has affected our present-day music, for there is some-

44

thing essentially *popular* about the music of this race which was brought to our continent against its will during the early days of the settlement and development of the country. The Negro is a natural musician: he possesses great talent, likes to sing and play, and whether he is singing a tune inherited from his ancestors or one that he has made up himself or borrowed from the white man, he always interprets it in a way that makes it different from anything else. His music is personal and vital, and it is no wonder that it has become an important element in American popular song.

For the original source of this music we must go to Africa, from whence the Negro was first brought to this continent in the early years of the sixteenth century. Historians have not yet done enough work in research and comparison to be sure, but it seems as if many of the traits that characterize the present-day music of the Negro came with him from Africa. The most important of these traits are: the predominance of rhythm over all other features, the union of song and dance, the alternation of solo lines and chorus refrains, the love of singing in harmony, and the astonishing ability to carry on simultaneous rhythms.

In a later chapter we will show how strong this Negro influence has been in shaping the folk and popular music of the Latin-American countries. In the United States, it was not until after the War between the States that native Negro singing and songs became widely known. Then, groups of singers from the great industrial schools that were established to help educate the emancipated slaves traveled through the country. In their programs these singers placed emphasis so largely upon the religious songs of the Negro called *spirituals* that his

45

The Nine Jubilee Singers who left Fisk University, October 6, 1871.

From J. T. Howard's *Our American Music*

THE FISK JUBILEE SINGERS OF 1871

equally fine secular music, found in work and play songs, dances, games, railroading and steamboating songs, was somewhat overlooked by the white man. All of these bear the stamp of the Negro's characteristic attitude toward life and are perfectly spontaneous expressions of a natural musical temperament (Sidelight 2).

It was this Negro music that inspired the well-known American folk songs of Stephen Foster. It became the model for the minstrel songs which were so very popular before the War between the States and so important in the development of the music of our theater. And, as we shall see, it was Negro music by way of ragtime and through jazz and swing which formed the basis of the popular style that represents the musical taste of a large number of our people. American composers as recent as Jerome Kern and George Gershwin, neither of them Negro, have used this type of music as their inspiration in writing some of the best popular music ever penned in this country. Such compositions as the song *Ol' Man River* from Kern's *Show Boat* and Gershwin's *A Woman Is a Sometime Thing* and *Summertime* from *Porgy and Bess* represent this

PAUL ROBESON, the famous Negro singer, as he sang *Ol'Man River* in *Show Boat*

47

American popular style, developed from the music of the Negro, at its very best.

Since jazz is such an important development of Negro music, two chapters will be devoted to it later in a discussion of its origin, spread, and various forms.

AMERICAN FOLK SONG

It is not always recognized that America has folk music; yet it really has not only one but many different folk musics. It is a vast land and different sorts of folk music have sprung up in different parts, all having validity and all being a possible foundation for development into an art music. For this reason, I believe that it is possible for a number of different styles to develop in America, all legitimately born of folk songs from different localities. Jazz, ragtime, Negro spirituals, Southern mountain songs, country fiddling tunes and cowboy songs can all be employed in the creation of American music, and are actually used by many composers now. — George Gershwin

In its broadest meaning folk music is music which is sung or played from memory by the people. Its composer may or may not be known, but if the people have taken it up and made it a part of their everyday lives, it is real folk music. We have a lot of such music in this country, for our people have always been hard-working and have sung a great deal to lighten the burden of their work as well as to relieve the monotony of their existence. Cowboys on the prairies, lumberjacks clearing

Pix, Inc. — Harriet Arnold

BURL IVES, a present-day folk singer

the forests, roustabouts handling the rough freight on the inland river boats, workers building the canals and railroads, soldiers fighting to save their country, backwoods pioneers seeking relaxation, all these have made original and important contributions to our American music. Their songs and dances, especially in recent years, have been taken up by professional writers and promoters and have become popular the country

49

over under the label of *hill-billy ballads, cowboy songs,* and the like. In most cases these are poor, synthetic imitations of the real thing, with no true flavor or individuality. It is not very hard to tell the counterfeit from the real in the case of these folk songs. The real thing, as someone has well said, never tries to get itself sung; it is a modest, unassuming product, but it eases itself into our minds and out of our mouths spontaneously, to stay singing around in our heads forever. If it doesn't, it isn't a real folk song. The popular hit goes in one ear, rings around in our head for a little while, and then flies out the other ear. But folk music, as Langston Hughes says, *sort of sneaks into your being and remains there with no effort whatsoever.*

Many of the traditional folk songs brought to this country by its original settlers have become naturalized and adapted to native conditions, and so they have become as American as baked beans, chewing gum, or chain stores. This is true of all types of songs in all parts of the country. Some of the music sung by the pioneers as they were beating back the American frontier were brought with them from the Old World, some were given new words suitable to their new surroundings, and some were made up on the spot. Such songs of the frontier as *Cumberland Gap, Way Down the Ohio, The Oregon Trail, The Devil and the Farmer's Wife, Chicken Reel,* and *Turkey in the Straw* tell the story of the American wilderness as well as any history book could. Some of our loveliest songs came over from England, Scotland, and Ireland with the people who settled in the backlands of the Blue Ridge and Smoky Mountains sections of the south. Because of the complete isolation of the descendants of these people from the rest of the coun-

50

Gies from Black Star

SINGING FOLK SONGS in the Appalachian
mountain country of Virginia

try, many of these Anglo-American songs have remained un-
changed to this day.

There are plenty of work songs typical of the men who have
helped make America — the sailors, miners, lumberjacks, river-
men, street vendors, cowboys, and the rest. In many cases as
rough and ready as the men who sang them, these songs contribute an interesting sidelight to the history of American life.
The topical songs of the first part of the nineteenth century
tell of the expanding life of the young United States and deal
with special events and conditions of the day. They sing of

51

election campaigns, city life, the building of railroads, oil spec-
ulation, and the like. All the growing pains of the young country are reflected in them. Then there are the sentimental songs
so popular around the middle of the century. To us they seem
filled with sugar and mud, but such things as *Rocked in the
Cradle of the Deep*, *The Old Arm Chair*, and *She Sleeps in
the Grave* show that the modern generation has no corner on
corny sentiment! It will have to be admitted that Stephen
Foster, greatest of all American songwriters, contributed his
share of these lachrymose effusions; but his best songs are so
fine that we are inclined to forget the large number of sob-
ditties which he wrote.

Foster's *Way Down Upon the Swanee River*, *My Old Kentucky Home*, and *Old Black Joe* are known and sung the world
over. Their unusual appeal comes from the fact that, as a well-
known psychologist has said, their composer was able to put
into music what every human being feels: a desire for the comfort, kindness, and understanding of his childhood home
(Sidelight 3). Foster wrote of the romantic South, of jasmine
and honeysuckle. He saw it only in his imagination, for there
is no evidence that he ever really lived in the South. The South
of which he sang was a dreamland synonymous with all his
longings as an adult to be back again in his childhood. Something of this lies deeply buried in all of us, and so his nostalgic
songs satisfy the universal desire of steadier, duller, and better-
adjusted mortals to return to happier days. Thus is great music
born!

Another abundant, but little known, source of American
popular music was the camp meetings which were held all over
the country as a result of the great religious-revival movement

of the early nineteenth century. Traveling from near and far, people would come in wagons or on horseback to hear the fire-and-brimstone sermons of the preachers and sing the camp-

JACOB NILES, a southern mountain singer of folk songs

meeting hymns that quickly spread over the countryside. Many of these hymns were set to dance tunes and were easy to sing and remember. There is little doubt that the Negroes borrowed many of them as the basis for their spirituals.

From the time of the American Revolution down to our own day, from *Yankee Doodle* to *Praise the Lord and Pass the*

53

When the war is ov-er we will all en-list a-gain

At 'em boys, —— Give 'er the gun!

Courtesy of A. M. Klum and Office of the Chief of Special Services, Dept. of the Army

AMERICAN SONG SHEETS from World War II, by B. Vincent

Ammunition, American songs have been an important accompaniment to our wars. In wartime, music always "suits for feasts, it suits for fun, and just as well for fighting," as a version of *Yankee Doodle* puts it. Such gripes of the soldier as his poor food, his demanding drill sergeant, and the easy life of his officers make ideal subjects for rowdy, eloquent songs. And we have them a-plenty, as well as lots of sentimental effusions. The private in World War II who sang about *Marlene* was not one whit more sentimental than the one in the War between the States who sang:

54

"SING OUT, SWEET LAND"

The years creep slowly by, Lorena,
The snow is on the grass again;
The sun's low down the sky, Lorena,
The frost gleams where the flowers have been.

This song, together with others of that time which tell about *Army Grub* and *Eating Goober Peas*, show that, after all, the soldier does not change a great deal. And they give us a more human picture of war than most records of military history provide.

THE MUSIC OF THE THEATER

In the early days of our country's life the energies of its inhabitants were largely given over to earning a living. Life was pretty grim and rugged, and there was little time for anything but the serious things of the world. What little music was known to these early settlers was that used in religious or social gatherings. But as the country developed politically and economically after the Revolutionary War and the people became more prosperous, they turned more and more to what they called amusements. The first native form of music for the theater was that written for the black-face minstrel shows mentioned above (Sidelight 4). This distinctively American form of entertainment could not have developed in any other country, and it was as popular in its time in both the United States and England as the movies are now.

Credit for starting this form of entertainment is generally given to a white singer, Thomas Rice, who around 1830 in Pittsburgh blacked his face, borrowed a Negro's clothes, and sang the famous *Jim Crow* songs on a stage. Later on, troupes of *Ethiopian minstrels* traveled all over the country. A letter

55

From The Albert Davis Collection

A MINSTREL POSTER OF 1867

written by a visiting German musician in 1852 shows how popular they were at that time:

...The so-called minstrels have the best business here. The companies are composed of six or seven individuals of the masculine gender. They paint their faces black, sing Negro

56

songs, dance and jump about as if possessed, change their costumes three or four times each evening, beat each other to the
great delight of the art-appreciating public, and thus earn not
only well-deserved fame but enormous money. I am of the
opinion that they look upon the latter as worth more than all
the rest.

Stephen Foster wrote some of his best songs for the famous
Christy Minstrels, and even so cosmopolitan an American as
Mark Twain said of the minstrel shows: To my mind they
were thoroughly delightful things and most competent laugh-
ter-compellers and I for one am sorry they have gone.

Later the more sophisticated variety and burlesque shows,
patterned after European models and produced in the eastern
seaboard towns, became popular. These in turn were followed
by the fashionable Gilbert and Sullivan operas, which during
the last quarter of the nineteenth century were almost as popular in the United States as they were in their native England.
American composers imitated them as well as their contemporary counterparts from Paris and Vienna, and there developed a real school of American light-opera composers. The
best of these was Victor Herbert, whose graceful and melodi-
ous music is still to be heard everywhere, especially on the
radio. Others were Reginald DeKoven, whose *Robin Hood*
became a model of its kind, and John Philip Sousa, who is
even better known for his marches than for his comic operas.
Indeed, it is impossible to find a better characterization of the
American spirit of optimism and patriotic fervor than this
composer's *Stars and Stripes Forever*. Later representative composers of this country's theatrical music are Rudolf Friml,

57

Sigmund Romberg, Jerome Kern, George Gershwin, Cole Porter, Irving Berlin, Richard Rodgers, Russell Bennett, and Leonard Bernstein. At its best, this type of American composition cannot be equaled by that of any other country.

FILM MUSIC

It is difficult for most of us who frequent the movies to realize what a recent innovation the combination of pictures and sound is. Prior to 1926 all moving pictures were silent. Whenever a musical background was necessary, it was furnished by players in the theater. Sometimes a large orchestra was used with instruments capable of imitating all sorts of natural sounds called for, such as thunder, hoofbeats, birdcalls, and the like. Sometimes a single pianist pounded away on a tinny instrument. When, after a great deal of experimenting, the problems of reproducing and amplifying mechanically recorded sound were successfully solved, the era of sound pictures arrived. From 1927 on, music was recorded on and reproduced from the same film as the picture itself, and many new possibilities were opened up for the movie producer and composer.

In some cases background music alone is called for. Much of this is adapted and arranged from works already existing, although recently it has become more usual for composers to write original music for the whole film. In musical-production films which employ the techniques of the Broadway musical shows, the music consists largely of hit songs. It is these that become popular wherever movies are shown and later are usually repeated over the radio. Some of this music is good, especially when a talented composer is engaged to furnish the score, as is sometimes the case in Hollywood. But the ironical feature of the whole situation is this: if the music is too good, it distracts attention from the picture and is therefore too dominating a feature of the whole. So a great deal of the movie music we hear is likely to be pretty much run-of-the-mill stuff, although composers are constantly trying to improve it (Sidelight 5).

Music has come to be such a commonplace thing in radio programs that we take it entirely for granted (Sidelight 6). All kinds of radio productions use music of one sort or another, the soap operas as well as the dignified documentary and historically descriptive programs. It is in the latter type of production that composers have achieved worth-while results, something that is beyond the stop-gap style that has become so familiar to present-day radio listeners. Two radio performances of this kind may be mentioned here as examples of this type of radio illustrative music: John Latouche's *Ballad for Americans*, with music by Earl Robinson, and Norman Corwin's *On a Note of Triumph*, with music by Bernard Herrmann. Both of these were originally broadcast over CBS and have been recorded for preservation in permanent form. They show the modern broadcast-with-music style at its best. The latter, given on the day which has gone down in history as V-E Day, hails the victory in Europe after World War II. It not only recalls the fighting and labor of Americans on the battlefield and the home front, but it stands, as someone has so well expressed it, *as a monument to those who are carrying on the fight for freedom and as a symbol of the power of the spoken word.*

59

CONTEMPORARY AMERICAN MUSIC

The greatest single influence in determining the style and content of that type of music which has come to be known the world over as American is undoubtedly Tin Pan Alley, that descriptive if not very elegant name given to the district of the popular music publishers in New York City. It is here that the different influences which shape and mold so much of our popular musical expression are strongest. Composers of dance music, hit writers of every race and nationality, singers and players and band leaders looking for new music, publishers anxious to plug their latest novelties, arrangers and orchestrators of all sorts, these have come to represent the Tin-Pan-Alley influences that have commercialized so much American musical production.

It was these influences that determined the distinctive features of such music as George Gershwin's, with its moods descriptive of life in a great American city — a peculiar combination of hectic gaiety and great loneliness. Irving Berlin, the Russian-born son of a Jewish cantor, successful composer and lyric writer, active theatrical producer and music publisher, could hardly have developed his peculiar genius in another environment. Ferde Grofé, one of the first arrangers to produce well-planned, carefully written symphonic jazz scores, the orchestrator of Gershwin's *Rhapsody in Blue* and the composer of a number of successful things in his own right, including the *Grand Canyon Suite*, is another typical Tin-Pan-Alley product. So also is Russell Bennett, brilliant orchestrator of many of Broadway's most sophisticated and successful shows.

60

Pix, Inc. — Karger

AN AMERICAN FOLK DANCE, as shown in the American folk play *Sing Out, Sweet Land*

But if Tin Pan Alley is responsible for the development of such real American talents as these, it is likewise responsible for some of the weaknesses that are to be found in American popular music. As a nation we are inclined to be rather sentimental, and this fact is often overemphasized in the mawkish longing and sickly yearning that is heard in many of our popular songs. (As we have shown, this is not a modern trait!) If a foreigner were to judge our national character by the words and music of such songs, he would be inclined to think us a weak-spined lot with no confidence in ourselves, suffering from

61

a national inferiority complex. This, we know well enough, is not true. Why, then, do we so often go *Dancing With Tears in My Eyes* or hope that *When You Want Somebody Who Don't Want You, Perhaps You'll Think of Me?* The titles of such songs change continually, but the sentiments are the same. It has often been said that the American is at least sure of one thing: he always wants to be somewhere else than where he actually is. To him the grass always grows greener on the other side of the fence. If this is true, it accounts for the great nostalgia that is found in so much of our popular music, for our longing to be carried *Back to Old Virginia* or to be *Deep in the Heart of Texas.*

The commercial producers of our popular music have been quick to take advantage of these national traits and to turn them to their own account. Instead of being content with pieces that have good, lively tunes, catchy rhythms, effective orchestrations, and decent sentiment, many present-day composers and arrangers go in for overexaggerated and rather cheap effects. These are apt to offend people of good taste and to turn them against this type of music. An occasional novel and unusual effect adds interest to all kinds of music. But when there is nothing but effect after effect, we soon become weary and turn away toward an expression that is more normal and usual and sane.

As we hear more music and learn more about art in general, we will come to realize that it is always the simple and sincere things which last. It is the cheap and tawdry and exaggerated ones that are bound to change. This is inevitable: the very fact that they are lush and overexaggerated makes us impatient to get on to something else, once the novelty has worn off. American popular music contains much that is valuable and good and sincere. It is a shame to have it cheapened by undesirable influences that have been introduced for purely commercial reasons.

SIDELIGHTS

1. In discussing Indian music Mrs. Boulton says:

The singing technique of the Indian is peculiar to their race. The Indian sings with his jaws only slightly open and there is very little change in the position of his jaws or lips while singing. The tone is forced out and has remarkable carrying power. The stress on the throat produces a special timbre (tone color). Sometimes special qualities of tones are used for certain kinds of songs.

2. In a recent interesting article in the news journal *Time* (on the singing of Negro music) by the great American artist Marian Anderson, the writer has some important things to say about the spirituals:

Professional musicians and musicologists are still locked in hot debate about the musical origins of the spirituals and the manner of their creation. One simple fact is clear — they were created in direct answer to the Psalmist's question: How shall we sing the Lord's song in a strange land? For the land in which the slaves found themselves was strange beyond the fact that it was foreign. It was a nocturnal land of vast, shadowy pine woods, vast fields of cotton whose endless rows converged sometimes on a solitary cabin, vast swamps reptilian and furtive — a land alive with all the elements of lonely beauty, except compassion. In this deep night of land and man, the singers saw visions; grief,

63

like a tuning fork, gave the tone, and the Sorrow Songs were uttered.

Perhaps, in little unpainted churches or in turpentine clearings, the preacher, who soon became the pastor and social leader of his wretched people, gave the lead:

> Way over yonder in the harvest fiel' —
> (The flock caught the vision too:)
> Way up in the middle of the air,
> The angel shovin' at the chariot wheel,
> Way up in the middle of the air.
> O, yes, Ezekiel saw the wheel,
> Way up in the middle of the air,
> Ezekiel saw the wheel,
> Up in the middle of the air.
> The Big Wheel moved by faith,
> The Little Wheel moved by the grace of God,
> A wheel in a wheel,
> Up in the middle of the air.

The Magnificat of their music has sometimes obscured the poetry of the spirituals. There are few religious poems of any people that can equal this one:

> I know moon-rise, I know star-rise,
> I lay dis body down.
> I walk in de moonlight, I walk in de starlight,
> To lay dis body, heah, down....
>
> I lie in de grave an' stretch out my arms,
> I lay dis body, heah, down.
> I go to judgment in de evenin' of de day,
> When I lay dis body down.

64

The problem of the white American and the Negro American has rarely been more simply evoked than in those last lines. The problem could be explained (and must in part be solved) in political, social and economic terms. But it is deeper than that, and so must its eventual solution be.

Well might all Americans ponder upon the fact that it is, like all the great problems of mankind, at bottom a religious problem, and that the religious solution must be made before any other solutions could be effective. It will, in fact, never be solved exclusively in human terms.

Dr. E. B. DuBois in his book *Souls of the Black Folk* calls their secular songs *Sorrow Songs* too. Those who sing them are apt to refer to them as *Sinful Songs*. In any case, most of these non-religious songs, like the spirituals, are the expressions of an unhappy people telling of their suffering and disappointment in their present existence and their longing for something better. In Africa, before he came to this country, the Negro had used music in his worship of the good and evil spirits. And so it is not strange to find him moaning:

> *Wake up dis mo'nin', blues all roun' mah head,*
> *Wake up dis mo'nin', blues all roun' mah head,*
> *Blues made me feel so low-down, wish's ah was dead!*

3. Dr. S. N. Wortis, director of the Psychiatric Division of Bellevue Hospital, New York, has made a careful study of Foster's career. He became interested in the life of this American folk-composer after coming across his medical record at Bellevue, where Foster died on January 13, 1864 after having been removed there from his miserably poor lodgings in down-

65

town New York. Foster died practically penniless and almost without friends — not a very pretty picture for those of us who love his songs!

4. Did you ever stop to wonder why the Negro occupied so much attention in the early amusement world of this country? In the flesh, he was subject to slavery on the plantations of the South and to an equally inferior social position in the North. But in imagination he inspired all sorts of impersonation and imitation. One musical historian explains it this way: *The Negro simply could not be overlooked. He contrasted too strongly with those who forcibly adopted him in appearance, manners, and ways of talking, thinking, and singing.* It is interesting to note that these Negro imitation acts on the American stage were preceded by similar performances in England, where Charles Dibdin, a popular songwriter of the day, put on a sort of musical entertainment, as early as 1789, in which he gave Negro impersonations.

5. The problems of the movie composer are unique, for he must limit and restrict his music to the direction and speed of the stories for which he composes, and this direction and speed are constantly changing. Here is what one movie composer has to say regarding these problems:

Suppose that a composer of screen music is asked to provide exactly 72 seconds of music for a love scene. He invents a melodic theme and sets to work on its development. Just about the time he gets into the middle of some really interesting composition, the action shifts to sea and his tender music is rudely interrupted by a foghorn or a ship's whistle. Then he must

66

return to the beginning and shape and trim his material according to the time pattern. He is very fortunate, indeed, if the length of the scene is not changed several times during the production, thus requiring his music to have rubber-band flexibility.

Because screen music must always follow the rhythm of action of the story, it is doubtful whether much music written for the movies will command serious attention and interest when performed apart from the picture. It simply lacks the continuity and logical development of music written for the concert hall. Movie music that is written to be given concert performance requires a complete re-arrangement of its conception and form.

The immediate establishment of a particular mood is one of the most important functions of motion-picture music. This usually can be done effectively through expert orchestration and scoring rather than through melodic and harmonic development. The same melodic statement may serve many moods through a variety of orchestration and treatment.

These and many other matters of technical construction have received long and careful study at the hands of the veterans who have been growing up with movie music for many years. They have had to solve not only the complex problems of fitting the right kind of music to stories but also the earlier difficulties of mechanical reproduction.

The composer of a concert piece may look forward to repeated performances of his work. It is studied and performed by one artist and then another. It receives critical study from many angles. Listeners may study the score and have opportunity for several hearings.

Not so with the music of the movie. It is played once and it is heard once. It must immediately be effective or it has no value. There is no time or opportunity for study and contemplation.

Despite all these limitations, movie music is an important part of American music culture. As it improves in content and technique, so does the taste and appreciation of the American public grow and improve, and in a subtle and unconscious manner that holds promise of true growth and improvement.

6. The role of the radio in our American life has not been a very inspiring one. No better mechanical means of dispersing music and literature and of cultivating taste has ever been devised. Yet see what Dr. Lee DeForest, the so-called "Father of the Radio" because of his inventions which made this device possible, has to say about the present state of radio broadcasting in this country in a letter he sent to the National Association of Broadcasters:

What have you gentlemen done with my child? He was conceived as a potent instrumentality for culture, fine music, the uplifting of America's mass intelligence. You have debased this child, you have sent him out on the streets in rags of ragtime, tatters of jive and boogie-woogie, to collect money from all and sundry for hubba hubba and audio jitterbug.

You have made him a laughing stock of intelligence, surely a stench in the nostrils of the gods of the ionosphere; you have cut time into tiny cubelets, called shorts (more rightly stains), wherewith the occasional fine program is periodically smeared with impudent insistence to buy or try.

The nation may have no soap, but soap opera without end or sense floods each household daily. Murder mysteries rule the waves by night and children are rendered psychopathic by your bedtime stories.

This child of mine has been religiously kept to the average intelligence of thirteen years. Its national intelligence is maintained moronic, as though you and the sponsor believe the majority of listeners have only moron minds. The curse of his commercials has grown consistently more cursed, year by year.

These are pretty bitter words from one whose inventions made possible the modern radio and motion-picture industries and much of electronics!

QUESTIONS FOR DISCUSSION

Draw a good-sized outline map of the United States and show on it where some of the most popular of the songs discussed in this chapter would be heard. What can be done in this respect can be seen by studying the Folklore Map of the United States issued by Hagstrom Company, 20 Vesey Street, New York 7, New York.

Can you think of any reasons why we in this country should have a very rich storehouse of folk music? Have any means been taken to preserve this kind of music for our descendants?

Do you remember any particular moving picture in which the music attracted your attention, either because of its unusual quality or because it was so poor?

How important an influence do you feel the radio to be in spreading music throughout the country?

Add as many examples as you can to the list of various kinds of American music (page 34).

A famous American musician once said that *unfortunately our popular music is full of Twentieth-Century kitsch*. Kitsch is a European slang word for something that is essentially cheap and designed to please poor taste. Do you agree with the musician? If not, why not?

A LIST OF AMERICAN MUSIC

Before examining in any detail the following list of American folk music available for listeners, we may well ask ourselves why it is that this music makes such an appeal to us today. The answer is quite simple: living as we do in the midst of an age of hurry and waste (the Age of Aridity and Agitation, Louis Bromfield calls it), an age far removed from the fundamental simplicity of earlier times, in a world in which "mechanical inventions and mass production have led man to worship the machine while it destroys his own higher capacities and makes a slave of him," we turn quite naturally to anything that gives us a "sense of the peace and confidence and satisfaction that comes of an adjusted and happy relationship of the individual to life and to the universe." These songs, sincerely felt and simply written, do this.

But we must hear them in their native state, without the false trappings and slushy sentimentality affected by so many music interpreters today. So we not only have chosen here some representative examples of American folk songs and dances but have suggested interpretations that are of the proper sort to bring this music to us in its real beauty. The list is a long one, but makes no attempt at being comprehensive or complete. The recordings by the commercial companies — Victor, Columbia, Asch, OK, Decca, Disc, and Keynote — may be ordered from any good record shop. Decca records may also be obtained through American Book Company. Records made in the field by folk singers in their native environment, for the archives of the Library of Congress, are sold directly by the Recording Library, Division of Music, Library of Congress, Washington 25, D. C. Full information and catalogues may be obtained by writing there.

THE MUSIC OF THE AMERICAN INDIAN

Indian Music of the Southwest (coll. by
    Boulton) [2]   V   P 49

THE MUSIC OF THE AMERICAN NEGRO

To show how wide the field of Negro folk music is, even if we exclude the later developments of the blues and jazz, Rudi Blesh has made the following classification of it in his book *Shining Trumpets*. The reader is referred to this excellent book for some fine descriptions of these various types of music.

RELIGIOUS

1. Congregational Preaching with Spontaneous Responses Shouted and Chanted (a spontaneous creative style coming almost directly from the African tribal practices, adapted to American Christian use)

[2] The symbols in the list of records may be interpreted as follows:

A	Asch	H	Hargail	LC	Library of Congress
C	Columbia	K	Keynote	MC	Musicraft
D	Decca	V	Victor	OK	Okeh

71

The Gambling Man   c
The Man of Calvary (Easter Day Service)

LC–AAFS 48

2. Congregational Singing of the Spirituals

I'm Gonna Lift Up a Standard for My King

LC–AAFS 4775

This record contains examples of "holy dancing" as well as congregational singing.

I'm Runnin' for My Life
I Am a Soldier in the Army of My Lord } LC–AAFS 49

3. Spiritual Singing by a Small Group

Jesus Goin' to Make Up My Dyin' Bed   OK

4. Solo Spiritual Singing

Deep River (arr. by Burleigh)
Dere's No Hidin' Place Down Dere (arr. by Brown) } V
Every Time I Feel de Spirit (arr. by Brown)

In these arrangements of the spirituals as sung by such artists as Marian Anderson and Paul Robeson, we get not only cultured singing in the style of the European art song but also conservatory arrangements that destroy to a large extent the real character of the music.

Meet Me in Jerusalem
When I Lay My Burden Down
In New Jerusalem } LC–AAFS 50
Steal Away

Ain't No Grave Can Hold My Body Down
Down on Me } LC–AAFS 47
Certainly, Lord

72

5. Ring-Shout Religious Dance

These are the earliest Afro-American religious dances, showing how strong the African influence still is in American Negro culture.

     Run, Old Jeremiah   LC–AAFS 12

SECULAR

1. Work Songs (devised for such occupations as cotton picking, hoeing, water carrying, chopping sugar cane, railroading, steamboating, etc.)

    Unloading Rails
    Tamping Ties
    Heaving the Lead Line   LC–AAFS 36
    Mississippi Sounding Calls

    Ol' Riley (sung by Lead Belly)   A

    Long Hot Summer Days
    Jumpin' Judy   LC–AAFS 13
    Long John

    Hammer Ring
    I Wonder What's the Matter   LC–AAFS 39

2. Street Vendors' Cries

    The Street Cries of Charleston   SOCIETY FOR THE
      Blackberry, Strawberries   PRESERVATION OF
      Flowers   THE   SPIRITUALS
      Blackberries, Watermelon   NOS. 13, 14
      (Various fish calls)

3. Rural Dances

    Green Corn   MC, A

    Corn Bread Rough   A

4. Play and Game Songs

We're Going Around the Mountain
Old Lady Sittin' in the Dinin' Room
Little Sally Walker
All Around the Maypole
Sissy in the Barn   LC–AAFS 45
Little Rosa Lee
Gwan' Roun', Rabbit
Satisfied

5. Negro Ballads

Stagolee (sung by Jelly Roll Morton)   LC–AAFS

John Henry   LC–AAFS 15

Stew Ball (sung by Lead Belly)
Gray Goose (sung by Lead Belly)   V

WHITE MAN'S SONGS ABOUT THE NEGRO

1. Plantation Songs

Old Black Joe (Stephen Foster)
Uncle Ned (Stephen Foster)   V

2. Negro Minstrel Songs

The Camptown Races (Stephen Foster)
O Lemuel (Stephen Foster)   V

3. Modern Developments of Negro Style

Ol' Man River (Jerome Kern)   D, C, V

THE MUSIC OF THE AMERICAN WHITE MAN

FOLK

1. Anglo-American Ballads

Anglo-American Ballads   LC–ALBUM 7
The Golden Willow Tree

74

The Rambling Boy
The Two Brothers
The Four Marys
The Two Sisters
Lord Thomas and Fair Ellender
Bolakins (Lambkins)
The Three Babes
Sanford Barnes
Claude Allen

Anglo-American Ballads   V
The Gypsy Laddie
Lulle Lullay
The Seven Joys of Mary
The Ballad of Barberry Ellen

2. Ballads of Early America

Early American Ballads   K
Patriotic Diggers
The Greenland Fishery
Ballad of Saratoga
Peter Parker's Song
Unfortunate Miss Bailey
Escape of Old John Webb
Nantucket Lullaby
Ballad of the Tea Party

3. American Ballads and Folk Songs

Ballads and Folk Songs of America   H
He's Gone Away
Old Bangum
Shucker of the Corn
A la puerta del cielo
Wee Cooper of Fife
Sourwood Mountain

American Folksong Ballads and Dances   A
> Good Morning, Captain
> Streets of Glory
> Dead or Alive
> Don't Lie, Buddy
> Cindy
> Who's Gonna Shoe Your Pretty Little Feet

Burl Ives Album   D
> Cockle Shells
> Dublin City
> (Ten other folk songs and ballads)

Hudson River Songs   DISC
> Blue Mountain Lake
> Tom Moore, or The Days of '49
> British Soldier
> Montcalm and Wolfe
> Bonnie Boy o' Biscay, O
> A Trip on the Erie

4. Frontier Songs

Sing Out, Sweet Land Album   D   A–404
> Blue Tail Fly
> Little Mohee
> (Many others)

Ballads from the Dust Bowl Album   DISC
> Pastures of Plenty
> Hard Traveling
> Rambling Blues
> Talking Columbia Blues
> When the Curfew Blows
> My Newfoundland

My Name It Is Sam Small
> (Carl Sandburg Album)   MC

5. Occupational and Work Songs

> Home on the Range ⎫
> O Bury Me on the Lone Prairie ⎭   V

> Away for Rio ⎫
> Blow the Man Down ⎭   V

> Casey Jones ⎫
> Cowboy's Lament ⎭   DISC

> *Cowboy Songs, Volume I* (sung
>   by Bing Crosby)   D
> *Home on the Range*
> *I'm an Old Cowhand*
> (Six other old-time cowboy songs)

6. Play Songs and Dances

> *Play and Dance Songs Album*   A
> *Parlez Vous*
> *Turkey in the Straw*
> *Darling Nelly Gray*
> *Lightfoot Bill*
> *Little Brown Jug*
> *Virginia Reel*

> *LC Album No. 9* (edited by Botkin)   LC
> *Haste to the Wedding, Off She Goes* (jig)
> *Irish Washerwoman*
> *Pigtown Fling*
> *Devil's Dream*
> *Nancy's Fancy*
> *Old Blue Sow*
> *Where'd You Git Yo' Whisky*
> *Pore Little Mary Settin' in the Corner*
> *Sally Goodin*

77

Old Sally Brown
Oh, Fly Around, My Pretty Little Miss
Soldier's Joy
Bile dem Cabbage Down
The Girl I Left Behind Me
Mississippi Sawyer

7. Sentimental Ballads of the Nineteenth Century
   Rocked in the Cradle of the Deep }
   Listen to the Mocking Bird } v

WAR SONGS

Chester (Revolution)
The Star-Spangled Banner (War of 1812)
Battle Hymn of the Republic (War
   between the States)
Songs of the North (War between the
   States)   D A 46
Songs of the South (War between the
   States)   D A 45
On the Banks of the Wabash (Spanish-
   American War)
Over There (World War I)
The Army Air Corps Song (World War II)

MUSIC OF THE THEATER

1. Minstrel Songs
   Silver Threads Among the Gold }
   When You and I Were Young, Maggie } v

2. Songs from Musical Comedies
   O Promise Me (*Robin Hood*, DeKoven)   v

   Ah, Sweet Mystery of Life (*Naughty
      Marietta*, Herbert)   v

78

Indian Love Call (*Rose Marie*, Friml) v

Begin the Béguine (*Jubilee*, Porter) v

FILM MUSIC

See the numerous entries in the 1948 Victor Record Catalog under the heading *Motion Pictures*.

RADIO BROADCASTS

Ballad for Americans (Latouche and
    Robinson) v
On a Note of Triumph (Corwin and
    Herrmann) c

BROADWAY ECHOES

The Sidewalks of New York (1894)
The Glow Worm (1905)
I'm Forever Blowing Bubbles (1919)
Rhapsody in Blue (Gershwin, 1923)
I Left My Heart at the Stage Door Canteen
    (Berlin, 1943)

POPULAR SONGS OF OUR TIMES

One of the most interesting developments in recording has been the preparation, by Decca, of a number of albums each containing the most popular songs of bygone years. So far this collection begins with the year 1926 and continues through 1933. These songs are sung with accompaniments on two pianos, the orchestra, or piano, guitar, and bass drum.

COLLECTIONS OF AMERICAN FOLK SONGS

Tom Scott: *Sing of America*. New York: Thomas Y. Crowell Co.

This book contains thirty-six of the best-known American folk songs.

Margaret Boni, editor: *The Fireside Book of Folk Songs*. New York: Simon & Schuster.

Included in the one hundred forty-seven songs in this collection are a number of good American ones; worth getting for the illustrations alone.

American Folk Music Series. New York: Decca Records, Inc.

The series consists of American folk-music collections of records with "sing along" booklets. It also contains folk dances with booklets illustrating the pattern of the dances.

Folk Song: U. S. A. New York: Duell, Sloan & Pearce, Inc.

The one hundred eleven best American ballads chosen by America's foremost authorities, John A. and Alan Lomax. It contains a fine list of record albums that should be consulted by every lover of Americana.

B. A. Botkin: *A Treasury of American Folklore*. New York: Crown Publishers.

A fine, encyclopedic collection of all kinds of folklore, including a great many songs with their tunes.

John A. and Alan Lomax: *American Ballads and Folk Songs*. New York: The Macmillan Company.

Many of these songs have been taken from the recordings made for the Archive of American Folk Song in the Library of Congress. An excellent collection.

"SING OUT, SWEET LAND"

Reed Smith and Hillton Rufty: *American Anthology of Old World Ballads*. New York: J. Fischer.

Twenty-five of the British ballads used in the United States as folk songs.

Carl Sandburg: *The American Songbag*. New York: Harcourt, Brace & Company, Inc.

One of the best collections, with interesting sidelights by the famous editor. The music is not too well arranged for easy playing.

AFRICAN DRUMMER, sculpture
by Malvina Hoffman

82

O F ALL the manifestations of the popular spirit in American music, the one which occupies the spotlight of attention today in this country as well as throughout the world is jazz. This is natural enough, for this type of music is an essentially American phenomenon, the most distinctly American phenomenon that has yet appeared in the field of music. George Gershwin has put this idea in these words: *Jazz is a powerful source of American music, since it is probably more in the blood and feeling of the American people than any other style of folk music.*

Just what do we mean by jazz? In this country most people think of it as the style or idiom in which our popular and dance music has been written for a good many years past — a sort of popular music dialect that has become understandable in all parts of our country. Although primarily designed for one purpose, the use of what we call jazz is no longer confined to dance halls, ballrooms, or night clubs. It is heard frequently (those who do not particularly care for it think much too frequently) on the radio. It is the staple item of juke-box programs throughout the land. And it is in demand whenever a lively, stimulating, rhythmic sort of music is wanted.

83

As we will see later, there have been a number of distinct developments in the field of jazz — developments, as one writer has well said, that are as bristling with class distinctions as the society pages of our newspapers. It started as a definite type of Negro folk music. It was later taken up by the whites and mixed with all sorts of foreign influences. For a long time all American popular music was called jazz, especially when it was somewhat rough or coarse in style. But now the experts insist that careful distinctions must be made between that kind of jazz which is supposed to maintain its folk origin and that which has been influenced by the commercial inroads of Tin Pan Alley. The devotees of one sort will have nothing to do with those of the other sort of jazz. All this seems very confusing to the intelligent musical listener who, although not a particular addict of this kind of music, realizes that it deserves serious attention as an important factor in the development of American music.

Then, too, there are certain peculiar activities associated with jazz that have little connection with its value as music. The violent likes and dislikes of those who follow the activities of some particular dance band or worship at the feet of some special leader make it seemingly impossible for these people to recognize the musical merits of anyone else. Fortunately this crazy sort of hero worship shows signs of diminishing. The enthusiasts who go scouring the country over for rare jazz records are more interested in collecting rare items than they are in artistic values. But there is no question that we as good Americans should know something of the history of this particular national contribution to the development of music and be aware of its proper place in our national life.

JAZZ BEGINS

Without trying to make too-fine distinctions, jazz may be said to be fundamentally a style of *musical performance*, derived largely from the spontaneous improvisation that is inherent in all folk music. In this case the basis happened to be the Negro and Creole music that had developed in the city of New Orleans around the beginning of the present century. This in turn had developed under a number of influences that were brought to bear upon the music of this fascinating old American city during the years following its settlement by the French in the early part of the eighteenth century. New Orleans, in its long career as a trading and social center, had gathered together in its shining crescent by the Mississippi a cosmopolitan citizenry made up of Frenchmen, Spaniards, Italians, Americans (including the exiled Acadians from Canada), and Negroes. The latter came at first directly from West Africa and then later by way of Haiti and other islands of the Caribbean. It is safe to say that in no other city of the world could such conditions have developed as those which shaped the beginnings of this particular style of American music in New Orleans during the years following the Emancipation. Let us see what some of these conditions were.

First and foremost was the background of African music brought with them to this continent by the Negroes. For centuries before they left that continent music in Africa had been a complex and highly developed art, an art which grew naturally out of the simplest fundamentals of rhythm and melody, perhaps even before European music began its similar development. Basically, of course, like all music everywhere, both African and European music started from a simple kind of dance and song, a kind of music in which the whole primitive

85

community could take part, making it up (*improvising* is the technical term) as occasion demanded. European music, however, became more and more specialized as it developed during the centuries. Composers and compositions and performers became important factors in it, and music became more and more a *fine art*, something that was separated from the activities of ordinary people and pursued by a group of carefully trained professionals.

With the Africans, however, music kept its original concept, that of a creative activity in which everyone was expected to participate. In Africa even today, as evidenced by the account of an American reporter who visited there with the American army during the years of World War II, "everybody is doing it" — dancing and singing, sometimes seriously, often humorously, as a part of their everyday existence (Sidelight 1). This attitude of music being a creative participative action was brought to America by the Negro when he first came here in the sixteenth century. It is one of his greatest gifts to our American civilization, a gift that is especially needed today when we are so apt to think of music as something which comes to us on records or over the radio or in concerts and which has little to do with our own personal lives.

So it was with the idea of music being a natural and spontaneous combination of drumming, singing, and dancing stemming out of the social and religious life of his African past that the Negro came to this continent. He has kept this idea ever since, wherever he has gone or wherever he has settled down. Underlying everything that he does in music is the idea of rhythm and its development. His music is a constant, continuous expression of rhythmic emotion, varied and

86

AFRICAN MUSICIANS OF THE BELGIAN CONGO, as
shown in the Tervueren Museum, Brussels

contrasted in different ways, often with sudden improvised changes, rising through repetition to a complete and exhausting expression. European music, on the other hand, has made use of other devices for its development. Rhythm is only one of the factors, a changeable and flexible feature rather than an underlying principle. Rhythm is combined (as we will see later) in European music with harmony and form to make the familiar musical patterns we know. As one writer has put it: European music, or Western music, is based on structure and balance; African music is one of free, continuous, creative energy. If we learn to understand these differences we will see why these two systems are constructed on entirely different principles and why jazz, which stems back to the African music in spirit and in technique, sounds so strange to ears that have been trained in the European style, and vice versa.

A contemporary account of the African slave trade of 1827–1847 tells of how *during afternoons of serene weather, the men, women, boys and girls were allowed on deck to unite in African melodies, which they always enhance by an extemporaneous tom-tom on the bottom of a tub or tin kettle.* It was thus that African music came to the New World, in the hearts and memories of the black man. As we have already seen, it was the horrible, inhuman institution of slavery that fostered the natural musical instinct of the American Negro. For out of his need to find some sort of beauty in the midst of oppression and suffering, and to create some sort of symbol of a spirit which refused to be conquered by trouble, came the spiritual. And this, together with its secular counterpart, the sinful song (as it was called by the Negroes), directly affected jazz. We have some accounts of the performances of American Negro

music, written years before the idea of modern jazz was even
thought of, which show that these African musical traditions
strongly affected all the music the Negroes performed in this
country as late as the end of the nineteenth century (Sidelight 2). And we know from contemporary accounts that African dancing and ceremonial music was still played in the famous Congo Square of New Orleans in the 1880's.

The very fact that this insistent rhythm of the Negro's
music is so appealing to all of us shows that it fulfills some
universal desire for rhythmic expression. As a popular writer
has said, "Everybody's got rhythm." Watch any group of people as they listen to music that is strongly rhythmic. Uncon-
sciously some begin to move their shoulders or head in time
to the music, or tap their feet, or clap their hands. Without
knowing just why, we have a longing to let the rhythm take
possession of us and work its will. This reaction to rhythm is a
perfectly spontaneous, natural one, and the Negro has never
been inclined to resist the temptation to give in to this over-
whelming urge. That is one reason why his music is so popular.

Because of the fact that dancing, like singing, has always
been a perfectly natural form of expression for the American
Negro, keeping as he has the concept of music possessed by
his African predecessor, when he began to put instrumental
accompaniments to his dancing and singing, these had a
strongly rhythmic character. Without doubt, the chief musical
contribution of the Negro to music is his complete mastery of
rhythmic effects. As one of his own musicians has said,[1] the
Negro loves to embroider and vary whatever basic rhythm is

[1] Dorothy Cole in *Negro's Contribution to Music in America* by R. K. Nelson
and D. J. L. Cole, Service Bureau for Intercultural Education, New York City.

89

set. He will double the time, skip beats, and introduce syncopations in a manner that is quite bewildering to those who do not respond to rhythm as naturally as he does. This accounts for the figures, rhythm, and tempo of Negro dances from the early breakdown, cakewalk, buck and wing, and soft-shoe shuffle to such forms as happen to be in contemporary favor — truckin', swing, and the rest.

Here, then, is the real genesis of jazz. This New Orleans of the end of the nineteenth century is the background out of which came such pre-jazz forms as the early ragtime and the blues. The actual transference of African characteristics into something that resembles modern jazz came through the medium of the street bands which for generations have been an important factor in New Orleans life. Every sort of communal celebration and activity was marked by the use of brass bands and parades — lodge and political meetings, weddings and funerals. The Negro copied the white man in this as he did in so many other things, and the Negro section of the city had its own bands, and mighty good ones they were, we can be sure. They probably started in by playing the white man's standard march tunes. But very quickly they began to transform these into something that had more of a rhythmic, personal character, just as they took the white man's hymns and folk tunes and turned them into the very personal spirituals. Buddy Bolden, the Negro barber of New Orleans who is generally credited with forming the first real jazz band, had an earlier brass band of this type. And there were plenty of other bands, the members of which received a good training in playing this lively Negro band music, even though they could not read a note.

Then someone had the brilliant idea of using these powerful and noisy brass bands for a purpose for which they were really ideal — that of playing dance music for social occasions. They supplanted the smaller string bands which up to that time had always played for Negro dances in New Orleans, bands which had played the more or less standard type of European dance music — French quadrilles, waltzes, Italian classics, and popular Creole tunes. Thus another influence came into jazz, for it is certain that many of the musical elements of these string dance bands flowed over into the march-style used by the street bands. And it is interesting to think that perhaps the first use of jazz (archaic jazz, the historians call it) was in street dancing during the great Mardi Gras Carnival or in some Sunday dancing in one of the parks where such bands as Bolden's often played. Later on, this social dancing to the music of these jazz bands became the rage. Halls were built all over town and in the summer resorts along the Gulf and at Lake Pontchartrain. The bands brought out ragtime in band form and the blues as well. Thus real jazz was born.

Ragtime made its appearance toward the end of the nineteenth century, the first published pieces being for the piano. They were such things as *Harlem Rag, Maple Leaf Rag,* and *Georgia Camp Meeting.* These were syncopated, lively pieces descended from the earlier minstrel-show tunes, the cakewalk, buck and wing, and jig, as well as from the early marches. It was Bolden's famous Ragtime Band of 1893 which first adapted these piano rags to band style. From the contemporary accounts he made a good job of it: *He had the town by storm and when the people heard Bolden, then you couldn't get in the place without you go early.*

The blues probably came into existence shortly after the War between the States. They were the result of carrying over into secular music many of the Negroid tendencies of repeated rhythmic effects, use of syncopation, and love for bemoaning fate. Although the blues were certainly sung long before in the hamlets and towns where wandering singers poured out their troubles to anyone who would listen, they first became known in the Negro cabarets of the cities — Birmingham, Atlanta, New Orleans, St. Louis, and Memphis — in the early 1890's. Originally they were always sung to words which, in the language of a Negro whose name has become closely connected with this form,

bolstered up the hope of the singer. He might be tired, discouraged, his family without enough to eat and with no money to pay the rent. But tonight he will go out and have a good time in an attempt to present to the world an appearance of unconcern, nay even of prosperity. So he sings the blues, adapting the words to an improvised tune.[2]

One of the technical features which distinguished the blues was the use of a more natural scale than the rather artificial one that has been adopted for so much European music. The Negro tends to sing the third and seventh tones of our scale in a way that sounds flat to our ears, accustomed as they are to a different scale. We have come to call these notes *blue notes*, and the natural scale in which they occur a *blues scale*. Moreover, many of the melodies used in the blues do not extend beyond the span of a five-toned (or pentatonic) scale of some sort:

[2] W. C. Handy in *Blues, An Anthology of Jazz Music.*

The Blues Scale   A Pentatonic Scale
often used in Negro music

Another distinguishing feature of the blues is the use, at
least in the earlier blues, of a natural form of verse and music
suggesting a statement and response. Many of these blues were
composed of three short lines, each of which was sung or
played to four measures of music in 4/4 time, the whole
thus making up what was called a *twelve-bar blues*:

> *If I had wings like Noah's dove,*
> *I'd fly up the river to the gal I love,*
> *Fare thee well, O Honey, fare thee well.*
>
> *'Member one morning, 'twas a drizzling rain,*
> *And round my heart I felt an aching pain,*
> *Fare thee well, O Honey, fare thee well.*
>
> *I had a gal, she was long and tall,*
> *She moved her body like a cannon ball,*
> *Fare thee well, O Honey, fare thee well.*
>
> *One of these days, and it won't be long,*
> *You gonna call my name and I'll be gone,*
> *Fare thee well, O Honey, fare thee well.*

There are also plenty of examples of the earlier eight-bar and
the more developed sixteen- and sometimes twenty-bar blues.
Each of these bars or measures is made up of a regularly recurring pattern of heavy and light beats, thus establishing the
fundamental pulse or rhythm of the music:

93

$\frac{4}{4}$ ♩ ♩ ♩ ♩ | ♩ ♩ ♩ ♩ | ♩ ♩ ♩ ♩ |

In music the term *pulse* is used to describe a succession of accents or beats, arranged in groups (the measures or bars) by means of a heavier stress which comes every so often. We feel this pattern strongly in such music as the blues and jazz, for their regularly recurring beats (in slow time in the blues, in faster time in jazz) form the basic structure upon which the other materials (melody and harmony) are arranged. In fact, the pulse of jazz is so prominent a feature of this music as to make it sometimes seem monotonous.

One of the most noticeable things about the blues is that this rhythmic pulse is often changed from where we expect it to where we do not. This shift of basic accent arouses our attention immediately, like everything that is different from what we ordinarily expect it to be. The musicians call this shifting of accent *syncopation,* and composers have realized that its use could greatly increase the listener's attention. It has often been used in European music, either the melody or the rhythm being syncopated. Syncopation came into jazz from ragtime as well as from the blues, and its use is more irregular than in most European classical music. Often both rhythm and melody are syncopated at the same time. The combination of two or more rhythms played simultaneously is called *polyrhythm* and is common to jazz, just as it is to the music of many primitive peoples:

$\frac{4}{4}$ ♩ ♩ ♩ ♩ | ♩ ♩ ♩ ♩ |

A Simple Kind of Syncopation
(Compare this with the fundamental pulse shown above.)

An Example of Polyrhythm

In traditional examples of the blues, we hear only a few basic *harmonies* arranged in a very definite way. The musician defines harmony as the simultaneous sounding together of tones in a group which he calls a *chord*, as opposed to their successive sounding in a tune, or *melody*. Both of these elements of music make use of the same materials of sound: melody gives shape and flow to the musical structure; harmony provides it with body and substance. If, for example, you listen to such a piece as *Mamie's Blues*, which the famous Jelly Roll Morton says was the first blues he ever heard, you will find that only four different chords are used throughout the piece:

These basic note groups, or chords, are used in a regular sequence, or pattern, which gives an unchanging harmony to the blues. The usual sequence of chords in the blues is this:

$$I - I - IV - I - V - I$$

In working out a jazz piece the players use such a chord sequence to accompany the principal melody, a melody that may be a traditional blues tune, a published Tin-Pan-Alley favorite, or a European classic. Sometimes it is improvised on the spot.

Of course, the real blues song varies with the temperament and desires of its singer. It is not written down, but passed

95

along from one singer to another. If we could be present at one of these improvisations of a regular three-line, twelve-measure blues, we would most likely hear the singer hold the last note and word of each line for several beats while deciding what he or she is going to do in the next line. This makes a *break* in the melody, during which some sort of instrumental improvisation on the accompanying instrument or instruments is heard. This give-and-take between the voice and the instruments, the latter filling in while the voice hesitates, is an essential part of the form of the blues. When the blues changed into instrumental jazz, these exchanges took place between the various instruments, and the part that was improvised during the break in the melody came to be known as the *jazz break*.

It was in New Orleans that these fundamental features of the blues came to be incorporated into the instrumental-vocal form we know as jazz. Paul Edward Miller, a well-known writer on jazz, describes it thus:

Perhaps no other city in the country could have provided just the fertile soil for this development that New Orleans did, a city composed of many races, of people accustomed to abandon and freedom in their personal lives; where all sorts of picnics, excursions, street dances, and festivals were a part of everyday living; a town which engendered an atmosphere conducive to easy ways of making money, of which music was the easiest for those who had talent.

The story of the spread of this form over the country will be told in the next chapter. In the meantime, the following outline showing the background of classic jazz may be of some help. It has been compiled from a number of sources:

96

JAZZ BEGINS

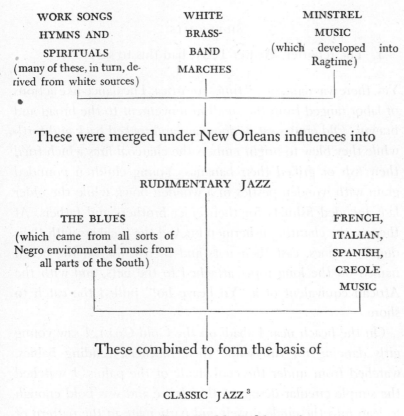

WORK SONGS
HYMNS AND
SPIRITUALS
(many of these, in turn, derived from white sources)

WHITE
BRASS-
BAND
MARCHES

MINSTREL
MUSIC
(which developed into
Ragtime)

These were merged under New Orleans influences into

RUDIMENTARY JAZZ

THE BLUES
(which came from all sorts of
Negro environmental music from
all parts of the South)

FRENCH,
ITALIAN,
SPANISH,
CREOLE
MUSIC

These combined to form the basis of

CLASSIC JAZZ [3]

in the bands of Buddy Bolden, 1893
and the white Papa Laine, 1892–3.

[3] There have been many and varied explanations of the derivation of the word
jazz, none of them very satisfactory. Some Negro musicians attribute it to the
name of a colored musician who, in the early days of the style, "played in a
certain raggy way." Others think it came from the use of the French word
jasser, "to chatter or cackle." Still others think it originated in the African
dialect of the Negroes in their native country.

According to the trumpeter Louis Armstrong, the name means little. He is
quoted as saying in 1934: "There'll probably be new names for this style of
playing, for there have been several names since I remember way back in the
old days in New Orleans, Louisiana, when Hot Music was called 'ragtime'
music. So you see, instead of dying out, it just gets a new name."

SIDELIGHTS

1. The reporter, Walter Terry, had this to say: [4]

Yes, there was dance at all times in Africa. The dance-like actions of labor ranged from the small in movement to the broad and brawny. Old crones sat in doorways and rocked back and forth while they blew to bright embers the charcoal fires which fried their fish or grilled their bananas. Young children pounded grain with wooden pestles in a wooden bowl, while the older lads mended fishnets for their elder brothers and fathers. At the sea, the chanting fishermen bucked the breakers with their dugout canoes, cast their nets and then those on the beach hauled on the long ropes attached to the nets, and with the African equivalent of a "Yo heave ho!" pulled the catch to shore.

On the beach near Labadi on the Gold Coast, I saw young girls dancing for fun while their mothers, tending babies, watched from under the cool shade of the palms. I watched the simple circular design of this dance and was bold enough to leap into the circle myself and participate in the pattern of action, much to the amazement of the Africans. Later, near dusk, I saw a group of women returning from work, their heads piled high with garden produce. An American GI started to conga along the road and in no time at all, the tired women, about twenty of them, had picked up the chant and were having the time of their lives in an African conga line, and none of the baskets fell off the heads! In a village deep in the Belgian Congo, I watched a minstrel play his harp (decorated on one

[4] In the *New York Herald Tribune,* July 28, 1946.

side by a colored print of the Holy Family and on the other with a fetish) and dance a shuffling measure of greeting. And in Accra, I caught a glimpse of a meeting of chiefs, a ceremony distinguished by gorgeous costumes, by an almost choreographed processional to the meeting place and by a ritual of etiquette both dignified and graceful. It is apparent, I think, that in serious dance, in folk dance, in labor and in plain horseplay, the African is an experienced and devoted master of the art of movement.

2. Here are two accounts of performances of American Negro music, both of which show how closely the character of this music which preceded jazz resembled in many respects the more finished product of today. The first, taken from *The Nation* of May 30, 1867, describes the singing of spirituals in a Negro congregation. The second, from *The Century* magazine (1885), tells of a Negro instrumental ensemble that had been heard by the writer that year.

I. But the benches are pushed back to the wall when the formal meeting is over, and old and young, men and women, sprucely dressed young men, grotesquely clad field hands — the women generally with gay handkerchiefs twisted about their heads and with short skirts — boys with tattered shirts and men's trousers, young girls barefooted, all stand up in the middle of the floor, and when the "sperichil" is struck up begin first walking and by and by shuffling around, one after the other, in a ring. The foot is hardly taken from the floor, and the progression is mainly due to a jerking, hitching motion which agitates the entire shouter and soon brings out streams of perspiration. Sometimes they dance silently; sometimes, as

99

they shuffle they sing the chorus of the spiritual, and sometimes the song itself is also sung by the dancers. But more frequently a band, composed of some of the best singers and of tired shouters, stand at the side of the room to "base" the others, singing the body of the song and clapping their hands together or on the knees. Song and dance are alike extremely energetic, and often, when the shout lasts into the middle of the night, the monotonous thud, thud of the feet prevents sleep within a half mile of the praise-house.

II. The drums were very long, hollowed, often from a single piece of wood, open at one end having a sheep or goat skin stretched across the other. One was large, the other much smaller. The tight skin heads were not held up to be struck; the drums were laid along on the turf and the drummers bestrode them, and beat them on the head madly with fingers, fists, and feet, with slow vehemence on the great drum and rapidly on the small one.

Sometimes an extra performer sat on the ground behind the larger drum, at its open end, and beat upon the wooden sides of it with two sticks. One important instrument was a gourd partly filled with pebbles or grains of corn, flourished violently at the end of a stout staff with one hand and beaten upon the palm of the other.

Other performers rang triangles, and others twanged from jew's harps an astonishing amount of sound! Another instrument was the jawbone of some ox, horse, or mule, and a key rattled rhythmically along its weather-beaten teeth. At times, the drums were reinforced by one or more empty barrels or casks beaten on the head with the shank bones of cattle.

But the grand instrument at last, the first violin, as one might say, was the banjo. It had but four strings, not six ... and for the true African dance, a dance not so much of legs and feet as of the upper half of the body, there was wanted the dark inspiration of African drums and thump and strum of the banjo.

And then there was that long-drawn cry of tremendous volume, richness, and resound to which no instrument within their reach could make the faintest approach. All the instruments silent while it rises and swells with mighty energy and dies away distinctly, "Yea-a-a-a!" Then the crash of savage drums, horns, and rattles.

To all this there was sometimes added a Pan's pipe of but three reeds, made from single joints of the common brake cane. Such was the full band! All the values of contrast that discord can furnish must have been present, with whatever there is of ecstasy in maddening repetition, for of this the African can never have too much.

MUSIC TO LISTEN TO

Fortunately there are many fine recordings which illustrate in detail the points made in this chapter. They are listed on the following pages. The listener should obtain as many of these as he possibly can in order to develop a real understanding of the backgrounds of modern jazz.[5]

---

[5] The symbols in the list of records may be interpreted as follows:

c	Columbia	CAP	Capitol
G	General	LC	Library of Congress
		V	Victor

CONTEMPORARY AMERICAN MUSIC

MODERN AFRICAN MUSIC

Modern African Songs and Dances

These records, made by the Denis-Roosevelt Expedition to the Belgian Congo, are dubbed from their excellent film *Dark Rapture,* a picture which should be seen by everyone interested in primitive African music and life. It will be interesting to compare these African songs and dances with the singing and playing of Negro congregations in Mississippi of

I'm Gonna Lift Up a Standard for My King	LC–AFFS 4775
I'm Runnin' for My Life	LC–AAFS 49

and the close connection between African tradition and American Negro practice described in the text will be clear.

SPIRITUALS

An Album of Spirituals	DISC
Blind Old Barrabas	
Jesus, I Love You	
I Love Traveling	
Jonah	
Motherless Child	
Charity	

NEGRO FOLK SONGS

Rock Island Line (sung by Lead Belly)	CAP
Gray Goose (sung by Lead Belly)	V

BAND MARCH-INTO-JAZZ

High Society	CAP
If I Ever Cease to Love	CIRCLE

Original Rags (played by Jelly Roll Morton)   G
Eagle Rock Rag (played by Lead Belly)   CAP

BLUES

See See Rider (verse with
    12-bar blues, sung by   UNITED HOT CLUBS
    Ma Rainey)   OF AMERICA
Careless Love (sung by Bessie Smith with
    Louis Armstrong)   C
Winin' Boy Blues (played and sung by Jelly
    Roll Morton)   G
Mamie's Blues (played and sung by Jelly Roll
    Morton)   G
Trouble in Mind (sung by Chippie Hill)   CIRCLE

These illustrations include examples of all the great blues singers.

MISCELLANEOUS

King Porter Stomp   G
Barney's Bounce   CAP
Tailgate Ramble   CAP

BLUES-INTO-JAZZ

I Hate to Leave You Now   G

(This record includes an imitation of the trumpet by the voice, breaks, etc.)

JAZZ KINGS ON THE LOOSE

The manifestation of popular spirit in American music which occupies the spotlight of attention throughout the world is jazz.

BEFORE outlining briefly the story of the spread of the jazz movement over the whole country, it will be well to summarize some of its outstanding characteristics. It must be remembered that we are dealing here entirely with jazz as it developed in New Orleans, what the connoisseurs call *hot jazz*. Its characteristics are:

1. the use of scales which employ and emphasize certain blue notes
2. the employment of a definite form, comprising a certain number of bars or measures
3. a strong rhythmic background in which the emphasis is constantly shifted by means of syncopation
4. a set of chords based on a regular, simple sequence which is understood by all the players
5. the use of breaks.

The real Negro players who established the instrumental-vocal form we call jazz improvised simultaneously upon a basic melody that was played by one or another instrument. The players always kept the same fundamental rhythmic beat and always followed the underlying chordal pattern of the music. Thus they were able to attain an artistic harmonious sort of improvisation in the small jazz-band group that would have been impossible in a more complex kind of music or with a larger band of players. This is what is meant by collective improvisation, recognized as another of the essential features of jazz. When a playing group numbers more than eight members, it means that some sort of music score must be written out. Thus the larger the band, the more it assumes the character of European symphonic music and loses its real improvisational character as jazz.

Another important characteristic of this early jazz was the *timbre*, or tone-color, of the instruments played by the different members of the band. The Afro-American music from which jazz developed — the blues, spiritual, and ragtime — has a peculiarly vital quality about it, to attain which the singer often uses a tone quality that is rough and harsh. So it is little wonder that in adopting the vocal blues to performance on instruments, the Negroes gave jazz this same peculiar tone quality suggesting strong emotion. Trumpets are forced and overblown until their tone is harsh and glittering; trombones sound hard and brittle; instruments are made to sound like voices; and voices, by "scat-singing," like instruments; the piano is made to sound as fantastic and monotonous as possible, oftentimes with a reiterated boogie-woogie bass. These characteristics, together with the absence of the stringed instruments (violin, viola, and cello), which create such definite color for the symphony, give the jazz band its peculiar timbre.

So, if we are to complete the list of hot-jazz characteristics with which we began this chapter, it will be necessary to add these two further items:

6. the employment of a type of improvisation that allows freedom of individual expression without too much incoherence of effect

7. the use of a characteristically rough, rather strident tone-color by the players.

We have already mentioned Bolden's Ragtime Band as the original of all jazz bands. Organized and dominated by a Negro bandleader-publisher-editor-cornetist, this band came to typify in time almost everything that real jazz means today, nearly sixty years after its founding. In the words of a hot-jazz enthusiast, this band, varying from five to seven pieces,[1] "established the classic repertoire, expanded the archaic technical style, and formulated the chief class instrumentations," the only change in which came about through the later addition of a piano. Other similar bands quickly sprang up throughout New Orleans, all of them keeping the same general instrumentation. The piano player who joined the ranks was recruited from the bars and gambling dens which thrived in the vicinity of North Basin Street in this rich, pleasure-loving city of the turn of the century.

This Negro style of jazz spread from New Orleans by means of the showboats which were retired packet boats, their careers as carriers of freight and passengers over because of the encroachment of the railroads, and which were fitted up as pleasure-excursion steamers. These showboats plied up and down the rivers, furnishing entertainment for local customers from river towns and villages. In this showboat entertainment there was much jazz, played by Negro bands; and gradually, by these and various other means, this new style of playing was

---

[1] Cornet, one or two clarinets, trombone, guitar, bass, and drums.

From The Albert Davis Collection

A SHOW BOAT AUDIENCE, as shown in the moving picture
Show Boat

carried far. afield. A good Negro band, the Original Creoles, traveled to California and later to Chicago. And then there followed a general migration of jazz players from the South, and Chicago became the center of the development of the style at the end of World War I.

In the meantime, some of the white players of New Orleans initiated what has come to be known as the Dixieland style, in frank imitation of the more spontaneous and rhythmic Negro playing of jazz.[2] The best-known of these early white bands was that of Jack Laine; and this Dixieland style of playing in its several variants was carried northward

[2] See Blesh: *Shining Trumpets*, p. 207 for an interesting and accurate account of the differences between Negro and white styles in jazz playing.

and first developed in Chicago and later in New York, which city became in turn the heart of jazzland. The progress of this style of playing in this country was thus from the South to the Middle West and then to the East. White and Negro bands, as well as mixed organizations, sprang up all over the country, the name-bands centering in the big cities, where the fast tempo of living, crowded conditions, and the tremendous struggle for existence gave a real vogue to their pounding rhythms and swinging melodies.

In the meantime, in contrast to this hot jazz, there developed from the same beginnings what is known to the trade as *sweet jazz*, a type which does not emphasize either the elements of improvisation or the extreme development of syncopation and dissonance. On the other hand, it tends toward the smoothness and melodiousness that are usually associated with musical interpretations in the mind of the common man. This, through the frantic and hectic efforts of certain bandsmen and their arrangers, became popular as commercial dance music. For the purist, this kind of jazz lacks the punch, vitality, and strong emotional expression that attracts them so strongly to hot jazz.

Another development that is strongly denounced by the hot-jazz addicts is *symphonic jazz*, music written for the theater and concert hall, and a compromise, they feel, between real jazz and the prejudices and tastes of the public. This kind of interpretation has been affected by the symphonic style of such standard composers as Debussy and Ravel. And it received its initial impetus by a famous concert given by Paul Whiteman and his band in New York in 1923, at which time Gershwin's *Rhapsody in Blue* received its first performance. Around 1926

109

Courtesy of The New York Times

THE DIFFERENCE BETWEEN SWING AND SWEET
JAZZ, as shown by Roy Doty's drawing

this style of jazz was so popular as to give Whiteman a lead over Beethoven in a poll taken in a western American university to determine the identity of the world's greatest musician. In spite of the compositions of Gershwin and the excellent arrangements of Grofé and Waring, symphonic jazz later lost much of its popularity in favor of a new development — swing.

Swing may be roughly defined as a commercial exploitation of a compromise between improvised hot jazz and the arrangements of sweet jazz. In the words of one writer it sprang from hot jazz but was attended with so much commercial exploitation that it became self-conscious from glamour. It received its greatest impetus through huge name-bands, the first one of which was formed around the famous clarinet of Benny Goodman in 1935. These big bands, which some time later seem to have fallen apart of their own weight, are in strong distinction to the small groups which had started the hot style. But the best of them were supposed to have preserved in their arrangements something of the zip and sparkle that is so much admired in the hot-jazz groups. Whether or not this is true is, of course, a matter of taste.

A further extension of the earlier diagram will make these jazz developments clear:

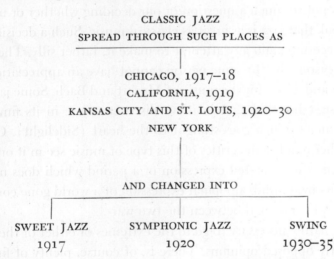

CLASSIC JAZZ
SPREAD THROUGH SUCH PLACES AS

CHICAGO, 1917–18
CALIFORNIA, 1919
KANSAS CITY AND ST. LOUIS, 1920–30
NEW YORK

AND CHANGED INTO

| SWEET JAZZ | SYMPHONIC JAZZ | SWING |
| 1917 | 1920 | 1930–35 |

The changes in jazz during the years of World War II were brought about by two divergent influences: (1) the desire for an increasing complexity on the part of both players and listeners, and an accent on skill and expertness of musicianship; (2) a

111

definite reaction, in turn, on the part of many jazz fans for a return to the primitiveness and forcefulness of the original New Orleans style and away from the commercialism that has been so marked a feature of this music since it moved out of the city that gave it birth. This latter influence is a good one; it has been aided by the increase in the number of records which show the particular advantage of the hot style in comparison with those styles which have been introduced under the influence of commercialism. The appreciation of the structure and meaning of jazz is growing, and listeners of all kinds are coming to realize that it has been an important factor in the development of American life. Just how important, each person has to decide for himself.

It is not so much a question of our deciding whether or not we think that jazz is as great as classical music. Such a decision is unnecessary; and any attempt to make it, rather silly. There is no reason why the same person cannot have an appreciation of jazz and a love for the music of Mozart and Bach. Some jazz enthusiast has said that in it we discover music in its finest state, music which goes straight to the heart (Sidelight). On the other hand, some critics of this type of music see in it only a violently exaggerated expression of a period which does not know its own mind, a popular expression of a world gone completely pleasure-mad between the two wars.

It is hardly necessary to go to the extremes of either of these violently opposed opinions. There is, of course, plenty of fine music other than jazz which goes straight to our hearts; and what is more to the point, it stays there. And we could easily point out to the jazz critic mentioned above that there have been plenty of other violently exaggerated expressions to come

Pix, Inc. — E. Colman

GENE KRUPA, famous band leader and drummer

out of the period between the two great wars. None, however, has given so much genuine pleasure to so many people as has jazz.

It is important, therefore, to realize that this music has been a strong social force, for it has given a large number of people a free and spontaneous means of expressing themselves through something they enjoy. As one of its admirers has well said, it has brought dancing back to music, where it belongs, and music back to those who make it and who dance it. It is, after all, a functional music with no aristocratic pretensions —

a music of, by, and for the people. And so it has helped dissipate some of the pretentious, rather "stuffed-shirt" attitude toward art which holds that it is something to be cultivated rather than enjoyed as part of life.

Most musicians would probably agree that the best jazz is that in which there is a real balance between its African inheritance and its European development. This balance should not lose the inexorable drive and momentum and flexible rhythm of its African origin in favor of an overindulgence in European harmonic developments and tricky instrumental coloring. If properly understood, real jazz seems a modern art, one that is closely allied to the noisy, rapidly moving, adventurous, highly mechanistic age in which we live. As a demonstration of American spirit, this, the only music developed in this country to be popularly adopted by the whole world, deserves serious attention. Whether we like it or not, or whether we feel that it has important significance as art, is quite another matter.

SIDELIGHT

The following rather characteristic comment on the nature of jazz from one of its rabid exponents shows why so much of the propaganda put out by the jazz intelligentsia is not very impressive to the "long-haired musician":

Written music is like handcuffs; and so is the pendulum in white-tie-and-tails up in the conductor's stand. Symphony means slavery in any jazzman's dictionary. Jazz and freedom are synonymous.... One-hundred-men-with-a-fuehrer, a music battalion hypnotized by a director's baton — that's no kind of a *set-up for a man's inspired soul to shake loose and jump out of his instrument in a flood of carefree, truth-speaking, right-from-the-heart music.*[3]

Mezz Mezzrow, according to his own description, was a youngster who, after World War I, devoted his life to trying to duplicate the qualities of the Negro New Orleans jazz as it came up from New Orleans to Chicago. Now he feels that he has solved the problem of how to produce pure, classical jazz: he has found the New Orleans secret.

QUESTIONS FOR DISCUSSION

Bring to class some records of your own choice to illustrate the various styles described in this chapter.

Define the following terms:

Style	Jam Session	Torch Song
Idiom	Obbligato	Corn
Jive	Jitterbug	Bebop

What makes a good piece of music last?

What is a jazz classic?

Which critic's viewpoint as to the importance of jazz seems to you most reasonable?

How typically American can a type of music such as jazz be, having originated in the Negro dance bands of New Orleans and developed largely by the metropolitan influences of great cities such as Chicago and New York?

An author has said that "jazz is the only music that has received recognition outside our own country as representing

[3] Mezzrow and Wolfe: *Really the Blues.* New York: Random House.

fundamental virtues and weaknesses of our American characteristics." Can you show how jazz does this?

Some time ago the members of a class in an American school were asked to "describe good music." The answers received included the following descriptions. Discuss them in the light of your own opinions on the subject:

a. Good music does not always have to be classical. *Rhapsody in Blue* by Gershwin is definitely good music. Even boogie-woogie is considered good by some.

b. Good music must be good enough to dance to — not too "jivey."

c. Music which the majority of people enjoy is good music.

d. Good music appeals to people and creates pleasure.

e. Music is good if it is appropriate and suited for the purpose which the composer intended.

f. Good music is strictly "out of this world."

g. Good music is what the critics praise.

h. Music must be good if it appeals to large masses of people.

i. Good music is not just entertaining but also educational — gets you thinking.

j. Music is good when it lives for a long period of time.

k. Good music has a purpose.

l. Good music is music which stirs your emotions and moves your feet.

MODERN BOOKS ON JAZZ

Since jazz is such a talked-about kind of music, a few books on it written by experts may be of interest. The authors of the books listed are enthusiastic on the subject, sometimes too much so for the good of their writing:

David Ewen: *Men of Popular Music*. New York: Ziff-Davis
  Publishing Company.

The evolution of American popular music during the last forty
years as told in the careers of fourteen composers and performers of jazz music.

Charles DeLauney: *Hot Discography*. New York: Commodore
  Record Company. 1940 edition.

A reworking and translation of a famous list of recordings published originally in France in 1938, of value especially to those
who go in for collecting jazz records.

Robert Goffin: *Jazz from the Congo to the Metropolitan*. New
  York: Doubleday & Company, Inc.

Not to be taken too seriously because of the overpartisan point
of view. Gives an interesting account of the history of this form
of music.

Paul Miller, editor: *Esquire's Jazz Book*. New York: Smith &
  Durrell, Inc.

These yearly collections are chosen from articles on jazz, its history, esthetics, and personalities, published in the well-known
magazine *Esquire*. Like so many of those who talk and write
about this subject, these writers seem to suffer from an unnecessary inferiority complex and so use overflashy paragraphs
in attempting to convey their enthusiasm and display a chip-
on-shoulder attitude toward those who are not as devoted to
the form as they are. But these collections contain good *Musicians' Bio-discographies*.

Charles Edward Smith: *The Jazz Record Book*. New York: Smith & Durrell, Inc.

Combines a history of jazz and jazz orchestras with a reference guide to the best recordings available.

Winthrop Sargeant: *Jazz, Hot and Hybrid*. New York: E. P. Dutton & Co., Inc.

One of the best all-around books on the subject, written by an impartial observer who knows well all kinds of music. Careful and authoritative.

Rudi Blesh: *Shining Trumpets*. New York: Alfred A. Knopf.

This is an enthusiast's book, written from a biased point of view. Yet it is one of the few which can be read with interest and understanding of the whole subject. Blesh writes as one who is thoroughly familiar with all kinds of music, and his viewpoint is understandable and well supported by evidence. We acknowledge with gratitude his fine list of recordings, from which suggestions have been taken for these two chapters.

Hoagy Carmichael: *The Stardust Road*. New York: Rinehart & Co., Inc.

The simple and eloquent story of a group of Midwesterners and their responses to jungle beat and plantation chant. It makes you aware of what jazz was to them: a glow of tonal perfection tinged with exaltation. It tells why they were ready to dedicate themselves to its realization, even through starving and defeat.

118

Rosenthal and Zachary, editors: *Jazzways*. New York: Greenberg.

A picture book of jazz and its people; some excellent photographs and short articles by experts.

MUSIC TO LISTEN TO

The development of jazz has been more or less contemporary with the gradual perfection of the process of recording music. Hence, although some of the earlier New Orleans pioneers were not recorded, there does exist in one form or another a particularly rich record of the development of the different jazz styles. Without pretending that this list is complete or authoritative, we give it here as a convenient reference for those who would learn to hear as well as read about jazz.

HOT JAZZ

NEW ORLEANS STYLE

Lulu's Mood (trio for clarinet, piano, drums) [4] CAP

This record is a modern rendering by an old-style jazz group of Negro veterans who worked in New Orleans three decades ago. It is a slow, instrumental blues, typical of its Tenderloin origin and a far, far cry from the modern style.

Sidewalk Blues (played by Jelly Roll Morton's
Red Hot Peppers)   V
Doctor Jazz (played by Jelly Roll Morton's
Red Hot Peppers)   BL

Here are two records often quoted to illustrate the classic New Orleans style. In the first there is an interesting section

---

[4] The symbols in the list of records may be interpreted as follows:
  c Columbia v Victor BL Bluebird CAP Capitol D Decca

done in the lush style of sweet jazz, as if the famous New Orleans pianist-composer-bandleader would contrast the Chicago style with the "beautiful, moving, flexible dissonance of hot jazz," as one of his admirers puts it. "The contrast," he goes on to say, "is breath-taking and utterly convincing."

The second record illustrates most of the devices used in classical jazz to give variety and secure contrast. The solo episodes (breaks) are especially numerous and effective. The hot-jazz enthusiasts feel that here Morton shows his greatness by expressing the whole meaning and possibilities of jazz.

DIXIELAND STYLE

At the Jazz Band Ball CAP

This is a modern recording in the manner of the Original Dixieland Band and composed by two members of that famous organization. This is characteristic of the period when jazz was moving up the Mississippi to St. Louis, Chicago, and then to New York.

HYBRID JAZZ

CHICAGO STYLE

Deed I Do (played by Jack Teagarden's Chicagoans) CAP

Here is the kind of jazz the Chicago bands played in an attempt to emulate the New Orleans players who came up the river to invade their city in the 1920's.

THE INFLUENCE OF WHITEMAN

Wang Wang Blues (played by Paul Whiteman's Orchestra) CAP

120

"JAZZ, HOT AND HYBRID"

This is a modern recording, by veterans of Whiteman's original band, of "arranged" music as developed by Whiteman and his followers. It is supposed to be the first song ever recorded by the famous bandleader. His more characteristic style is shown in the big-band treatment of

San (played by Paul Whiteman's Orchestra)   CAP

THE INFLUENCE OF ELLINGTON

Mood Indigo (played by Sonny Greer
    and the Duke's Men)   CAP
The Mooche (played by Sonny Greer
    and the Duke's Men)   CAP

These two classic compositions by Ellington, played by men most of whom knew the Ellington style and formulas, prove, according to Ellingtonians, that "time has proved the Duke's influence on jazz has been and still is more far-reaching than Whiteman's and the Chicagoans'. For the Negro of New York had just about the same thing to say about jazz as his cousin in the South." Many would not agree with such a statement and feel that Ellington lost all contact with the African origin of jazz and brought his music thoroughly under the European tradition.

SWING

According to the proponents of this almost hysterical development which swept Benny Goodman and other top-money leaders into popularity in 1935 and 1936, swing is actually jazz with New Orleans roots. "Musicians didn't really care what the public called their product so long as it was a good product." (And, we might well add, so long as it brought in good money!) Others are not so sure. Blesh calls swing an "abandonment of the truly Negroid elements of jazz in favor of white elements more intelligible and acceptable to white society." Whatever it is, here is a good example:

Riffamarole (played by Dave Baxter's International Jazzmen) CAP

BENNY GOODMAN'S CASE

An interesting comparison showing what has happened to Goodman in ten years can be made by listening to

Let's Dance V
Benny Rides Again CAP

The first album was recorded in 1935–1937, when Goodman was not yet the financially secure "King of Swing." The second album was recorded after Goodman had become the capitalist of 1945–1947. According to one of his enthusiasts, these examples "strongly support the theory that the Goodman of 1935–1937 really played good jazz, while the later Capitol-ist just doesn't have the stuff of which jazz is made — no matter what the reason."

SYMPHONIC JAZZ

Rhapsody in Blue (played by Paul Whiteman's Orchestra) D

No matter how much we may like this music, we have to admit that it is not jazz at all; it is simply an artificial and sophisticated arrangement of some jazz characteristics. And yet *Rhapsody in Blue* remains the most popular of all Gershwin's contributions to the symphonic style, perhaps because of its meaningful attempt to combine singable tunes with "proper" structure.

"JAZZ, HOT AND HYBRID"

Lady, Be Good (played by Billy Butterfield's
    Orchestra)   CAP
Love for Sale (played by Henry Carter's Or-
    chestra)   CAP

The big-band orchestras are far cries from the early jazz style,
for they make use of elaborate composed tunes by popular
Broadway composers, such as Cole Porter and George Gershwin, and they use all sorts of complicated instrumental effects,
achieved by well-trained and carefully polished musicians.

THE USE OF JAZZ IN SERIOUS MUSIC

Gershwin: *Concerto in F*   D, C
Milhaud: *La Création du Monde*   C
Copland: *Music for the Theatre*   V
Stravinsky: *L'Histoire du Soldat*   C

One well-known critic feels that this last piece shows the
whole technique of jazz, "particularly that of percussion, in the
service of a genuine intention of composing which reveals, as
it were, the hidden meaning of jazz itself." Whatever this may
mean!

EL JALEO, a Spanish dance as painted by one of America's
greatest artists, John Singer Sargent

CHAPTER VI. *POPULAR MUSIC IN THE AMERICAS SOUTH OF US*

ONE hot summer afternoon not so long ago the thousands of travelers who pass every day through the Pennsylvania Station in New York City were startled to hear the lively strains of some good Latin-American dance music echoing through the wide spaces of this great terminal. The sound of *rumbas, zambas,* and *guaraches* might have been familiar to many of these people if they had heard them in dance halls or night clubs, but it seemed rather bizarre, to say the least, to listen to them in a metropolitan railway station.

And yet the Pennsylvania Railroad did a very natural thing in providing Latin-American popular music for the inauguration of a new train service between New York and Mexico City. We are becoming more and more conscious of the fact that those of us who live in the United States are not the only Americans in the Western Hemisphere. And we are beginning to see that the more opportunities we have of traveling through these other American countries and learning something about their people and their customs, their history, and their cultural backgrounds the better neighbors we can all be in the critical years that lie ahead of us. There is no better way of learning to know the Mexicans, Guatemaltecans, Colombians, Brazilians, and Argentineans than through their music. And, as has been shown time and time again in the history of the development of music, it is the popular music of countries that is best known beyond their borders. This Latin-American dance music, even in the diluted and commercialized form which we hear in this country, is so different from our own that its sources will be well worth some investigation.

Most of us think of American civilization as beginning in the latter part of the fifteenth century, when the intrepid explorers who sailed under the flags of Spain, Portugal, France, and England discovered the American continent and staked out claims to large shares of land in the name of their respective sovereigns. Actually, however, there were Americans here long before the coming of the Europeans. These native inhabitants probably crossed to this continent many thousands of years ago from Asia, coming on the frozen ice or a land bridge which then may have connected Alaska with Siberia. During succeeding centuries, other groups may have come in canoes that traveled along the coast or drifted in with the ocean currents from Asia. In the North, where the cold climate prevented any great cultural development, these Asiatic natives have remained in much the same stage of culture as their ancestors were when they first landed on the American continent. They constitute our present-day Eskimos and Indians. In Central and South America, however, the descendants of the original settlers, favored by better climate and richer land, had developed great agricultural civilizations as early as a century before Christ.

126

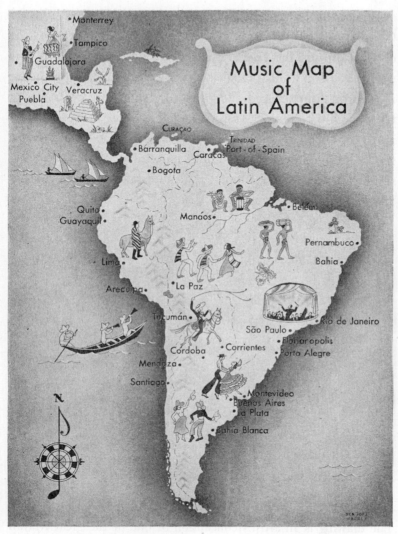

Music Map
of
Latin America

Monterrey
Tampico
Guadalajara
Mexico City Veracruz
Puebla

Curaçao
Barranquilla
Caracas
Bogotá

TRINIDAD
Port-of-Spain

Quito
Guayaquil

Manáos

Belém

Pernambuco
Bahia

Lima

La Paz

Arequipa

Tucumán

São Paulo
Corrientes

Rio de Janeiro
Florianopolis
Porta Alegre

Córdoba
Mendoza
Santiago

Montevideo
Buenos Aires
La Plata
Bahia Blanca

N

In drawing this music map the artist has tried to depict, in the
proper places on the map, something of the characteristics of the
different songs and dances. See the list on pages 145–148.

127

It may be that some new influx of people from cultured China came to these shores (Sidelight 1); or perhaps this civilization was the result of new local developments. Whatever the reason, rich and cultured civilizations came into being in Central America and along the coasts of Peru at about the time of Christ. The Mayas, who lived in what is now Mexico and the Yucatán peninsula, numbered some twenty million souls and lived in large, well-built cities. They had a phonetic system of writing, possessed a profound knowledge of mathe-

Courtesy of the Brooklyn Museum

TIKAL, GUATEMALA, a drawing by Louis Kurtz

The drawing is an artist's conception of one of the great Mayan cities in the northern part of what is now Guatemala, reconstructed from modern excavations. These great cities, with their magnificent sculptured stone palaces, temples, and public buildings, represent one of the world's greatest civilizations, flourishing before the seventh century, A.D.

matics and astronomy, and were deeply concerned with the fundamental questions of the nature of God and man. These people of Central America were untiring workers and patient craftsmen, as well as skilled decorators and builders. The design of their buildings was bold and massive; and they have left behind them, from Yucatán to Arizona and Colorado, ruins so stupendous that even modern builders regard them with awe.

Later on, the Aztecs conquered these earlier people and, like the Romans in Europe before them, built a civilization on the ruins of an earlier one. They set up their capital at Mexico City and dated their rule from the first king in A.D. 1370. They, too, were fanatically religious, and their gorgeous ceremonies and magnificent rituals made extensive use of music (Sidelight 2).

In South America, the pre-Columbian civilization centered in the Incan city of Cuzco, situated high in the Peruvian mountains at an elevation of eleven thousand feet. From this great and beautiful capital paths were built through the mountain passes and carried over great chasms to unite the empire of the Incas, at that time stretching from modern Colombia to the Argentine.

It was in the early years of the sixteenth century that the Europeans came. Under the leadership of the Spanish *conquistadores* (Hernando Cortes, who conquered Mexico in 1519, and Francisco Pizarro, who conquered Peru in 1535) ruthless alien conquerors subdued the natives. They destroyed the impressive civilizations, robbed the lands of gold, silver, and precious stones, and massacred the people. All Europe became excited and envious of the report brought back

AZTEC WARRIORS, a mural by José C. Orozco

These militaristic representatives of the proud Aztecs carry
banners of silver and feathers. Tribal emblems, the eagle
and tiger, are also seen in this mural.

by these devastators, and large numbers of expeditions were
sent out to discover and exploit the New World. Thus sadly
ended the great and colorful chapter of pre-Columbian Ameri-

CUZCO, PERU, a woodcut by Camilo Blas

can history, a chapter which certainly does little credit to the white man.

In spite of the fact that scholars from time to time discover hitherto-unknown Mayan and Aztec ruins, the mechanical and architectural perfection of which are hardly equaled anywhere else in the world, the most impressive surviving records of these great early American civilizations are to be found in the vocal

Courtesy of American Museum of Natural History, New York

MACCHU-PICCHU, PERU, the remains of a great Incan stronghold

and instrumental music which they left behind them. This music is still played and sung by the Indians of Central and South America, lineal descendants of the people who flourished in these countries long before the Europeans came. Few who have not been fortunate enough to visit these regions can realize what a great proportion of the modern population of the Latin-American countries is Indian. Some seventeen million Indians live there today, all of them taking an essential and vital part in the life of the countries in which they were born.

So we find a great stream of Indian music reaching from the Rio Grande on the north to Tierra del Fuego on the south, a stream which stretches along the whole western coast of Central and South America, reaching out into the east along the Amazon and touching many other parts of the continent. This

Courtesy of American Museum of Natural History, New York

SNAKE TEMPLE at Macchu-Picchu, Peru

is music, as one historian has pointed out, that speaks of great civilizations, tells of magnificent festivals and stately rituals, shows how the Mayas, the Aztecs, and the Incas lived, worshiped, and died. Because the Indian way of life in the lonely Mexican hinterland and the Andean highlands has changed very little since pre-Columbian times, there has been but little European influence affecting their music. And experts agree that it is among these Indians that we find the purest examples of music that has kept its native character throughout the centuries. Here again it is the art which has survived through the centuries that tells us more about the life of bygone generations than all the more tangible relics they happen to have left behind.

This music, as Irma Labastille has pointed out in her study of it, speaks of religions deeply felt, of ancient gods awed and

133

revered; it recalls great dance ceremonies and martial enter-
prises, victories won and high social occasions. Or it echoes in
our ears the gentle, plaintive melodies of loves that have long
been lost. Here is a musical tradition that was so strong, so
firmly rooted that the European conquerors could not and did
not combat it or overcome it. It has remained, passed on from
father to son, from generation to generation, is expressed still
today in the tonalities of old, in the same Indian tongues, with
the same instruments, drums and rattles, rasps and shell trumpets, flutes and panpipes.

A prominent Mexican composer, Carlos Chávez, after considerable study has written a piece of music which he thinks
gives an idea of what this early American music sounded like.
He has written a piece for large orchestra to which he has
given the rather jaw-breaking title *Xochipili-Macuilxochitl*.[1]
In it are woven the sounds and melodies which the old Aztec
instruments, now carefully preserved in Mexican museums,
could produce. These possibilities have been developed in the
light of what Chávez knows about the general culture of these
early peoples — the architecture, literature, and sculpture
which they left behind them. Weird-sounding as this music is,
it gives a sort of general impression of what this ancient American music may have sounded like.

The best way of learning something about the early music
of the American Indian, however, is by hearing some of the
traditional music that has survived through successive generations of his descendants. Authentic traces of this music are to be

[1] This is not as difficult to pronounce as it seems; its very sound, with the x
sounding like s, and the i and e made long, seems to suggest the flavor of the
old Indian culture: sō-khē-pē-lē-mah-kwēl-sō-khē'tlc.

found in the songs and dances still used by the Indians of Peru, Bolivia, Argentina, Paraguay, and Equador. Such melancholy songs as the *yaravi* ("lamentation" in the language of the Incas)

NATIVE FLUTE PLAYER, a painting by Julia Code-
sido, Peru

are to be heard everywhere today in the highlands of South America. And dances such as the lively *huaino*, which probably is the direct descendant of the dramatic dances used at the Incan court at Cuzco, are still popular with the Indians today. Although somewhat affected by European musical instruments brought in by the Spaniards, these haunting rhythms and melodies are strongly suggestive of the pre-Columbian era of the Indians. The character of this native Indian music is shown in the pictures on this page and pages 140 and 159.

135

Another influence upon the modern popular music of the other Americas has been the music of the Negro, a music which takes us away back to the mysteries of the Dark Continent of Africa. Black slaves were first brought from Africa to the New World in 1512, when they were introduced into Haiti, thus initiating the process which has brought us our large Negro population. Most of us have forgotten that there are records showing a Negro culture which goes back more than five thousand years in Africa and that it was this culture which was transplanted to the New World during the centuries of slavery.

With him, as almost his only possession, the African brought music to America (Sidelight 3). This music, like that of all the oppressed peoples of history, was filled with a strong religious fervor and a wonderful, magical presence of rhythm. This rhythmic, emotional music united song and dance and showed a strong tendency toward the use of harmony and an ability to carry on several rhythms at the same time. It was a great comfort to the black man far away from his native land, and its peculiar traits have strongly influenced much of the music of the Western Hemisphere. We have already seen how important Negro music was in the formation of our North American styles of popular dance music. In the central and southern regions of the American continents this native African style and the dances that have developed with it are still a component part of the Negro's religion.

Nowhere is this primitive use of religious music and dances by the Negroes so easily observed as in Haiti, that French-speaking republic of the West Indies, the great majority of whose three million inhabitants are Negroes. Here it is associated with *vodun*, more commonly known as *voodoo*, a sort of black-magic kind of religion. In the primitive rites of his religion, which originated in Africa, the Afro-American has evolved gods that are strangely comparable to those of classic

From the Collection of Mme. Helena Rubenstein

THE COFFEE BEARERS OF BRAZIL, a painting by
Portenari

Greece and Rome. Katherine Dunham, the dancer-anthropologist who has traveled deep into the mountain fastnesses of Haiti to study these religious ceremonies, has given us some strangely fascinating pictures of voodoo. The worship of the supreme god, the Loa of the Haitians, is really the worship of the beautiful in nature, and his services — as well as the services of the other gods and goddesses — make full use of drum rhythms and wild chanting (Sidelight 4).

137

It is this strong predominance of rhythm over every other feature that makes Negro music so fascinating and irresistible. It will be found in the music of all those countries where the population of African origin is proportionately large. And it most certainly is the Negro's great contribution to the art of his adopted lands.

The third strong influence in shaping modern Latin-American popular music was that exerted by the European explorers and settlers. It was the discoveries of Columbus that gave the Spanish a footing in Cuba and Santo Domingo. From thence they sent out expeditions which, in something like seventy years, implanted Spanish rule on the American continent from Chile and Argentina through Mexico and eventually as far north as California, Colorado, and Florida. The only important exception to this Spanish domination was Brazil, which by a queer trick of fate was discovered by the Portuguese Admiral Cabral in 1500 while he was searching for a route to the fabulously rich India. The intrepid Spaniards, who conducted their schemes of colonization on strictly business principles, brought with them all the customs and ideals, the religious and cultural backgrounds, as well as the powerful desire for amassing wealth and power that were to be found in their homeland.

So it was that European music came to our shores. The missionaries brought their chants and religious music. The settlers and colonists had their dances and *romances*, a kind of Spanish ballad. On feast days, the Spanish and Portuguese blended their long-established European traditions of music and dancing with the native customs peculiar to the regions in which they had settled. This was in accordance with the general practice of the Catholic Church in lands where it colonized.

THE COMING OF CORTES AND THE CROSS, a mural by
José C. Orozco

By one of those occasional coincidences of great historical moment,
Cortes and his small band of adventurers arrived on the American
continent at a time set by legendary prophecy for the return of the
god Quetzalcoatl. The coincidence provides, in large degree, explanation of the historical marvel of the conquest of the native
thousands by Cortes and his few hundred Spanish followers. In
this panel the conquering figure of Cortes appears against the
background of his burning ships, destroyed by himself, and of a stern
cross both supporting and supported by an ascetic priest. Under-
foot are ghastly heaps of slain and subjugated natives and the
wreckage of a despoiled civilization. In the figures of both Cortes
and the priest are represented the mixture of positive and negative
values inherent in the conquering European culture.

It was wise in the way it adapted its requirements to the
habits of the people. The result was the Latin-American *fiesta*,
a celebration resembling a great Fourth of July on the loose,

but an institution like no other in the world. It is a grand public festival combining religious rites, colorful native customs and dances with lots of fun and diversion. As early as 1698 a French priest, observing the Negroes of Santo Domingo, tells of them dancing the *calenda* (a dance that originated on the Guinea coast of Africa) in celebrating one of the great festivals of the church. *It is so popular, he said, that it became a part of their religious devotions. They dance it in the processions and in the churches, the nuns performing it on Christmas Eve.*

This European musical tradition has been especially strong in Cuba and Brazil, where it has combined with the rhythmic vitality of the African music to produce the most popular of all topical music of Central and South America. The music historians use this term, *topical music*, to designate the popular music of the cities as distinguished from the music of the lonely and isolated people in the rural and mountainous districts. This urban type of popular music is played and sung in the streets, in the cafés, and in the ballrooms. It is the type

A SOUTH AMERICAN FOLK DANCE, a drawing by Camilo Blas

Photograph by Bill Gottlieb

THE RHYTHM SECTION is most of the body
as well as the soul of popular Latin-American
music.

which is best known beyond the borders of the land that
gave it birth. Some of these topical songs and dances are
the *pasillo, punto, guaracha, guajira, zapateo,* and *bolero,* all
of which retain the stamp of their Spanish ancestry; the
habanera, a very popular one that originated in Spain, in spite
of Cuban claims to the contrary; and the *conga* and *rumba,*
with definitely African suggestiveness. The *son,* somewhat
similar to the rumba, shows a nice balance between Spanish
and African backgrounds.

To sum up, the popular and serious music of the other
Americas is a peculiar mixture of three components:

141

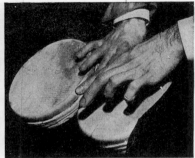

Photographs by Bill Gottlieb

TYMBALES, twin snare drums, often used with bass drums, cymbals, and cowbells

BONGOS, small twin drums, struck with palms, fingers, or sticks

1. the music which survived from the early original inhabitants, the Indians
2. the music that was brought in from Africa by the Negro and developed by his vivid imagination, his natural artistic temperament, and his strong rhythmic sense
3. the music that was imported by the Spanish-Portuguese colonists.

Out of these elements has come, in the course of the generations, a music that is strikingly original in character and very distinct from the European style of music. It is rich in emotion, simple in content, rhythmically complex and fascinating, melodically haunting and, above all, peculiarly alive. That is why we North Americans like it and have taken to it so strongly in recent years.

Naturally in such great centers as Mexico City and Rio de Janeiro, with populations running into the millions, and Buenos Aires, the world's sixth largest city, life is as cosmopolitan and sophisticated as in any city on earth. The term

LATIN–AMERICAN POPULAR MUSIC

CLAVES, two hardwood sticks, key instruments of the rhythm section

MARACAS, gourds filled with shot to give a peculiar swish-swish effect to the rhythm

popular music in such cities would be taken to mean much the same as it does in New York or London — ballroom and theatrical adaptations of Latin-American rhythms, as well as of North American jazz and swing. But real Latin-American popular music is something quite different. A genuine South American tango, for instance (not the commercial imitation we almost always hear in this country), is one of the most interesting and graceful of all dance rhythms. Originating in a Negro dance that was known as the *tangano* and that was popular in Central America during the sixteenth century, whence it had been introduced by the Negroes from Africa, the modern tango developed in the slum districts of those great River Platte cities, Montevideo and Buenos Aires. There its Negro background was strongly influenced by the habaneras, boleros, polkas, and other popular Spanish dances. The result seemed wild and shocking on its first introduction into the ballrooms of the world and brought severe and open denunciation from all the conservatives. Much the same sort of

143

thing had happened when the waltz was first introduced into European society at the end of the eighteenth century (Sidelight 5). As time passed, however, the tango became more tame, and from 1910 it has been cultivated by good society the world over, making its way to Europe and North America and ousting all other similar dances in popular favor.

Now, it is only natural that the tangos we hear played by our own dance bands do not have the same flavor and character as those directly imported from the land of their birth. Many of those played in this country have been greatly diluted by popular taste, affected by syncopation and other devices of our own dance music, and standardized and streamlined for commercial consumption. What we hear is something quite different from the cadenced Argentinean rhythms which express so well the melancholy that is an underlying characteristic of the people of that great land.

So it is with other Latin-American dances. The habanera, whose rhythms are much like those of the tango; the conga, originally used in the carnival fiestas of the Cuban cities, with texts of local political significance; the rumba, also of Cuban origin — all have been colored and influenced and complicated by the sophisticated and standardized expressions of modern popular composers. And in the process, they have lost much of their flavor (Sidelight 6).

The following table of popular songs and dances from Latin America shows the various influences that have helped make them as we hear them today. The mixing of so many different influences makes this music of the people especially attractive and gives it an exotic and foreign flavor that cannot but intrigue us. Moreover, if we take the trouble of learning some-

144

thing about this music, we come to a better understanding of the peoples that produced it. And understanding them better will in turn enable us to realize something of their peculiar problems and national differences. So music can be of real assistance in enabling us to become Good Neighbors to the hundred and twenty-five million people living to the south of us.

A TABLE OF SOME OF THE MOST IMPORTANT LATIN-AMERICAN SONGS AND DANCES

DANCE NAME	PRINCIPAL INFLUENCES
MEXICO	
Corrido	Spanish; descended from the romance plus Indian narratives; has topical words, often relating to political events
Jarabe	Spanish (from zapateado); combines 3/4 and 6/8 meter
Huapango	Spanish and African; lively dance with many combinations of polyrhythms
GUATEMALA	
Son Guatemalteco	European
TRINIDAD	
Calypso	African; topical ballads sung in English
MARTINIQUE AND SAINT LUCIA	
Béguine	African and Spanish (from the French béguin, a flirtation)

145

DANCE NAME	PRINCIPAL INFLUENCES
CUBA	
Habanera	European, introduced into Cuba at Havana and reintroduced into Europe as a Cuban dance
Guaracha	Spanish and African; lively song dance
Guajira	Spanish country dance
Punto	Spanish
Bolero	Spanish; Cuban bolero in 2/4 meter in contrast to Spanish bolero, which is in 3/4 meter
Rumba	African
Conga	African; named after a drum and used in carnival street parades
Nañigo	African; savage tribal music in 6/8 meter; religious in origin
Son	African; perhaps imported from Haiti; slow, very rhythmic, in 2/4 meter
Danzón	African; syncopated; not strenuous
Zapateo	Spanish tap dance

146

A TABLE OF SOME OF THE MOST IMPORTANT
LATIN-AMERICAN SONGS AND DANCES (*continued*)

DANCE NAME	PRINCIPAL INFLUENCES
BRAZIL	
Samba	African; many varieties; duple meter; lively dance in major keys
Maxixe	African and Spanish
Batuque	African
Modinha	Italian and Portuguese
Coca	African
Lundú	African
Tirana	Portuguese, from the Azores
Aboio	Portuguese herdsman's song
ARGENTINA	
Tango	African and Spanish
Milonga	Spanish city dance
Gato	Argentine gaucho dance (cowboy dance)
Ranchera, Chacarera	Argentine gaucho dance
Chamamé	Argentine gaucho dance; Indian origin
Pericón	Argentine gaucho dance
Zamba	borrowed from Chile (Zambacueca)
URUGUAY	
Milonga	Spanish
Pericón	Country dance

CONTEMPORARY AMERICAN MUSIC

A TABLE OF SOME OF THE MOST IMPORTANT
LATIN-AMERICAN SONGS AND DANCES (*continued*)

DANCE NAME	PRINCIPAL INFLUENCES
CHILE	
Zambacueca	Spanish; national air of Chile
Cueca	Indian; lively
Tonada	Indian; popular country dance-song
PERU	
Cachua	Indian; popular country dance-song
Yaravi, Triste	Indian and European
Huaino	Indian
Marinera	Spanish; coastal dance
ECUADOR	
Sanjuanito	Indian; religious dance
Pasillo	Spanish
VENEZUELA	
Tono Llanero	Spanish; dance-song
Joropo	Spanish and African
COLOMBIA	
Bambuco	African
Pasillo	Spanish
Torbellino	Indian

SIDELIGHTS

1. We do know that the Chinese emperor who built the Great Wall, which for many centuries represented "the most

148

colossal tide-mark of the human race, sent expeditions across the eastern seas in search of a drug that would produce immortality." This was in the third century. Recall Ponce de Leon, the Spanish discoverer of Florida, who came centuries later in search of the Fountain of Youth.

2. Some of the early European chroniclers of the New World have left interesting accounts of the importance of music and dancing among the Indians they visited. One of these, the sixteenth-century writer Gonzalo Fernández de Oviedo y Valdés, says of the Indians of Santo Domingo in the West Indies:

On this island their songs, which they call Areytos, are the only memorial that is passed on from parent to son and from the living to those yet to come.... These people had a good and gentle custom of remembering things past; and this was done through their songs and dances performed in the following manner: When they sought pleasure, to celebrate some noble feast, to celebrate a victory over their enemies, to rejoice in the marriage of their chief, or just to pass the time, a great number of Indians, male and female, gathered (sometimes the men only, and sometimes the women by themselves). In order to express their joy and pleasure, they take each other by the hand or link their arms, or form a line or circle, one of them, either a man or woman, acting as leader; the leader takes some steps forward or backward, the group measuring and taking the same steps as the leader, singing loud or soft at his direction, and fitting the rhythms of their steps to the verses or words which they sing. Following the leader's performance, all of the

149

others answer with the same steps and words, and in the same order; and, when they answer him, the leader remains silent but continues to dance. And when the answer has been made, the leader proceeds without pause or interval to sing another verse, which the chorus in turn repeats; this process continues for three to four hours or more until the master or leader of the dance finishes his story. Sometimes this performance goes on from one day to the next.

Many times they accompany their songs with a drum, which is made from a hollowed trunk of a tree, often as large as a man and sounding like the drums made by Negroes. There is no parchment on the drum but, rather, holes or slits are made, from which the sound emanates. With this imperfect instrument or without it, they describe in song the death of many past chiefs, and many things which they do not wish to be forgotten. Sometimes the leader or master of the dance is changed; when this happens, the melody and figures of the dance are also changed, but the story is continued if it has not been completed by the first leader. When a new story is begun, the melody may or may not change.[2]

3. One of the earliest references to African melodies brought over from Africa, *Captain Canot or Twenty Years of an African Slaver*, says this:

During afternoons of serene weather men, women, girls and boys are allowed on deck to unite in African melodies which they always enhance by an extemporaneous tom-tom on the bottom of a tub or tin kettle.

[2] From *Historia General y Natural de las Indias y Tierra-Firme del Mar Oceano*, quoted in *The Musical Quarterly*, January, 1945.

4. Professor James G. Leyburn of Yale University has written a most understanding book, *The Haitian People* (New Haven: Yale University Press) in which he has a great deal to say about vodun, the religion that answers for these simple people the questions that arise in the world as they know it, while giving them confidence to face the crises of life. Professor Leyburn says:

Vodun is a true religion in the same sense that Mohammedanism, Buddhism, or Christianity are all true religions. That is to say, it is a set of beliefs and practices which claim to deal with the spiritual forces of the universe, and attempt to keep the individual in harmonious relation with them as they affect his life.... Using the greatest number of criteria available for the definition of religion as distinct from superstition, religion may be said to be a set of beliefs about spirits or gods and their nature, about the origin of the world, about good and evil, about man's relation to the universe he knows; it includes a set of practices of worship, it is an attempt to ward off misfortune and get good; it treats of what happens after death; it is a system of seeking security, solace, and support in the face of a supposed supernatural. Vodun is all these....

Its worship consists of services which employ a great deal of ritual borrowed from the Catholic Church, followed by sacrifices of animals for the purpose of restraining or pacifying gods who may have been pursuing with misfortune or gratifying those who have made happiness. Then a dance follows, expressing the joy of the worshipers at dangers averted and gratitude for blessings bestowed. While the service is private in character, the dances are in the nature of social events. To quote again from Professor Leyburn,

Drums are not always used at the earlier service, but no dance could be held without them. The crowd drifts in slowly, so that the dance may be long in getting under way. The best drummers in the community may not arrive until after two or three hours. Three drums of different sizes, all properly baptized, set the rhythms, and sometimes gourd rattles embroider a commentary upon the beat. Whereas at the service possession (the seizing of a worshiper by some one of the gods, making him completely uninhibited and unrestrained in his actions and ideas) comes as a result of the priest's invocations, at the dance it is inspired by the drumming. Each Loa or god has his own particular rhythm, so that as soon as it is determined what god has seized upon a dancer, the drummers take up the rhythm of that god. . . . The dancers do not embrace each other as at a white man's dance; the climax of a successful dance is a religious experience. . . . Creed and practice go hand in hand in Haiti. The Vodun worshiper believes in the Loa of his faith and does the necessary things to get in touch with them. These conceptions are the major part of his creed, as the corresponding actions form the bulk of his religious activity.

Melville J. Herskovits' book *Life in a Haitian Valley* (New York: Alfred A. Knopf) has also a good deal to say about this particular use of music in the rites of voodoo.

5. According to Burney, the English musical historian, writing in *Rees' Cyclopaedia* around 1805, the waltz was:

a *riotous German dance of modern invention. The verb
waltzen, whence this word is derived, implies to roll, wallow,
welter, tumble down, or roll in the dirt of mire. What analogy
there may be between these acceptations and the dance, we
pretend not to say. But having seen it performed by a select
party of foreigners, we could not help reflecting how uneasy an
English mother would be to see her daughter as familiarly
treated and still more to witness the oblidging manner in which
the freedom is returned by the females.*

Somehow this all has a very familiar ring, and quite a modern one!

6. The question of the supplanting of local cultures by a
standardized, commercial product which represents the taste
of the United States in other countries is one that needs serious consideration, although there is probably little that can be
done about it. Recently a well-known New York music critic,
Paul Bowles, who loves the popular music of Central and
South America and has wandered far afield in search of real
examples of it, wrote an article on this subject. It was published in the New York *Herald Tribune* on August 19, 1945
under the title *Notes on an Unpleasant Subject*:

*The sudden taking on of our popular culture by peoples who
have not recently been in connection with the Occident involves in some measure a repudiation by them of their own.
This would not be inevitably so if ours had anything at all in
common with theirs, but the incompatibility is complete.
Theirs are carefully elaborated human necessities; ours is the
streamlined broadcast that advocates our national product, industrialism. And they rather like the idea of the product and*

153

Courtesy of Associated American Artists Galleries

PUERTO RICAN FOLK SONG, an etching by Irwin D. Hoffman

The scene depicted in the etching is one that is quite common in the hill country. Here are gathered a group of neighbors enjoying a singfest of their old folk songs. There is a constant ebb and flow to the audience, with neighbors dropping in for a few minutes to listen.

are completely sold on its smart programs. Thus it is not surprising that in the case of music, at once the most emotionally direct and intellectually abstract of the conventions of human expression, systematic disparagement is directed by various peoples of the world toward their own folk musics, while these same spirits are placidly or even eagerly receptive to our commercial anti-music.

154

LATIN-AMERICAN POPULAR MUSIC

It is of course only to be expected that those countries which have been carefully creating themselves in our image should carry out their imitation of us to the point of being one up on us in the production of kitsch, musical, literary, and graphic trash. But folk culture in Europe, with the possible exception of a few backward countries such as Spain, Greece or Albania, is pretty much lost anyway. The period of a quick cultural death exists particularly for those parts of the globe peopled by races other than the Caucasian, but where Western civilization enjoys more prestige than the indigenous. In Latin America, Africa, the Far East, progress is taken seriously, and this fact ineluctably entails the destruction of the present system of thought and artistic expression.

Local culture is in ill repute. In 1934 I went to Colombia to hear the music of the Indians of the Goajira Peninsula. What happened is difficult to appreciate unless one is accustomed to the violent hatred of most Latin-American officials towards their own native cultures.

I was in Santa Marta, waiting for the weekly boat that used to sail to Riohacha. The company was openly incredulous when I explained why I wanted passage and proceeded to notify the police, who quickly arrested me and went through my luggage. All the while they kept repeating, as if trying to convince me by hypnotic suggestion: "There is no music in the Goajira," and even "There are no Indians in Colombia." I was forbidden to purchase a ticket and finally had to go back to Barranquilla without having heard anything more indigenous than some bambucos and cumbiambas.

I went to buy Panamanian records in Panama and found several mejoranas I like, but the clerk almost tearfully insisted

155

that those outlandish things were from Ecuador. And so it goes. All through Central America, and particularly Mexico, the musical styles which were easy to find ten or fifteen years ago are nearly extinct, thanks to the ubiquitous and urbanizing radio, whose talent scouts in the last-named country corral rural musicians, carry them to the capital, and ruin their delicate collaborative technique, which is to say their tradition, in literally a few days.

A case in point is Cuba, a land where one might reasonably expect to hear, at least in the cheaper dance halls, a certain amount of that Afro-Latin music which, along with her cigars, the world has come to consider Cuba's most typical export. By Cuban music most of us mean rumbas, congas, pregones, guarachas, and sones. We have also got used to expecting a varied and active percussion section in the performing group. What do we find in July, 1945? In the first place, looking for a rumba in Cuba is almost tantamount to instigating a search in this country for a turkey trot: the answer to one's inquiries is likely to be amused and condescending explanation that the rumba is an outmoded dance form that everyone knows perfectly well is passé. If you do by chance find an orchestra playing one, it is likely to be in a place frequented by Americans, and the conjunto is certain to lack the percussion, save for one person who occupies himself indifferently with either maracas or guiro. One can scarcely object to a dance or song-form's going out of style; it happens to the best of them — of all the afore-mentioned, the only one still functioning is the guaracha, a Cuban counterpart to the Mexican corrido — but what comes up in its place? American commercial music for one thing. "Triste Lluvia," recognizable to our ears as "Stormy Weather," seems to be the island-wide hit this year. And secondly, something worse: Latin swing, a new hybrid commercial idiom being propagated in the radio studios of the torrid zone. Its words, prosody and harmonic sequences are likely to be roughly on the Argentine side, its melodic devices are often Mexican-inspired, while underneath is an insistent but dull simplification of Cuban rhythm. The idiom, which is consciously being pushed in order to destroy the international barriers normally preventing foreign consumption of any given country's product, is as meaningless as our own commercial music, and if possible even less engrossing. Now, wherever you may be in Latin America, you can hear the same pseudo-music, the same poisonous clichés of melody and harmony, the same empty purple lyrics. It has all been made digestible for the radio and film audiences of the Latin-American republics, and presumably everyone is happy.

The Cubans are almost as loath as the Americans to admit that their folk music, at least that part of it which can be called distinctive, is primarily of Negro origin. They constantly point out Iberian turns of melody much as people here insist on the modes from the British Isles. In the music which receives public encouragement (radio, theater, dance hall) there is as little as possible of the African element. Even those numbers now distinguished by the adjective *afro-cubano*, circumspectly Europeanize the Negro elements.

Along the waterfront in Santiago or Havana, a group of Negroes will begin a vigorous bit of true Cuban music, complete with marimbula, bongo and antiphonal estribillo. They seldom get very far. The police saunter past and suggest silence. Reason: Such music provokes "scandals." Or you, a foreigner,

157

may happen by and catch them singing and playing something quite relaxed. Shamefacedly they will hurry to finish it and begin something from the radio. Reason: The other is "old-fashioned," or even "backward"; you might deduce that Cuba is not that thing they have been taught is the ultimate good: a modern country. The same pattern prevails all over the world; the uprooting of natural culture for the implantation of an ersatz culture which can be controlled from headquarters. There is obviously no remedy.

MUSIC TO LISTEN TO

Much of the so-called Latin-American music that has been recorded is southern in name only. Most of it is simply southern in rhythmic suggestiveness, with no feeling for real style or understanding of how this music is played south of the Rio Grande. Many of the men who play it for recordings or radio have never been south of the Battery, the southernmost tip of Manhattan Island; and many of the native players and band-leaders who play it here have been so imbued with our dance-band techniques and styles that they have lost a great deal of whatever natural manner of interpreting this music they may once have had.

The following list will be helpful in understanding something of the real style of the popular music of the Americas to the south of us. In some cases it is difficult to disassociate the many influences — folk, music hall, dance band, radio — that have gone into the making and interpreting of this popular music. There is here a great deal of what our southern friends call typical music (canciones típicas), a term they use to describe popular city-bred music. This is in strong distinction to

SOUTH AMERICAN NATIVE MUSICIANS, a woodcut by José Sabogal

the folk style — music of the people themselves, away out in
the mountains or on the plains, sung as they work or dance.
We have tried to keep the distinction clear in the brief descriptions given.

Typical Latin-American Melodies (played
by Los Andrinis Orchestral Ensemble)

ALPHA VOL. II

Tico Tico No Fuba (samba from Brazil)

This is the less violent *city samba* used in Brazilian dance
halls and quite different from the wilder, rural African-
influenced samba.

159

Alma Llanera (jorope from Venezuela)

This is perhaps the best-known of all Venezuelan joropes.

Tango Verde (from Ecuador)
Andalucía (from Cuba)

These are from Lecuona's *Andalucian Suite*.

Recuerdos (pasillo from Colombia)

The pasillo is a popular refined ballroom dance akin to the waltz.

18 de Septembre (cueca from Chile)

This, the most popular native dance of Chile, is danced by a couple waving handkerchiefs over their heads.

Sol y Sombra (paso doble)

The paso doble is a dance in 2/4 meter with a marchlike theme.

These are all played in real Latin-American style and with good, characteristic instrumentation.

Two other interesting, well-played volumes of typical native Latin-American music, under the supervision of Stokowski, are:

Native Brazilian Music, Volume I [3]   c   SET c 83

Macumba de Ochócê
Macumba de Inhançan
Samba Cancão
Caboclo do Matto

[3] The symbols in the list of records may be interpreted as follows:

B	Bost	G	General
c	Columbia	H	Hargail
v	Victor	k	Keynote

Seu Manè e Luiz
Bambo du Bambu
Sapo no Saco
Ke Ke Re Ke Ke

Native Brazilian Music, Volume II   C   SET C 84
Zé Barbino
Tocanda pra Você
Pelo Telefone
Passarinho Baleu Aza
Quem Me Vé Sorrir
Teirú, Nozani-Na
Cantiga de Festa
Canide Ioune

Latin-American Folk Songs   B   ES 3

In this excellent volume Irma Labastille has provided some
fine examples of both folk and typical songs; she differentiates
carefully between them. Included are some yaravi, dating away
back to Incan times, accompanied by the ancient flute, or
quena. One of the best features of this album is that the music
has been arranged for voice and piano, with original texts and
English adaptations, and published under the title *Memories
of Latin America*. New York: E. B. Marks Corp.

Mexican Folk Songs   G   16, 17, VOLS. I, II

These are typical songs, recorded on the spot, with real local
flavor. The best are these:

La Mujar de Cuchu
La Potranca
Jarabe Chiapas (marimba)
Toro Coquito
El Ranchero

La Julia
Pina Maclura
El Qualite
Tu Ya No Soplas
Zacatecas (marimba)

Brazilian Folk Songs (sung by Elsie Houston)   v

Bahia Characteristic Song
Dansa de Caboclo ('The Frog Song) (from Coco)
Benedicto Pretinho (A Little Pickaninny)
Bia-ta-ta (from Coco)
Tayêras (Song and Dance of the Mulattresses)
Bambalelê (from the northern interior)

These songs are of special value, for they are authentic folk songs, sung in an authentic manner by the late Elsie Houston, perhaps the most gifted of all Brazilian singers. The Bahian Tayêras is a good example of a song containing blends of African fetish rituals and Christian doctrine.

Native Brazilian Songs   H   MW 700

Incan: *De blanca tierra*
        Kurikinga mapanawi
Spanish: *Canción Andaluza*
          Nina Nana
Brazilian: *Dem Bau*
            Queha o coco menina
            Rei mandon me chama
            Bambalelê

Indian Music of Mexico (collected by Boulton)   v

This is real, primitive folk music of the isolated Indians in the hinterlands of Mexico.

Zapotec-Teotitlan, Oaxaca: *Fireworks Music*
Otomi-Honey, Puebla: *Flying Pole Dance*

Yaqui-Tlaxcala, Puebla: *Deer Dance and Pascolas*
Matachines and Pascolas
Ancient Instruments, Mexico City: *Tones*
Maya: *Ticui* (from Yucatán)
Merida (from Yucatán)

Yaqui Indian Music (recorded on location)   G   18

Tarascan Indian: *Dances of Birth, Marriage, Death*
Los Viejitos (The Little Men)
Yaqui Indian: *Pascola* (Masked and Unmasked
Dances)
Coyote (Song of an Old War Society)
Chapuyeka Procession; Matachini
Dance
The Deer Dance
Chichimaca Indian: *Huehuenche Dance*
Alahamza a Guadaloupe

The Yaqui Indians, who live in Sonora, the state farthest to the northwest in the Republic of Mexico, are the descendants of practically the only North American Indian tribe to survive unsubdued through the centuries. They have remained quite out of touch with the white man's civilization, and their music is thus of unusual interest.

The Tarascan Indians now live in Michoacán, the state directly west of Mexico City and the most romantic of all the Mexican states. Local customs and ancient religions survive here without much change, and the popular art of dancing and music have remained alive and vigorous among the Indians. Danced to the music of the *teponaxtle* (wooden drum), a flute, and sometimes a violin, these dances are taken very seriously. One of the most original and characteristic of them is

163

Courtesy of the Albright Art Gallery, Buffalo, New York

CHALCHIUHTLICUE, the Aztec Goddess of
Flowing Water

the dance *Los Viejitos*. Although really a rain dance, it has a
sense of humor not often found in these ceremonies. According to one who has seen it, the dancers wear very low-crowned,
wide hats with bright-colored ribbons and cover their faces

164

with clay masks which, although they represent old men, have a strangely healthy look and a laughing expression.

Vodun Music from Haiti   G   12

> *Ibo-Lélé* (Ibo Song)
> *Joué Kanga Joué* (Kanga Song)
> *Djá Keke Djá* (Corn Grinding Song)
> *Ciyé ciyé Ti Bobine Carré* (Conga Ciyé Song)
> *Jean Pierre Poungue* (Congo Song)
> *Soleil Malade* (Rada Song)
> *Erzulie nainain oh* (Jenvalo Song)
> *Moundongue Oh yé, yé, yé* (Rada Song)

These are genuine songs connected with the rites of the natural Haitian religion. They are evidently sung in the Creole language and show the influences which have so strongly affected this religion: African and Roman Catholic.

A *Calypso Album* by Sir Lancelot   K   126

> *The Century of the Coming Man*
> *Trinidad Is Changing*
> *The Young Girls Today*
> *Ugly Woman*
> *Night in Central Park*
> *Scandal in the Family*

The titles of some of these calypsos indicate readily enough that they have been strongly influenced by events far from Trinidad, their original home!

Photograph by Hoyningen-Huene

THE ART OF GREECE: TEMPLE OF APOLLO
EPICURIOS

In that fair clime the lonely herdsman, stretched
On the soft grass through half a summer's day,
With music lulled his indolent repose. . . .

166

INCE we have just been speaking about the differences between *art* music and *popular* music, this may be a good place to find out what these differences are. You may remember that in Chapter III there was a quotation from George Gershwin in which he used the term *art* in connection with a type of music which he felt could be developed from the various kinds of folk music that have sprung up in this country. Let us see what he meant by the term *art* music as he used it in distinction to the type of music we have been considering.

To the average American, art is a disturbing word. It means to him something elaborate and fussy, something far removed from everyday life, produced by impractical individuals and acquired by rich and powerful people in order that they may seem more magnificent and cultured. Or it is something out of the past that has been collected and placed in huge museums where the common people can go to see it and be educated. Or it suggests to him the queer and mysterious conceits of an individual who delights in being as much out-of-this-world as possible and does not care very much whether anyone understands these conceits or not.

167

Courtesy of Colonial Williamsburg

AN AMERICAN BUILDING OF THE EIGHTEENTH
CENTURY: The Governor's Palace, Williamsburg, Virginia

Somehow the average person in this country cannot realize that art is an essential element of life; he is either inclined
to consider it as completely useless or else as something that
can be tolerated if there is money on hand to pay for it, and
something that should be dispensed with when times begin
to be hard. And, unfortunately, art often suggests a means
whereby "unpleasant individuals educated beyond their intelligence" can show how much better they are than the average
man who knows little about art except that he doesn't like
it. We can be pretty sure that Henry Ford had some such
conception in mind when he made his famous statement, "I
wouldn't give five cents for all the art in the world."

168

ART AND MUSIC

In spite of the fact that art is an extremely difficult term to define, we can state very definitely that such conceptions about it as these are entirely wrong. Art is not something that is intensely unsocial, nor is it a mysterious activity that can be understood by only a few. On the contrary, it has a daily impact on the lives of everyone and should form an integral and significant part of living. It is a field of human activity in which men use their talents and abilities to communicate to their fellows the meaning of the experiences through which they have lived. And these artists are thus able to transform the common materials of life they find all about them — words, sounds, colors, etc. — into something that makes for better living and a better world. Art, moreover, is not an activity that is peculiar to our time but has been an essential factor in man's existence from the earliest times of which we have definite knowledge. Some sort of interest in that which is beautiful has occupied a good deal of his attention ever since.

This may be as good a definition as any we can find of what art really is: the result of a natural love for the beautiful which has always possessed man, a love that has impelled him to shape his activities in such a way as to bring some sense of order and some shade of meaning into the world in which he lives.

In the earlier and less-specialized periods of man's development, his love for the beautiful was something that he took more or less for granted, without feeling that there was any great need for emphasizing it. Our earliest human ancestors, when they needed tools for tilling the soil or utensils from which to eat and drink or weapons for protecting themselves from beasts and for hunting animals for food, took what nature had provided them. A bent tree branch served as a plow, a hollowed-out gourd was good enough for a bowl, and a stone picked up from the ground made a serviceable weapon. But it was soon found that by shaping and modifying the things used in everyday life, they could be made more service-able; and that, as an object became better suited to do the things for which it was intended, its form and appearance became more pleasing.

Men soon learned to make colored pigments from plants and animals and minerals. Then they began to decorate and color the objects used in ordinary living — their clothing, their utensils, and even their bodies, and found a great deal of pleasure in doing so. They painted pictures on the walls of the caves in which they lived, molded and whittled little statues to propitiate the gods they worshiped as well as to give themselves pleasure in something that was well shaped and beautiful. When it became necessary to build houses to protect themselves from the weather, they quickly learned how to make these good-looking as well as useful. And the indiscriminate bangings on hollowed-out tree trunks and the primitive vocal sounds which they made to communicate ideas or feelings later gave way to ordered music that afforded our early ancestors pleasure as well as served them in religious rituals and tribal dances.

By the time of the Greeks of the fifth century B.C., a love of beauty was as natural to man as the air he breathed or the sunlight which flooded his beautiful land. The imposing legacy of beauty left behind by these Athenians is proof enough of this. It is some of the finest art ever created by man. The Christian Church in the greatest period of its develop-

170

ment (from the fifth through the sixteenth centuries) did not hesitate to use art for its own purposes, to proclaim its doctrines and explain its beliefs. And during this time it acted

Courtesy of Colonial Williamsburg

THE FORMAL GARDENS of the Governor's
Palace, Williamsburg, Virginia

as sponsor for all the great painters, architects, sculptors, and musicians. During the Renaissance a delight in beauty of all kinds absorbed such a large part of man's attention as to produce a fair share of the world's finest literature, painting, architecture, and music.

171

It is only in these later, more practical years that the process of earning a living has been completely separated from the necessary part which beauty should play in that living. The Athenian of the fifth century B.C. would certainly have been puzzled by the peculiar misconceptions of art that we have described above. So would the architects and builders of the great cathedrals of twelfth-century France (which, we must always remember, were erected through the faith and labor of the people themselves) and the Italians of the Renaissance.

The term *art* is used, we may say, to refer to those things which man has created during his centuries-old search for beauty — the churches and temples, the paintings and sculptures he has left behind him. Or to refer to the communication of the artist's experience and feelings that have been made through literature and music; or to such adaptations of the things used in ordinary life as make them more beautiful and effective. In this sense a cathedral, a statue, a symphony, and a lovely porcelain bowl are art. The word is also used to describe the manner in which the activities which have brought these special things into being have been performed. If we look in the dictionary we will find that one of the definitions of art is the "application of skill and taste to the production of things of beauty, especially by painting or sculpture." So when we speak of the art of architecture, we mean not only the beautiful churches, palaces, houses, and buildings that have been built through the centuries, but also the means by which these buildings have been created. The art of painting refers as well to the technique and processes used for putting pictures on walls, canvas, or wooden slabs as to the millions and millions of paintings thus produced.

172

Courtesy of Museum of the American Indian, Heye Foundation, New York

AN EARLY AMERICAN STONE BOWL

So we see that when he spoke of the possibility of American art music developing out of the different types of our folk music, Gershwin had a special kind of music in mind. He meant that sort of music which a composer sits down and writes intentionally in such a way as to achieve certain planned effects and to carry definite *meanings* to those who listen. It is thus quite different from the folk or popular music that is the real possession of the masses of a people within a country. Folk music belongs to them not only because it is the expression of their common ideas but also because it is easy for them to sing and play. A tune or dance is a popular folk tune or dance because it is the sort that the average person can sing or dance easily and, moreover, one that he enjoys singing or

173

Castleton's Modern Museum Shape
Approved by The Museum of Modern Art, New York
Designed by Eva Zeisel

GOOD MODERN CERAMIC ART

dancing. Art music, on the other hand, has been composed; that is, it has been designed and put together in a manner that fits its ideas to certain forms of expression and plans its construction according to certain laws of balance and proportion and effect.

A good description of the differences that exist between these types has been given by the English folk-song expert Cecil Sharp:

Art music is the work of the individual; it is composed in, comparatively speaking, a short period of time, and being committed to paper it is forever fixed in one unalterable form.

174

Folk music is the true product of a race and reflects feelings and tastes that are communal rather than personal. It is always in solution; its creation is never completed, while at any moment of its history it exists not in one form but in many.

A great deal of the world's finest music is art music, but we should not necessarily consider it any greater than folk or popular music. Nor do we need to think that popular music is the only kind worth listening to and that all classical (what is really meant by this term is *art*) music is long-haired, dull, and unnatural. Each kind of music has its own particular place and importance in the world.

QUESTIONS FOR DISCUSSION

Show how art, in the sense in which the word is used in this chapter, can help solve some of the problems of human needs (1) in the home, (2) in the community, and (3) in industry and commerce.

Bring to class some examples of art created by the Christian Church in order to proclaim its doctrines and explain its beliefs. Can you illustrate the statement in the text that during the Renaissance an interest in art absorbed such a large proportion of man's attention as to produce a fair share of the world's great literature, painting, and architecture?

MUSIC TO LISTEN TO

Dubensky: *Stephen Foster, Theme, Variations and Finale*   V   DM 912

The songs of Stephen Foster, written in the middle of the nineteenth century, are some of the most beautiful folk music we have in America; they are known and loved the world over.

175

None of them is more widely sung wherever the English language is understood than *Old Folks at Home*, sometimes called, from its first line, *Way Down Upon the Swanee River*. It is a song wonderfully suited for singing either by soloists or large numbers of people, with simple banjo-like accompaniment or a large orchestral background. Everyone agrees that it is a folk song of the universal type even though it expresses the peculiar longing and sadness associated with a particular kind of American life, that of our southern states before the War between the States.

A few years ago Arcady Dubensky, an American composer even though he was born in Russia and received most of his musical training there, used this popular tune as the basis for an effective bit of art music, written for the symphony orchestra, which he called *Stephen Foster, Theme, Variations and Finale*. He constructed this piece, which takes about fifteen minutes to play, according to the tradition of a *form* that has been used by writers of instrumental music for centuries. This theme-and-variations form is based upon the simple principle of presenting an idea (in this case Foster's tune) in a number of modified versions, each of them called a variation. While we recognize the underlying musical idea to be the same throughout the work, there is a change in each variation that holds the listener's interest and makes him wonder just what is coming next, without confusing him too much or making him feel that he is lost at any time. After several of these variations, Dubensky adds a Finale made up of two other Foster tunes (can you recognize them?) and finishes the whole thing with a last playing of the tune which we heard at the very beginning. Thus a simple tune is molded and stretched and developed into an extended and elaborate and more sophisticated piece of music suitable for playing at a concert or on a radio program of serious music.

Gould: *Latin-American Symphonette* v M 964

Another good example of how a composer may develop folk or dance tunes into a form of musical art is this music by a young American composer. According to Morton Gould's plans (he has written a number of American symphonettes), he believes in mixing contemporary American *idioms*, such as jazz or swing, with classical forms and structures. That is to say, he has tried to develop, just as Gershwin prophesied would be done, an American art music out of popular American tunes and rhythms. In composing the fourth of these symphonettes he has used some of the dance rhythms that are peculiar to Latin America. Let us see how he has planned his music.

The composition is divided, like most of the classical symphonies, into four parts or movements, each of them based on a different Latin-American dance rhythm. The First Movement uses that most popular of Spanish-Negro dances, the rumba. But instead of simply playing a rumba tune over and over again as would be done for dancing, the composer, after he has once made us feel the fundamental rhythm upon which the music is based, lets us hear two contrasting themes and proceeds to *develop* them. *Development* consists of treating the themes in such a way as to make them grow logically, increase their intensity of expression, and work them up to an effective climax. It is one of the most familiar ways by which a good composer evolves his music and was widely used by such men as Haydn, Mozart, Beethoven, and Brahms.

The Second Movement is a real Argentine tango and shows what a talented composer can do in the way of revealing the symphonic possibilities of popular tunes. Little parts of the fascinating tango tune are echoed back and forth by the different string instruments, and the movement ends with an effective, wide-sweeping arpeggio.

The Third Movement, a guaracha, in strong contrast to the quiet, languorous tango, is a nervously rhythmic exploitation of this Cuban dance rhythm. It has two easily distinguished themes and contains some fine rhythmic effects in which strange gourd-like, rattling instruments are used.

This, quite short, leads into the Fourth Movement, a conga, which builds up gradually, by the addition of more and more instruments and the increase of rhythmic stress, to a tremendous climax. The final sharp chords on drums and cymbals make a wonderful effect.

In this delightful composition, a talented American composer has tried to do with typical American dance rhythms what Bach and his contemporaries did with the dances of their time — the gavottes, sarabandes, gigues, and the rest. He has thus written something that has more value than mere entertainment music and consequently gives these rhythms a permanent place in the music of our time.

Delius: *La Calinda* from *Koanga*   V   11–8644
                                                      C   1143

Some sixty years ago a well-to-do woolen merchant of Bradford, England sent his talented son to the wilds of Florida to grow oranges, in the hope that he would thus forget his foolish ambition of becoming a musician and settle down to a steady, responsible business career. Instead, Frederick Delius, for that was the young man's name, learned in the hard way how important music was in his life and decided then and there that he was to be a composer and nothing else. Solano Grove, where Delius lived in solitude, was an old Spanish plantation where slaves had been employed and where Negroes still worked. Their singing so fascinated the young musician that in later years he wrote several pieces suggestive of his remembrance of this Negro music. Among them was an opera, *Koanga,* based on the story of Creole life in Louisiana. One of the attractive numbers in this opera is a Negro dance, calinda, full of rhythmic appeal and rich color. An early trader to New Orleans describes the calinda as one of the favorite Negro dances, based primarily on the primitive dances of the African people, but with copious borrowings from the dances of the French. Delius catches this atmosphere in his orchestral episode.

Still: *Scherzo* from *Afro-American Symphony*

C 11992 D

As a last example of American art music based on a popular folk pattern, we cite this scherzo, or Third Movement, from the leading work of William Grant Still, probably the best-known Negro composer in the United States. Like Gershwin, Still started his musical career in the field of popular music. Some foreign critics have said that his *Afro-American Symphony* is the most "characteristically *indigenous* music to have come from the United States." Whether or not this is true, the music has lusty power and strong rhythmic appeal. It really says something and is not, like so much present-day music, merely an experiment in tonalities and sonorities.

179

LOWER MANHATTAN, 1921, a painting by Stefan Hirsch

180

E MUST not think that all American art music has had a folk or popular origin. Ever since the New England tanner William Billings published in 1770 his *New England Psalm Singer,* a church music book which contained tunes, as he said, that "were twenty times more powerful than the old slow tunes," our composers have been busily at work producing serious original musical compositions (Sidelight 1). Many of these have been inspired by and copied after European models, as we would expect to be the case in a new country. It is only in quite recent times that our composers of serious music have learned to stand entirely upon their own feet and to write music that is unmistakably original and American.

In the early days many of the settlers in New England, as well as those farther to the south, were musically inclined, their interests being largely devoted to psalm and hymn singing in church and social gatherings. The second book [1] to be published in this country, the *Bay Psalm Book,* printed in Cambridge, Massachusetts in 1640, was prepared for use in church;

[1] The first work published was called *Freeman's Oath.*

and for many years afterwards the Puritan colonists were not very enthusiastic about using music for any other purpose.

The Pennsylvania colonists, many of them from Germany, were much more liberal in their views, although even here church music predominated. A German, Conrad Beissel, was the first-known composer on American soil. He established a communistic settlement at Ephrata, near Philadelphia, in 1735 and wrote a number of hymns and chorales for use in its church services. And later the German Moravian colony which had been founded at Bethlehem, Pennsylvania developed into the first important music center in the United States (Sidelight 2). When George Washington visited Bethlehem in 1782 he was greeted, as so many other visitors have since been greeted, by the Moravian trombone choir. Five years later we find a little girl writing from her school at Bethlehem: *I play the guitar twice a day; am taught the spinet and forte-piano, and sometimes I play the organ.*

Philadelphia has also the honor of producing the first native-born composer of American music. His name was Francis Hopkinson (1737–1791), and he was an important man in his day, a signer of the Declaration of Independence, a judge of the Admiralty, and a great friend of Washington. He was one of a group of musical amateurs which used to meet regularly in its members' houses to play and sing together, and it may well have been for such a meeting that he wrote the first song to be composed by a native-born American: *My Days Have Been So Wondrous Free.*

After the American Revolution there came a flood of well-trained artists and teachers to this country, men who easily crowded out all the native musicians in the artistic life of the young republic. The most original of these (his admirers did not hesitate to call him the Beethoven of America) was a rich Bohemian amateur, Anton Philip Heinrich (1781–1861), who came to America in 1820 and settled in the Kentucky wilderness. There he composed a great number of instrumental and

Bettmann Archive

SINGING IN AN OLD AMERICAN CHURCH

orchestral works under the title *The Dawning of Music in Kentucky*. These compositions, which call for a large orchestra to play them, were mostly *program works* dealing with such subjects as the American Indian or descriptive of such American scenes as Niagara Falls. Very probably if they should be played today, we would find them strange and rather amusing. It was William Henry Fry (1813–1864), the composer of the first American grand opera to be produced (*Leonora*, 1845), who said that "until the American public shall learn to

183

support American artists, art will not become indigenous to this country." This is a statement as true, and unfortunately as largely disregarded, today as it was when it was written in 1852.

There was one stalwart figure who did help somewhat in bringing the native composer into prominence during these middle years of the nineteenth century — Lowell Mason (1792–1872). He was a bank clerk who turned musician and wrote a great many hymn tunes that are still used in our churches. He also succeeded in persuading the Boston school board in 1836 to make the study of music a regular part of its school curriculum, thus starting a movement the full effects of which are not yet visible. Louis M. Gottschalk (1829–1869), born in New Orleans, trained in Paris, started the fashion in this country for artists to affect glamorous backgrounds and foreign manners. These have been features of our musical life ever since. As a composer he was not particularly important, although he wrote a great number of rather sentimental piano pieces based on Creole backgrounds.

The first United States composer to write big-scale music for performance by a symphony orchestra was John Knowles Paine (1839–1906). His *First Symphony* was played by one of the great pioneer American orchestras, that of Theodore Thomas, in 1876. Trained in Germany, Paine was the first professor of music in an American college (at Harvard). He had a number of famous pupils, who, together with some other composers living in that vicinity, formed what has been called the Boston Group of American Composers. This group has had a strong influence upon the development of our styles and tastes in music. Strongly contrasting with these New Eng-

184

EDWARD MACDOWELL, America's first composer of international reputation, an engraving by Howard Simon

landers was Edward MacDowell (1861–1908), a New Yorker of Scottish descent and a man of great musical imagination and high purposes. He is thought by many to be our outstanding composer so far. MacDowell's short piano pieces and orchestral works are still played today and are thought to be typically American.

185

Courtesy of Phillips Memorial Gallery, Washington, D.C.

SUNDAY AFTERNOON, 1926, a painting by Hopper

There have been many other important composers whose works have become known mostly in the twentieth century. Since the country has grown more and more musical and there are many more opportunities for performing good music, it is natural that our composers should become better. Some of the best-known of these later men are Deems Taylor (b. 1885), Howard Hanson (b. 1896), Roy Harris (b. 1898), Aaron Copland (b. 1900), Samuel Barber (b. 1910), and William Schumann (b. 1910). It is always difficult to form final opinions regarding the work of contemporary composers such as these, but the very fact that these men have written so much good

186

music and that it is being played is sufficient proof that the country is coming of age musically. This music has something original to say, something that has not already been said by foreign writers. Perhaps when the people of our country become better integrated as a nation and learn more about what music can mean in their lives, they will see the necessity for cultivating more and better American music (Sidelight 3). And then it may well come to pass that we will produce some of the world's great composers. There is every reason to believe that events, as they are now shaping, will bring about such results.

SIDELIGHTS

1. William Billings was born in Boston in 1746 of humble parents and apprenticed as a tanner. Later he became interested in music and its development and became not only an important native composer but also one of the most original characters in eighteenth-century America. From 1770 on (the year of Beethoven's birth) Billings issued a number of church tunes in "fuguing style," through which he maintained "the audience is entertained and delighted, their minds surprisingly agitated and extremely fluctuated, sometimes declaring for one part, sometimes for another." He concludes his description of these tunes with the characteristic line, "Oh ecstatic! Rush on, you sons of harmony!"

2. Olin Downes, in *The Treasury of American Song*, tells the story of how the town of Bethlehem received its name. On Christmas Eve, 1741, the neighbors from miles around had gathered to celebrate the holiday in the first house built

Courtesy of Rosenberg Galleries

NEW YORK AT NIGHT, a painting by Max
Weber

in the little village, a house which served both as a place of
worship and as a defense against the Indians. There was a
question as to whether the town should be called Jerusalem or

188

Bethlehem, and Count Zinzendorf, the leader and founder, at this Christmas Eve service was inspired to improvise a song to the effect that it was Bethlehem, and not Jerusalem, that gave Christ to save us. The settlers were so moved that then and there they decided to call their new settlement Bethlehem. The famous Bethlehem Bach Choir of today is descended from the Collegium Musicum, a body of vocalists and instrumentalists which was founded in 1748 for playing the works of Haydn and Mozart.

3. Here is what Deems Taylor, the well-known American writer and radio commentator, has to say about this:

We Americans are not a race. America is a club, not a motherland. Her people have almost no common thoughts and feelings and instincts. We talk a good deal about the Spirit of '76 and the ideals of the Founding Fathers. They once existed, too; but that was long ago, when we were a race of transplanted Englishmen. By now, our blood is such a conglomeration of diverse racial strains that we have hardly any nationalistic feeling at all, in the European sense.

All of which does not make for a national school of music or any sort of art. It is not easy to find in our painting or poetry or music any unmistakably American characteristics, to isolate, as it were, an aesthetic bacillus that flourishes in our own culture. Edward MacDowell, George Chadwick — German composers, both of them with a deliberate touch of Amerindian. Sargent was a superb painter of the French school.... Our best novelists seem purely American — frequently for no other reason than that their subject matter is American. But read a

189

Collection of The Museum of Modern Art, New York

THE SENATE, 1935, a painting by William Gropper

poem by Edna Millay or Archibald MacLeish without knowing the poet's name and (disregarding geographical allusions)
tell me the poet's nationality.

The great American music of the future will be a music to
which America will listen and respond. But it will not be the
music of Sitting Bull or Booker T. Washington or even George
[Gershwin]. It will belong to us because one of us made it;
but it will, like all great music, belong to the world. And the
world will not be curious regarding the name and address of
the composer.[2]

[2] From *Of Men and Music.* New York: Simon and Schuster, Inc.

190

OUR OWN ART MUSIC

Here are some qualities that may help you determine whether music is "American" or not:

1. Must it be based on native tunes, or may it be based on tunes from other countries?
2. Is it American simply because the composer has lived here most of his life?
3. Must it express some phase of life, some aspect of feeling that can be definitely recognized as American?
4. Is music American because it contains new ideas created by an American resident or peculiar to the American people?
5. Can a composer who has put native feeling into old forms be called American?

Bring to class some good examples of real American poetry. How does this compare, in your estimation, with the quality of American music?

Illustrating this chapter are four pictures illustrative of different types of modern American painting. Can you find their parallels in music and poetry? Which seem to you the most characteristically American? Why?

MUSIC TO LISTEN TO

William Billings: *Fuguing Tunes*   C M 434

Does this music have the effect designed by its composer? (See Sidelight 1.)

Edward MacDowell: *To a Wild Rose* }
                 To a Water Lily }   C   4279–M

            Sea Pieces: A.D. *1620*   C DB 1235

These short pieces for the piano show MacDowell's genius at its best.

Deems Taylor: *Through the Looking-Glass,*
    Suite for Orchestra   C M 350

We have already mentioned this work in an earlier chapter as a wonderful example of fantasy in music. It presents five pictures from Lewis Carroll's immortal nonsensical fairy tale. The two best are *Jabberwocky*, the poem which Alice found so mystifying until it was explained to her by Humpty Dumpty, and the *Looking-Glass Insects* that bothered Alice so — the Gnat, the Rocking-horse-fly, the Snap-dragon-fly, the Bee-elephant, and the Bread-and-butter-fly. Does this humor seem English or American? What would be the difference?

Roy Harris: *Symphony No. 3*

Thought by many critics to be this composer's best work, this symphony conveys much of the wide sweep and breezy manner of the Middle West, where Harris was born. Instead of being divided, as most classic symphonies are, into separate movements, this is in one movement. Compare this with the European influences shown in MacDowell's works.

Aaron Copland: *Music for the Theatre*   V M 744
               El Salón México   V M 546
               A Lincoln Portrait   V M 1088
               Appalachian Spring   V M 1046

It is not often that we are able to trace the development of a composer as readily as in the case of this Brooklyn-born American. The first of these four pieces was written in 1925 and frankly adopts the jazz idiom, with many direct allusions to Tin Pan Alley. The second, composed in 1936, is marked by a great simplicity and directness. We will treat this in more detailed fashion in Chapter XVIII, but it is interesting to note here that Copland makes use of a number of Mexican folk tunes to give the proper atmosphere to his description of a famous dance hall in Mexico City. Compare his treatment of the folk tune *La Paloma Azul* with that of Chávez (page 203).

The third piece is written somewhat in the style of the modern radio treatment of music, with a narrator and musical background. In the last number Copland has shown that he can express himself with deep feeling and real poetry. Thus we have glimpses in these examples of how a rather hard-boiled American experimentalist developed gradually into a sensitive, imaginative poet.

PROPHECY, a mural by José C. Orozco, suggesting the combining of the Conqueror and the Cross in the subjugating of America

194

OST people have the idea that the European style of music was transplanted to the shores of North America by the English settlers who came to Virginia in 1607 and the Pilgrims who founded the Plymouth Colony in 1620. Actually, however, European music in the United States may be said to have begun in that part of the country settled by the Spaniards in the sixteenth century, later (in 1845) ceded to us, and now comprising the states of Texas and New Mexico. A full hundred years before the Pilgrims set foot on Plymouth Rock, the intrepid Spanish explorer Hernando Cortes battled his way with more than five hundred men, some horses, and cannon inland from Veracruz, where he had landed on Good Friday, 1519. Arriving at Tenochtitlan (now Mexico City), the powerful capital of the Aztec empire of Montezuma, he conquered it in 1521. This achievement resulted in the complete destruction of the great Aztec civilization which had flourished throughout Mexico up to that time, with the loss of its art, its religion, its social customs, and even its language. The era of Spanish colonial domination in the Americas had begun.

Included in Cortes' forces were at least ten musicians, whose names are still known today. These men helped bring about a development of music in Mexico earlier than elsewhere in the *Nuevo Mundo*. Within a few years after the fall of the Aztec capital, monks opened schools which included music in their instruction; and some of the Spanish soldier-musicians quickly started schools for teaching dancing and secular music in the new Spanish city. By the middle of the century an organist and choirmaster had been appointed for the church which later became the Cathedral (a magnificent building whose cornerstone was laid in 1573). And in 1556 the earliest-known book with musical notation printed in the Western Hemisphere was published at Mexico City, eighty-four years before the *Bay Psalm Book* of the New England Puritans appeared. So we see that American music had an early and an important start in the lands lying to the south of the Rio Grande.

At the time when our forefathers in the United States were singing their crude hymns published in the early psalm and hymn books or the vigorous, but also crude, anthems of Billings, the Boston tanner, the choristers of Mexico City Cathedral were already singing the masses and motets of the Spanish and Italian masters. And soon these pieces, brought from Europe by church musicians and musical missionaries, were sung in the other cathedrals of Latin America and served as models for similar compositions that were written by native Mexican, Venezuelan, and Brazilian composers.

In the field of music for the theater, the composers of the southern countries have certainly outdistanced their northern colleagues. We have had no opera composer like the

196

Brazilian Gomes (1839–1896), whose operas were performed again and again in foreign theaters. And a recent compilation of operas and ballets by Spanish- and Portuguese-American composers whose works have been played on European stages

Courtesy of the Brazilian Govt. Trade Bureau

THE OPERA HOUSE IN RIO DE JANEIRO

shows that there are more than fifteen hundred such works — a record that we in the United States cannot begin to equal. Of course, this is partly due to the fact that opera and dramatic music found a ready and natural home with the Spanish and Portuguese colonials. We find that many of the operas of the well-known Italian composers were given in Havana, Rio de Janeiro, or Buenos Aires before they were heard in New York, which we like to think of as the musical capital of the

197

New World. And so important was Brazilian music during the reign of Emperor Dom Pedro (a descendant of the royal family of Portugal, which came to Brazil for a time to escape Napoleon) that Richard Wagner thought seriously, in 1857, of giving the world première of his *Tristan und Isolde* in Rio de Janeiro.

Today all the countries to the south of us are bustling with musical activity. In Mexico, Carlos Chávez is trying to write music that is expressive of the Mexicans themselves and yet takes full advantage of the experiences of the outstanding European composers. This music is, as one of the critics has said, strangely somber and fantastic, "music which refuses to smile and yet which possesses strange power." It speaks of the past greatness of the Indian as well as of the European influences that have affected all Mexico and Mexican art so strongly. Another important Mexican composer was Silvestre Revueltas (d. 1940).

Brazil has a parallel figure in Villa-Lobos (b. 1884), an energetic, largely self-taught composer who has written the almost unbelievable number of over fourteen hundred works of every kind imaginable. He, too, tries to instill a feeling of national Brazilian backgrounds into his music; and the listener easily recognizes in his music the savage throb of primitive peoples, the life of the steaming jungles, as well as the sophisticated polish of the art of Brazil. A well-known Brazilian has said of the art of his country: "Its outstanding trait is that artists have ceased to be snobbish imitators of European fashions. They have stepped down to earth and joined hands with the common man in this universal crusade for a better world of peace, brotherhood, and freedom" (Side-

Courtesy of The Museum of Modern Art, New York
Oscar Niemeyer, Architect

THE MINISTRY OF EDUCATION AND HEALTH IN RIO DE JANEIRO

This building is a splendid example of what many architects have called the most advanced public architecture in the world.

light). This is a good description of the artistic aims of Villa-Lobos. Can you think of any better ambition for an artistic creator? Other prominent Brazilian composers are Fernández, Mignone, and Guarnieri.

199

In addition to these well-known men, there are many others in Venezuela, Colombia, Peru, Chile, Argentina, and other Central and South American countries devoting their lives to the writing of music. Working together, these men have produced a great musical heritage, one which will have important results for the future. And we who are so proud of the expanding developments in music and poetry and architecture and painting that are taking place within our own country must learn to correlate these with the work of the artists who live to the south of us; as we must learn to think of all those living in these continents as Americans in the real sense of the word.

SIDELIGHT

One of the few Brazilian authors whose work has become known in this country, Erico Verissimo, whose novel *Crossroads* has been published in English, has this to say: [1]

Brazilians are generally a simple kind of people. Of course they have many defects, but I believe that when all is said and done you will find in them a residue of virtues. They hate war and violence, and they have no color problem. They are hospitable and kindly, even when their passionate nature causes them to seem intolerant or aggressive. Brazilians are Bohemians; they do not care very much about growing rich or having colossal buildings, plants, or cities. They love to loaf, and they have a wonderful sense of humor. They live more by the heart than by reason. Friendship is a magic word down there.

[1] From Erico Verissimo: *Brazilian Literature*. Copyright, 1945, by The Macmillan Company and used with their permission.

ART MUSIC IN LATIN AMERICA

A recent writer on race relations puts the whole matter of international co-operation in this way:

There is mainly one way that people can learn to know each other better, and that is to enter upon co-operative fields of cultural and commercial interest. It is very simple and has been expressed over and over again by those people working for world unity — knowledge is the key to understanding anything, and above all to the understanding of other people of different races and cultures.

In order to accomplish this, there must be a dissolution of the ignorance which swirls between people, and the future appreciation of each other as individuals will see the dissolution of prejudice and the growth of knowledge and understanding.

MODERN BOOKS ON LATIN AMERICA

A *Guide to Latin-American Music* edited and prepared by Gilbert Chase. Concerning this *Guide*, a government publication says:

As an important initial step toward the systematic organization of bibliographical materials which may form the basis for the study of music in the Americas, the Library of Congress has published A *Guide to Latin-American Music*. Prepared by Gilbert Chase, this 274-page volume was compiled and published by the library as part of the program of the Interdepartmental Committee on Scientific and Cultural Co-operation of the Department of State.

Fundamentally, the *Guide* is a detailed bibliography of both literary and musical materials referring to our expounding the art of music in the sister republics south of the United States.

Included is also an important section on parts of our own country where Spanish and Portuguese musical influences have been felt. Musicologists, historians, sociologists, and all other scholars interested in the musical and social activities of Latin America, in the flourishing of its folk music or the growth of its art music, are expected to find this *Guide* an important tool for further study and investigation. Those exploring the field for the first time will look upon it as a benefit denied their predecessors.

The *Guide*, arranged geographically by country and thereafter systematically by carefully selected topics, includes material published as late as 1943. The larger countries have of course wider topical coverage than the smaller, but a general pattern prevails throughout. For example, under Brazil there are the following main sub-divisions: introduction; general and miscellaneous; biography and criticism; lyric theater; education; instruction and theory; national anthem; folk and primitive music; popular music; collections of music (general). Included in the bibliographical compilation are 2,699 entries for entire books, pertinent book chapters and sections, and periodical articles. A preface and an introduction to the *Guide* afford insight into the problems of the field and disclose their extent and ramifications. At the end there are a key to periodicals, an index to authors, and an index of names and subjects.

A *Guide to Latin-American Music* is obtainable by purchase from the Superintendent of Documents, U. S. Government Printing Office, Washington 25, D. C. This is only one of a number of valuable books published by our government for the promotion of better Pan American relations.

ART MUSIC IN LATIN AMERICA

Slonimsky: *Music of Latin America.* New York: Thomas Y. Crowell Company.

This is a standard reference book on the subject and contains accounts of both folk and standard Latin-American music. Written in a personal, interesting way.

Selected References in English to Latin-American Music prepared by Fern. Washington, D. C.: Music Division, Pan American Union.

For those who want to know the vast amount of reading material available in English on the subject of Latin-American music, this reference list will be invaluable.

MUSIC TO LISTEN TO

Chávez: *Danza a Centeotl* from the ballet
Los Cuatro Soles [2]   c   70334–D

This dance, in adoration of the Indian goddess of maize, Centeotl, is really a dance of-praise for the abundance and fertility of the earth. It is taken from a modern ballet and makes use of musical themes which its composer heard used by Indians in their religious dances of our own times.

Chávez: *La Paloma Azul*   c   70333–D

A beautiful arrangement of a well-known Mexican folk song for chorus and orchestra.

[2] The symbols in the list of records may be interpreted as follows:

c	Columbia	con	Continental Records
v	Victor	hmv-	His Majesty's Voice (English Victor)
h	Hargail	b	Bost

Villa-Lobos: *Bachianas Brasileiras No. 1*   v   DM 773

Do you feel any particular Brazilian characteristics in this music by the country's most important composer? In it he attempts, he tells us, to transmit the universal spirit of Bach (one of the greatest of all composers, revered by musicians the world over) into the soul of Brazil. Written for eight cellos, this work is in three movements: Introduction; Prelude; Fugue. Villa-Lobos appropriately calls the last movement a conversation. Can you see why?

Villa-Lobos: *Bachianas Brasileiras No. 5*   c   71670–D

Here, in one of the loveliest pieces of music to come to us from Latin America, we can feel much more readily the soul of Brazil. How beautifully the soprano voice of Bidú Sayão, a native Brazilian who has won fame in the Metropolitan Opera in New York, combines with the tones of the orchestra!

Latin-American Piano Classics   CON ALBUM A 103

This is a group of short piano pieces by some of the best-known composers of Latin America. They show how the piano style can be adapted to the rhythms and color of the lands to the south of us.

> Vianna: *Corta — Jaga*
> Villa-Lobos: *Brasileiras No. 2*
> Mignone: *Mocrobinho*
>   *Congada*
> Lecuona: *Andalucía*
>   *Malaguena*
> Fernández: *Valse Suburbaine*

Fernández: *Batuque* from the ballet *Il Rei-
sado do Pastoreio*   V   11–8608
Batuque from the opera *Malazarte*

                                                                 C   M–588

These very effective evocations are from the more primitive aspects of Brazilian folklore.

Mignone: *Cantiga de Ninar*   V   10–1181
Lenda Brasileira, Nos. 1, 2 ⎫
Tango Brasileiro   ⎬   B   BA 2
Quasi Modinha   ⎭

The first of these is a lovely lullaby with piano and cello accompaniment. The last three are popular Brazilian piano pieces played by the composer.

Guarnieri: *Queha o coco menina*   H   MW 700
Dem Bau

Intriguing songs with guitar accompaniment.

Respighi: *Impressions of Brazil*   HMV   DB 4643–44

Three vivid impressions written by an Italian under the spell of this Latin-American country:

Tropical Night
Butantan, A Garden in São Paolo
Canzone and Danza

A HIGH-SCHOOL GROUP MAKING MUSIC

CHAPTER X.   *IN CONCLUSION AND*
RETROSPECT

EVERY so often in a learning process such as this one, it is wise to stop and take stock of what has been accomplished before going on to further discoveries and new ideas. Here is a very brief summary of what has been covered in the first nine chapters of this course. Use it to make your own review of the material and as suggestions for short essays to be written on the different subjects discussed.

We have been concerned so far largely with the development of music on the American continents, but we will find that many of the concepts that we have learned and the experiences we have had with American music will be valid for the more general European style to be studied next. It makes little difference whether we are talking about Europeans or Americans when we divide men into two general classes and label one imaginative and the other practical. And it is perfectly obvious that, although the practical people are needed if we are going to exist at all here upon earth, much of the satisfaction we get out of living comes from our contact with the imaginative class. It is through realizing that there are things that are beyond the eating and the drinking, the walking and the talking, that we get a sense of how great and strange and beautiful human existence can be. And it is the artist, a man who feels this more keenly than do most of us and who has expressed it more clearly, who has constructed out of his dreams the most endurable record we have of man's existence here upon earth. This record, as we get to know it through our study of music, painting, literature, sculpture, and architecture, can enlarge our own experience, increase our own joy in living, and give us some idea of how we may attempt to plan our future upon what has transpired in the past. Art, in a word, is a great matter, and its function in the world a most important one.

Because of the peculiar circumstances of our historical development and the facts of our physical environment, we who live in the United States of America have not been as conscious of the importance of art in our lives as have the people who have lived for hundreds of generations in Europe. And now that we have emerged with little harm, comparatively speaking, from the terrible struggles of World War II and possess in addition so much of the world's present and potential wealth, people outside our boundaries are looking more and more to us as leaders. This is as true of artistic matters as it is of economic and social and political matters. Are we ready for such leadership? What are our artistic assets and liabilities? These are important questions that need answering before we can take the place expected of us in the guidance of the world.

We have found that we do possess a considerable musical heritage, not as great as that of Europe, to be sure, but one of which we can nevertheless be proud. There is especial vigor in our popular music, the music which, to use the words of one of our best American poets, gives the feel and atmosphere, the layout and lingo of our national regions, of our kinds of men, of our customs and slogans. A number of influences have been strong in this shaping of our musical heritage, none of them stronger or more significant than the music of the Negro. As a people, brought to this continent originally against their own will and in circumstances that do little credit to the white man, they are great natural artists and have contributed strikingly to American artistic life both north and south of the Isthmus of Panama. Much can be said, too, for the strong faith in the future and the hardy endurance of our pioneer ancestors who expressed themselves in homely but sincere ways in music and literature. It is a strong condemnation of our own times that so many of these simple means of sincere artistic expression have been commercialized to such a degree as to cause them to lose much of their real character and significance.

This is certainly true of jazz, that peculiarly American style of musical performance, which has become popular the world round; and which, together with the movies, seems to represent to most countries our ideals of culture. Starting with a perfectly sincere, spontaneous expression of real value artistically, this kind of music has become so standardized and commercialized as to lose its original flavor and importance. So there has arisen a strong movement to get back to the primitive qualities of the original hot jazz as evolved in New Orleans.

Anyone who has ever visited any American country beyond the borders of the United States will realize well enough how strongly the people of these countries resent the idea that we are the only Americans worth consideration. And quite rightly, too. For not only were these countries discovered and settled before the United States, but they possessed significant and important cultures of their own before the white man came from Europe. And they have succeeded in many cases in amalgamating the various elements of their culture into a more unified and characteristically American expression than have we.

This is particularly true of music. Serious music has been cultivated and loved throughout Latin America since the time of the early Spanish settlers. But it is the folk music of these countries south of the Rio Grande that has attained a blend of European, Negroid, and Indian elements that has not been achieved here in the United States at all. There is little wonder that we have become so fascinated by these Latin-American songs and dances; they are among the most colorful, rhythmical, and expressive folk music ever evolved. But here, too, mechanical standardization has had its bad effects, and some of this individuality and freshness has already disappeared.

Art, although a suspicious and disturbing word for many Americans, can be shown to be something that is immediately and importantly concerned with the processes of everyday living. For it is in essence the adaptation of the things we use in ordinary life so as to make them more beautiful and effective. In this sense we have developed a real American type of art music, music which has been consciously planned and written to achieve certain effects and to carry certain definite meanings to its hearers. In this it differs from folk or popular music, which is the real possession of the people within a country. There is a place, and it is a most important one, for this kind of art music in America. We need not think that popular music is the only type of musical expression that is worth listening to, or that classical (art) music is long-haired and dull. Our rising generation of serious American composers is writing excellent music, and it deserves our enthusiasm and support unless we are to think of music as simply a museum-like exhibition of the great things that have come out of Europe in the past. Certainly this would be no way to assert our confidence in the future of American leadership in the arts!

PART TWO

BACKGROUNDS FOR LISTENING

THE GREEK THEATER AT EPIDAURUS

Built in the fourth century, B.C., this is the best example of the Greek theater. In the center is the circular *orchestra*, where the chorus danced and sang; behind it are the remains of the stage buildings. This auditorium held about 15,000 spectators.

214

CHAPTER XI. *EUROPE, A BRIDGE BETWEEN*
ASIA AND AMERICA

THOSE of us who listen to music today are apt to take a great deal for granted. We are able to sit at a piano and play any kind of music we please; we put on a record and listen to the phonograph reproduce the interpretation of some great player or singer; or we turn on the radio and enjoy a great orchestra's interpretation of a symphony or concerto. Without giving much thought to how our music came to be what it is today, or how long a period of experiment was necessary before it developed as we know it, or even how the instruments which produce this music at the present time evolved from primitive beginnings, we enjoy listening. All of this is natural enough, for music is an art created for sensory enjoyment rather than for thought. But if we can learn something about the great effort that has been required over a long period of the world's history to make our music what it is, we will be able to appreciate it the more and realize how fortunate we are in having it so easily available.

In talking about music today, we often try to make a distinction between *classical* (meaning music that appeals to people of serious tastes) and *modern* (meaning music that is in a light vein — jazz, swing, etc.). As a matter of fact, such distinctions are neither exact nor necessary. One of the usual definitions of classical art — music, painting, sculpture — that is often given is that it is art which conforms to some already established form or pattern. In this sense we might say, of course, that the famous *St. Louis Blues* is a classic piece. And anyone who knows anything at all about music will realize that there are many serious composers who write what is properly known as modern music in great quantities, such composers as Copland, Harris, and Shostakovich, for example. But none of this music could be called popular in any sense. So these terms are confusing and inexact.

We have already suggested in another place what the differences are between the more serious, composed, *art* type of music that is generally spoken of as *classical* and the popular, folkish kind of music that is so easily enjoyed by the average person. And we have also said that although much of the world's finest music is of the composed sort, this music need not necessarily be thought of as being *greater* than folk or popular music any more than we should think of all classical music as being dull and unnatural. There is, we must never forget, a time and place in the world for both these kinds of music and art.

If we want to make distinctions, it would be much more useful to think of both *classical* and *popular* music as being European or Western in character and very different from the music used by the peoples of Asia and Africa. This European music is the result of long centuries of experiment and development which have taken place in Europe, where so

216

many of the great roles in history have been played. It differs in so many respects from the great musical systems that are in use today by millions of people living in India, China, and Arabia that we who are used to it can hardly listen with any

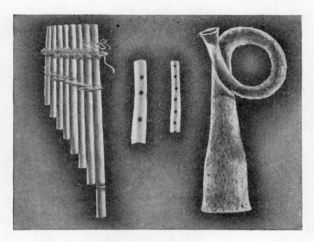

PANPIPE, FLUTES, HORN

We are indebted to Europe, too, for the development of crude, primitive instruments like these into the fine wood winds used in modern symphony orchestras.

pleasure at all to Chinese, Arabian, or Indian musicians. The history of our European music is an interesting one and worthy of long and detailed study, but even a brief outline can show enough of its main features to enable us to trace the steps by which the simple, crude music of our prehistoric ancestors became the complicated, expressive art which is used today in Europe and America.

An astronomer looking at our world from Mars would probably consider the continent of Europe as being nothing

more than a peninsular extension of the continent of Asia
(see map). And he would be more than ever confirmed in
such an opinion if he could learn something of the history of
these regions. Practically everything that we are today, including the fact of our existence, came originally out of Asia. It
was there, unless all present speculations as to racial origins

218

are wrong, on the western plains not far from the shores of the Mediterranean, that the branch of the human race to which we belong had its beginnings. And it was those valleys of the Tigris and Euphrates that gave us the rudiments of the sciences and arts and the first glimmerings of moral principles that set man apart from the rest of the animal world. Later on, Asia was to give the world its great religions — Judaism, Christianity, Mohammedanism, Buddhism — as well as the fundamentals upon which were later constructed the entire framework of our present civilization. In reality, a great deal of the much-vaunted progress of the West is merely a continuation of the progress begun in the East. And it is the opinion of many geographers and historians that, as Van Loon has put it, it is highly doubtful whether Europe could have produced what it has if it had not learned the rudiments of everything it knows in the schools of the East.

This is as true for music as for the other branches of art and science. The detailed knowledge of mathematics and astronomy and medicine possessed by the Greeks was the result of long centuries of slow growth and painful thinking, a great deal of which was originally done along the banks of the Tigris and Euphrates rivers. Even such "native" Greek arts as architecture and sculpture, arts in which this people achieved results that have never been surpassed, were built upon the techniques and ideas borrowed from the older nations to the east of them.

We are accustomed to think of European music as reaching its first great peak of achievement in Greece; but, as a matter of fact, Greece acted as a connecting link between the music of the older Asia and the newer Europe. The elements out of which the Greeks built their musical system, a system that was to determine the destiny of Western music for two thousand years, were mostly imported. Not a single musical instrument originated in Greece, and many of the scales the Greeks used were borrowed from Asia Minor. But, being a people possessed of great imagination, outstanding as thinkers and artists, the Greeks greatly improved upon the achievements of their predecessors. And the well-organized musical systems which they handed on to their successors included definite, fixed scales and a real system by which music could be written down (notation). With them, choral singing was a highly developed art, used in their religious ceremonies and combined with great theatrical dramas. Instrumental music was largely subordinated to it, although the people loved to play the *kithara* (lyre) and the *aulos* (reed pipe). And the great athletic contests such as the Olympic and Pythian games often included competitions in instrumental music.

In 586 B.C. a famous piper at the Pythian games in Delphi represented on his aulos a battle between Apollo and the dragon. This long descriptive piece had a program that included the first meeting of the contestants, the contest itself, the triumph following victory, and, at the very end, the death of the dragon. This certainly sounds like modern *program music!*

Another race whose music furnished the foundation upon which our modern European system was built was the Hebrew. A group of wandering shepherds, they entered the region known as modern Palestine somewhere around 1500–1300 B.C. Some of them sought refuge in Egypt when drought and famine attacked their own land, were imprisoned, and

220

finally rescued by Moses about 1200 B.C. Music to them was a means of expressing their joys and sorrows. The Bible, which tells their story so eloquently, describes how Moses, after he had led his people through the Red Sea, sang to glorify the Lord, and all the people joined in. When their later leaders, Saul and David, returned from victorious battles against their enemies, they were welcomed with singing and playing and dancing.

Later on, these Jehovah-worshiping people settled down and established their own civilization centering in Jerusalem, a civilization which copied that of their neighbors — the Egyptians, the Philistines, and the Canaanites. Then it was that the practice of music in Israel became professional. King David, a musician himself, founded the first official body of musicians for the temple he was building. These musicians, or Levites, were trained in instrumental playing and in singing; and later, under David's son Solomon (reigned c. 973–935 B.C.), some four thousand of them were selected as students in a sort of academy of sacred music. A little of the glories of this music provided for Solomon's temple may be learned from this description given in II Chronicles 5:12–14:

...the singers...with their sons and their brethren, being arrayed in white linen, having cymbals and psalteries and harps, stood at the east end of the altar, and with them a hundred and twenty priests sounding with trumpets: It came even to pass, as the trumpeters and singers were as one, to make one sound to be heard in praising and thanking the Lord; and when they lifted up their voice with the trumpets and cymbals and instruments of music, and praised the Lord, saying, For he is *good; for his mercy endureth for ever: that then the house was filled with a cloud, even the house of the Lord; So that the priests could not stand to minister by reason of the cloud: for the glory of the Lord had filled the house of God.*

It was this tradition which, carried down through the ages, survived in the Jewish synagogues until after the time of Christ and was incorporated into the musical practice of the new Christian sect during the first century A.D., where it combined with the Greek-Roman ideals of the period.

The Roman civilization which flourished for something less than a thousand years, beginning with the sixth century B.C., acted as the medium by which its own contributions to politics, law, philosophy, literature, and art, as well as the ideas it had gained from the Greek and other Eastern cultures, were passed on to the West. Thence they came down to us by direct descent through the Middle Ages and the Renaissance. In so far as music is concerned, it was a most fortunate circumstance that the rise of the Christian Church coincided with the decline of the Roman Empire. For as the Church increased in strength and power, especially after Constantine the Great became a Christian emperor in 312 A.D., it adopted to its own needs and purposes the music and art which it had inherited from the past through Rome. And by the time of Pope Gregory the Great (540–604), when Rome became the center of the Christian Church, a well-developed set of vocal chants had been written and collected. They were based upon the traditions of the past but suited to the Church's needs at the time. With the exception of a few minor changes, these *Gregorian Chants* have remained in use until today.

Thereafter for many centuries — until the time of the Renaissance, in fact — music was cultivated largely under the auspices of the Church and its connected establishments (the monasteries and universities), although the people had their own songs and simple instrumental tunes. This music of the Church was largely vocal in character, consisting first of chant-like melodies that were sung in unison by choir and congregation. Later, beginning in the eighth century, other melodies were added to these, thus making what we have come to know as *part music*. This developed rapidly until, around 1600, it became a most amazing series of intertwined and complicated vocal melodies, weaving in and around each other and producing an elaborate *contrapuntal* texture. Instruments, which seem to have been introduced into Europe directly from Asia, if they were used at all, played along with the voice parts.

Thus we can imagine what the music was like which resounded through the great spaces of the Gothic churches, so many of which were built during the thirteenth century. This music consisted of elaborate, intricate contrapuntal melodies, spun together in a tonal web that seems most confusing to modern ears and supported at times by string or brass instruments playing along with the voices. To present-day listeners, this music would indeed sound *Gothic* in the original sense of this word — something that seems rude and barbaric.

During the Renaissance (roughly, the fourteenth and fifteenth centuries), with its new attitude toward life and its interest in beauty and humanity rather than only in religion and the future life, music, like so many of the other activities of man, escaped from the bondage of the Church. It became simpler, easier to make, and more enjoyable to listen to. No

223

longer was it constantly associated with sacred texts, but many pieces were written for secular use, to be sung in castle and hall, for the amusement and pleasure of the people.

Before 1400, players on instruments were limited to accompanying the singers. After that time they slowly began to make themselves independent musicians, at first taking over the popular dance tunes of the people and adapting them to their own use or to playing on their viols, shawms, flutes, etc. the music originally written for voices. For a long time, even as late as the seventeenth century, a piece of music was often labeled: *To be either sung or played.* Finally composers produced compositions that were entirely different in style from those written for voices; and the great instrumental period of music, in which we are still living, began. These developments of secular vocal and instrumental music may be thought of as originating in Italy, that most artistic of all countries and center of general humanistic ideals. But they quickly spread to other countries: France, which at this time was just beginning its great role of guardian of civilization; England, which we must think of as just beginning its great period of expansion and development; Spain and Germany, the latter hardly much more at this time than a miscellaneous collection of unimportant states.

After this, developments came thick and fast. Opera, a happy combination of vocal and instrumental joys, set to a dramatic story and mounted on an elaborate stage, was invented. It spread rapidly over all Europe. There arose a new generation, which demanded that music appeal not only to the souls and minds of listeners but to their hearts as well. Composers tried to put feeling into their music; and it was

Photograph by Philip Noble

THE GOTHIC INTERIOR OF WINCHESTER
CATHEDRAL, ENGLAND

told at the time that, when in one of the new operas the leading lady sang a heart-rending lament telling of her being for-
saken by her love, the audience burst into tears (Sidelight).

In furthering this idea of expressing emotion in music, the
older contrapuntal, weaving style of music was gradually
changed for one which emphasized the importance of one
single part (usually the melody on top) as being better able

225

From the National Gallery, London

A THEATER OF THE RENAISSANCE, from a painting
ascribed to Ferdinando Bibbiena

European opera enjoyed its popularity in such elegant, aristocratic
surroundings as this. It was originally written for the enjoyment
and amusement of the aristocrats.

to express man's emotional outcries. New instruments were
developed, especially the agile, powerfully-toned violin family;
and others (such as the keyboard instruments) were greatly
improved, thus making instrumental music more popular than
ever. The idea of combining instruments into orchestral
groups possessing different tone qualities, with definite parts
assigned to specific instruments, began to be popular. A uni-
form standardization of tonal intervals in the scales made up
of tones and half tones was generally adopted. This system,
or method, made possible easy and frequent changes of key.

226

EIGHTEENTH-CENTURY
ORCHESTRA AND SINGERS

Bass and stringed instruments are at
the left; the organist and drummer,
in the center. The conductor uses a
roll of music as a baton.

It opened the door to the whole modern style of composing. During this time music was largely supported by princely patrons and wealthy families. The people had their own ideas of singing and playing and dancing, ideas which were strongly rhythmic in character and were later to influence the more serious music of the professionals.

Still later on, during the latter years of the eighteenth and all of the nineteenth century, there was a further increase in the desire of composers to put feeling into their music. Spurred on by the political ideals of such movements as the American and French revolutions, with the insistence upon the personal rights of individual men, art became less and less aristocratic and more and more popular. The small salons and private theaters of the nobility, where so much earlier European music had been heard, were supplanted by large concert halls and opera houses, thus making it possible for large numbers of people to hear and enjoy music. More and more instruments were added to the orchestras, so that every shade of human feeling could be expressed. Opera houses became more elaborate and spectacular, thus appealing to much greater numbers of people. Whole flocks of virtuosos arrived on the musical scene, men who were interpreters of real genius and could popularize and glamorize the music which had been written for them by contemporary composers. These musicians, like Liszt, Chopin, and Paganini, made use of instruments that had reached their height in development after long years of painstaking care and experiment on the part of the instrument makers. In a word, the nineteenth century saw music change from an aristocratic to a democratic art, from something that had been created for and participated in by a

228

Press Association, Inc.

THE INTERIOR OF THE METROPOLITAN OPERA HOUSE, NEW YORK

Huge theaters such as this were built in the eighteenth and nineteenth centuries to give opportunities for a large number of people to enjoy elaborate and spectacular productions of opera. Several rows of boxes were provided for those patrons who could afford to pay for them. Support of the opera came largely through such means.

favored few to an art of the people — something which expressed their moods and feelings, delighted their ears, and enriched their lives. The works of the Romantic composers — Beethoven, Schubert, Schumann, Chopin, Wagner, Brahms, Tchaikovsky, Dvořák, Sibelius, and the rest — became known everywhere.

229

By the end of the nineteenth century such music became the common heritage of all the countries of Europe and had been transplanted to the new worlds of the Americas and Australia. It had even permeated as far afield as Japan, where it succeeded to a large degree in supplanting the native music. This tendency toward popularization was further strengthened during the twentieth century by the invention and development of such instruments as the phonograph and the radio, which make it possible for music to be heard anywhere and at any time the listener desires.

Thus the music lover on a South Sea island can hear a tolerable reproduction of the playing of the Boston Symphony, the London Philharmonic, or the Philadelphia orchestras even though he cannot hear the real thing in the concert halls of the United States or Europe. As was to be expected, such widespread interest in music on the part of people everywhere has emphasized certain of its popular elements, particularly those of rhythm and percussion. The underlying pulse that we feel in all music, expressed by certain arrangements of strong and weak beats, constitutes one of its strongest appeals. This underlying pulse is present in the most primitive as well as the most complex compositions. And the inclusion of all sorts of percussive instruments in our modern orchestras in order to emphasize these rhythmic beats is only a sign that this primitive *motor impulse*, which had long been rather suppressed in favor of melody and harmony, is alive today.

Jazz and swing, as we have seen, are simply glorified manifestations of this universal love for rhythm and percussion. Unfortunately, they also tend to emphasize the general desire that people seem to have for oversentimental expression. The

230

gradual introduction of feeling and sentiment in music, which we have just described, has finally resulted in such an over-exaggerated sentimentalism and ready-made sentimentality as

Photograph by O. Rothschild

HOLLYWOOD BOWL, CALIFORNIA

Hollywood Bowl in California accommodates 20,00c people hearing music at the same time, without any amount of distortion. In surroundings such as these, music now appeals to great numbers of people. Sometimes music is combined with the other arts, as in the ballet. Things are so arranged as to appeal to the tastes of the largest number of people.

to disgust the true lovers of music. As a sort of protest against this overpopularization of their art, many contemporary composers of serious music have adopted a strange, dissonant kind of writing, strongly at variance with former styles but closely

231

attuned to the mechanistic existence in which they find themselves. How future developments will affect music, only time can tell. The one thing we can be reasonably sure of is that we in this country will have a great deal to do with whatever happens.

There was a time in Europe when we may say, in general, that art was greater than politics. This was the Golden Age. And then politics rose, occupied the center of the European stage, and finally strangled art. *With art died good-will, tolerance, inspiration, and ecstasy.* We today have inherited the full results of this terrible period in Europe's development and know only too well what agony and suffering and destruction it has brought to the world. European civilization and the art it created almost passed from the earth. As some of the German musicians said when they learned that Hitler had come to power in Germany in 1933 and that the Nazis had burned the Parliament building in Berlin, *It's all over with Europe.* Today it seems as though they were right in their prophecy. But we must always remember, as a great German conductor and interpreter who saw Europe's glories go down in dust, Bruno Walter, reminds us: *The political leaders of Europe's destiny — such men as Napoleon, Kaiser Wilhelm, Hitler — are dead, but Beethoven still lives.*

SIDELIGHT

It was in Monteverdi's *Arianna*, sung in 1608 at the Court of Mantua. The Lament is:

> *So let me die.*
> *Why must I, who have trusted in thee,*

EUROPE, A BRIDGE

Feel the blows of such a cruel fate
And suffer so bitter a fortune?
Ah, let me perish, let me die!

QUESTIONS FOR DISCUSSION

In what particular respects does Western (European) civilization owe a great debt to Greek culture?

What systems of music other than the European are used today? Can you show how they differ from the European system?

Explain why the music of the Romantic period — that composed during the nineteenth century — is more pleasant to listen to than that written earlier.

Which of all the European countries has produced the greatest music? Can you suggest any reason for this fact?

What do you consider were the political events that brought "Europe's glories down in the dust"?

What are the differences between sentiment and sentimentality? Illustrate your explanation by giving examples.

MUSIC TO LISTEN TO

(The quotations are taken from this chapter.)

1. With the Greeks, "choral singing was a highly developed art, used in their religious ceremonies."

Hymn to Apollo [1]   v   24549

---

[1] The symbols in the list of records may be interpreted as follows:
        c   Columbia   d   Decca   v   Victor
    as   *Anthologie Sonore*, Gramaphone Shop, New York City

2. "It was this tradition which, carried down through the ages, survived in the Jewish synagogues."

Traditional Hebrew Prayers D A–41

3. The "chant-like melodies" of the early Church.

Any record from the *Solesmes Collection of Gregorian Chant* V M 87

4. Music that is "Gothic in the original sense of the word — something that seems rude and barbaric" to our ears.

Credo and *Sanctus* from *Mass* by Guillaume de Machault AS 31, 32

5. Renaissance music, with its "new attitude toward life and its interest in beauty and humanity rather than only in religion."

Madrigals: Pilkington: *Rest, Sweet Nymph* } Morley: *Sing We and Chant It* } C 5716

6. Early European dance music, "popular dance tunes of the people" taken over by musicians.

French Dances of the Sixteenth Century AS 5

7. Eighteenth-century music that was "largely supported by princely patrons."

Bach: *Brandenburg Concerto No. 4* C 68440/1

8. Music which illustrates the "desire of composers to put feeling into their music." There are many good recordings of these; for instance:

Beethoven: *Eroica Symphony* C MM–449
Wagner: *Prelude to Tristan und Isolde* C 12132–D

234

9. Nineteenth-century music of the virtuosos, who were "interpreters of real genius and could popularize and glamorize music."

Chopin: *Polonaise in A Flat*, Op. 53 ⎫
     Polonaise in A Major,   ⎬   v   DM 353
       Op. 40, No. 1   ⎭
    Sonata in B Flat, Op. 35   v   DM 1082

10. "An overexaggerated sentimentalism and ready-made sentimentality."

Tchaikovsky: *Solitude* ⎫
       Humoresque (arr. by ⎬   v   11–9187
       Stokowski) ⎭

11. "A strange, dissonant kind of writing" used by contemporary composers "closely attuned to the mechanistic existence in which they find themselves."

Hindemith: *Mathis the Painter*   v   DM 854

12. European music "differs in so many respects from the great musical systems that are in use today by millions of people living in India, China, and Arabia."

Hindu: *Tabla Taranga* ⎫
    Danse Kartikeyya ⎰   v   M 382
Chinese: *Chinese Instrumental Music*   v   24549

A SCENE FROM A HAYDN OPERA

The orchestra is made up of thirteen violins and violas, one cello, two basses, two flutes, and a bassoon. Haydn himself is at the cembalo on the left.

CHAPTER XII

THE ORCHESTRA AS A MUSICAL INSTRUMENT

I N WEBSTER'S dictionary, one of the definitions of *instrument* is a *contrivance by which
musical sounds are produced*. In this sense, during the long
story of the development of music, there have been many different instruments that have been popular with players and
listeners. If we look back at Bible history, we find that King
David was a most enthusiastic player of the harp. The Greeks,
perhaps the most really civilized of all ancient peoples, used
the lyre and reed pipe for their music. At the time of the establishment of the Christian Church during the early centuries
of our modern epoch, large choirs and congregations sang the
music of the liturgy. The eighteenth-century composer Johann
Sebastian Bach loved the organ above every other instrument.
During the eighteenth century the string quartet and other
small instrumental groups became popular, largely because
they sounded well in the salons and music rooms of the aristocrats, who were then the principal patrons of music and the
other arts. The nineteenth century was a period when the
individual player began to assume musical importance.

237

THE SAN FRANCISCO
ORCHESTRA
Pierre Monteux, Conductor

And so it is not strange that single instruments such as the piano and violin were played by great artists, became very popular in the musical life of that time, and are still popular today.

For those who listen to European music today the symphony orchestra is *the* instrument. In fact, for many listeners the word *music* means *symphonic music;* that is to say, music produced by a combined and unified group of from sixty to a hundred players, all of them under the command of a single leader, the conductor. Such a force is capable of producing

Courtesy of The Musical Association of San Francisco

almost any musical effect as well as giving listeners unlimited musical pleasure and satisfaction.

The nature of this great musical instrument is suggested by its name. In Greek (the language from which our present name for this instrument has come) *symphonia* means *simultaneous sound*. Hence the term is naturally applied to such a happy musical family as an orchestra or band, a family in which all the members possess real individuality and yet, because of their cordial feelings for each other, are capable of sounding together in harmony. The orchestra is really a

239

modern instrument, for its development did not start until late in the eighteenth century; and it did not reach its present high state of technical perfection until the end of the nineteenth century.

This is not to say, of course, that there have not been orchestras of various types from earliest times. We have, for instance, an excellent description of an early orchestra in the Bible: the third chapter of Daniel describes a musical performance at the court of the Babylonian king, Nebuchadrezzar, who lived in the first half of the sixth century before Christ. This performance started out with a blaring trumpet signal, quickly followed by music on reed instruments, stringed lyres, and harps. These were all played together, as the Bible describes it, producing *all kinds of musick*.

Those musicians who have traveled to the vast peninsulas and islands to the east and southeast of India tell us of orchestras made up entirely of numbers of various-sized gongs. These *gamelans*, as the gongs are called, have come down from earliest times. Sometimes sounding together in powerful tonal crashes, sometimes with solemn, silvery chime effects, these orchestras are certainly very different from our European ideals.

Still another primitive sort of orchestra is described in a large collection of poems written in China during the Shang Dynasty, the earliest family of rulers known to that very ancient land:

> *In what unison sounded the drums and bells!*
> *What joy was there in the hall . . .*
> *The lizard-skin drums rolled harmonies,*
> *As the blind musicians performed their parts.*

Courtesy of The Metropolitan Museum of Art, New York

A BURMESE ORCHESTRA

And many centuries later, during the time of the European Renaissance (in 1568), from some instructions that were written out for a court wedding of the time we learn of an orchestra made up of three groups of players: one of gambas, the instruments from which developed our present-day violins; another of flutes; and the third of a combination of a bassoon, flute, pipe, and cornet. This kind of orchestra, which was very often used at that time, would certainly sound peculiar to our ears today.

These examples, chosen at random from widely different times and countries, show that the idea of a group of musicians playing in ensemble is by no means a modern one or one that has been limited to Europe and America. But the symphony orchestra as we think of it today, that is, as a large band of

241

instrumentalists capable of producing many different shades of tonal color and playing with great skill and unanimity, dates from the end of the eighteenth century. A good description of a famous orchestra of that time has come down to us, so that we know just what these orchestras sounded like. This description was written by a famous English traveler and music lover of that period, Sir Charles Burney. It tells of the musical establishment of a rich German prince, Karl Theodore, at his palace in Mannheim:

I found [this band] to be all that its fame had made me expect: power will naturally arise from a great number of hands; but the judicious use of this power, on all occasions, must be the consequence of good discipline; indeed there are more solo players and good composers in this than perhaps in any other orchestra in Europe; it is an army of generals, equally fit to plan a battle, as to fight it.

But it has not been merely at the Elector's great opera that instrumental music has been so much cultivated and refined, but at his concerts, where this extraordinary band has "ample room and verge enough" to display all its powers, and to produce great effects without the impropriety of destroying the grandeur and more delicate beauties peculiar to vocal music. . . . Every effect has been tried which such an aggregate of sound can produce; it was here that Crescendo and Diminuendo had birth; and the Piano, which had before chiefly been used as an echo . . . as well as the Forte, were found to be musical colours which had their shades as much as red or blue in painting.[1]

[1] From Burney's *Present State of Music in Germany, Netherlands and United Provinces*. London: 1773.

THE ORCHESTRA AS INSTRUMENT

Prince Karl Theodore spent much money on music; and the palace where he lived in the summer employed over fifteen hundred persons, all of them kept at his expense in a village near the summer palace. *To a stranger walking through the streets this place must seem inhabited only by a colony of musicians, who are constantly exercising their profession: at one house a fine player on the violin is heard; at another, a German flute; here an excellent oboe; there a bassoon, a clarinet, a violoncello, or a concert of several instruments together.*

Thus Burney wrote concerning the most important experimental laboratory out of which came our modern orchestra. There were a number of these eighteenth-century court orchestras. Haydn was the experimental composer who had most to do with them in laying the foundations upon which the modern organizations have been built. If we look at a picture of one of these, we will find that the instruments can be described as being divided into four great groups of families, or choirs:

1. String Choir: violin, viola, cello, bass
2. Wood-wind Choir: flute, (piccolo), clarinet, oboe, English horn, bassoon, bass clarinet, contrabassoon
3. Brass-wind Choir: trumpet, French horn, trombone, tuba
4. Percussion Choir: kettledrums, bass and side drums, cymbals, bells, celesta, etc.

These groups are usually placed on the stage of a concert hall in the following order: strings in front (with the exception of the basses, which are lined up along the back); winds in the center (wood winds first, brass winds last); and the percussion instruments in the back. On the next page there is a seating plan typical of that used by most orchestras:

243

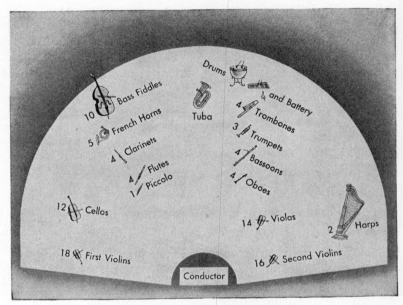

Drums
and Battery
10 Bass Fiddles
Tuba
4 Trombones
5 French Horns
3 Trumpets
4 Clarinets
4 Bassoons
4 Flutes
4 Oboes
1 Piccolo
12 Cellos
14 Violas
2 Harps
18 First Violins
16 Second Violins
Conductor

SEATING ARRANGEMENT OF THE ORCHESTRA
UNDER ARTURO TOSCANINI

QUESTIONS FOR DISCUSSION

Can you see any reason why the symphony orchestra should be the typical instrument of our time?

Who were the most important writers of music for the symphony orchestra as we know it?

Do you think the jazz orchestras as developed in this country will have any important influence upon the larger symphony orchestra? If so, why?

Name the symphony orchestras in this country that are generally considered the most important.

THE ORCHESTRA AS INSTRUMENT

Dohnányi: *Suite in F-sharp Minor*, Op. 19   D 433

This work, written by one of the more conservative Hungarian composers, Ernst von Dohnányi (b. 1877), is a fine example of music that we can describe as being popular in the best sense of the term. It has good tunes, plenty of rhythmic changes, fine orchestral contrasts and, in addition, is well put together.

The First Movement of this suite is in the form of a series of variations on a tune that is played first by the entire woodwind ensemble, with the oboe, clarinet, and flute taking the upper harmonies, and the English horn (really an alto oboe) filling in, while the bassoons furnish the foundation for the whole. The peculiarly bitter-sweet, sharply pungent tone of the wood-wind choir is heard here at its very best. A moment later you will hear it in contrast and in blend with the string choir.

If you listen carefully to the different variations, you will find that the fifth one gives opportunity for the use of the kettledrums in the percussion group; and that the last variation displays the brass choir to wonderful advantage in a broad, very dignified version of the main tune, above which float the strings and wood winds. This whole movement clearly and unmistakably contrasts the essential characteristics of the various tonal groups of the orchestra: the pungency of the wood winds; the broad, singing quality of the strings; the strength and dignity of the brass; and the pulsating, rhythmic help of the instruments in the percussion group.

Listen to the Third Movement of this fine piece and you will hear the oboe of the wood winds in strong contrast to the cello of the strings. The Fourth Movement is also very worth while, with brilliant and vigorous tunes and strong rhythms.

Britten: *The Young Person's Guide to the Orchestra*   c   703

In 1947 the English composer Benjamin Britten wrote the music for a film devoted to the orchestra. In it he introduced the listener to the sounds of the instruments shown in the moving picture, first as they are grouped in choirs and then singly, one at a time. This music is sometimes played without the accompanying film, and no better way of being introduced to the sound of this magnificent instrument — the orchestra — can be imagined. If you listen to the first part of this music, a theme from the early English composer Henry Purcell (c. 1659–1695), you will hear this great tune played first by the whole orchestra and then taken up in turn by each of the four groups, or choirs, of instruments:

Notice the change in the character of the theme as it is heard on the wood winds, then on the brass, strings, and even percussion instruments alone. In securing these great changes of mood, Britten, who is one of England's most promising present-day composers, shows great technical skill in orchestration.

246

After it is heard on the wood winds, brass, strings, and percussion in turn, the whole orchestra plays it again. Then comes a succession of thirteen variations, one for each kind of orchestral instrument. These will be discussed on page 286 of Chapter XIV.

Here are a few more places in orchestral pieces where the sounds of the different choirs are sharply differentiated:

In the beginning measures of Beethoven's *First Symphony* the strings have most to say, with the violins on top sounding the melody. They are joined occasionally by the wood winds, but the chief color is that of the strings, which form a background for the characteristic tone quality of the other groups. If you would hear the strings alone, listen to Mozart's use of them in his serenade *Eine Kleine Nachtmusik*, written for some social occasion when a stringed orchestra was available.

Someone has said that the brass, with its impressive choir of trumpets and trombones, can *roll up the heavens like a scroll*. This is certainly true of such places as the last movement of Brahms's *First Symphony*, where the effect of the music is given by the golden quality of this important family of instruments.

In the Second Movement of Beethoven's *Ninth Symphony*, the work which many believe to be the greatest this composer ever produced, there is marvelous use made of the tympani as solo instruments. Another place where this composer used the tympani to great effect is in the connecting passage between the Third and the Fourth Movement of his *Fifth Symphony*, which is built up on a long, swelling roll of the drums.

AN AFRICAN DANCE, accompanied by native musicians

CHAPTER XIII. *THE EARLY ORIGIN OF INSTRUMENTS*

T HE instruments used by the players in a modern symphony orchestra are beautiful to look at, for they are shining, slick, and streamlined. Yet they are descended from some very primitive instruments used by our ancestors centuries ago. In fact, each of the four great orchestral families just mentioned is well represented in those instruments which were devised by primitive man in order to make a kind of music that was different from the sound of his voice. We know this from the study and researches that have been made into the life and activities of ancient peoples by modern scholars and historians.

Some of these men, whom we call archeologists, have not been content to sit at their desks and read about the life and customs of the peoples who lived here on this earth before our time; they have traveled over the whole world, digging up and examining the relics, monuments, and everyday utensils left behind by these early peoples. Thus very definite conclusions can be reached from the work of these archeologists as to how early man lived, fought, and died.

249

From Dalzel's History of Dahome, 1793

MUSIC AND DANCE IN AFRICA

This early drawing shows a ceremonial dance with music. Note the
drums and the horn made of an animal's tusk. The bound seated
figures and the horses in the background are sacrificial victims.

Another group of these scholars, the anthropologists, by
using such information can give a further description of these
primitive races by comparing them with certain stages of
primitive existence to be found in Africa, Asia, the Americas, and on the isles of the seas. For example, an archeolo-
gist may discover the ruins left behind by some tribe of
prehistoric hunters who lived in an out-of-the-way place in
Europe. The anthropologist can then show a similar culture among some present-day Australian aboriginal tribes

using the same weapons and instruments. Thus, by comparing the dead with the living, the scholar can give us a
fairly accurate idea of how our prehistoric ancestors lived and
thought.

The experts, using all the information they can get, have
decided that one of the earliest musical instruments used by
man was the rattle. This was a contraption made of sounding
materials such as nutshells, seeds, or stones strung together or
placed in a gourd container. When shaken by the player, this
rude instrument makes a sharp, percussive sound; and when
suspended from the ankles or the waist of a dancer, it responds
to his movements with a sharp noise. Thus rattles became
closely associated with rhythmic pulse. The next time you hear
one of the many gadgets used by dance bands to mark out the
rhythmic pulses of the music, think of it as being the modern
representative of one of the earliest instruments devised by
man for making music.

Another rhythmic instrument used by prehistoric man was
the stamping-pit, again a device that was used to indicate the
rhythmic beats that accompanied the dancing. This is the way
it was built: a big hole was dug in the ground and covered
with a bark lid; the musicians stamped on this lid with their
feet, thus producing what we have come to call a *drum beat*.
A recent traveler in the Solomon Islands describes the sound
of this instrument as follows:

*Sometimes as many as forty women and girls danced around a
pit, while two women stamped on a board fixed in the pit about
halfway down; this made a dull, hollow sound to which the
women of the circle timed their dancing.*

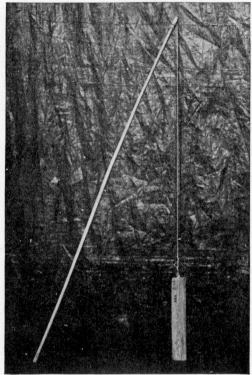

Courtesy of The Metropolitan Museum of Art, New York

A BULL ROARER

The player uses this instrument by whirling it over his head to suggest the sound
of wind.

A somewhat later development of this drum idea was the
substitution (for the bark lid) of a tree trunk hollowed out
like a boat, thus giving a stronger and more resounding tone.
It was soon found that if the skin of some animal was stretched
over the hollow trunk and struck with the hands, it would
increase the usefulness of this primitive drum still further.

252

Finally drums were made much smaller and more portable, with wooden frames which were especially designed to keep the skin taut.

Thus the percussion instruments were developed first, which is what we would naturally expect. From these earliest days drums seem to have had a symbolic and magic significance for man. They were used (and still are used in such parts of the world as the African jungles) for all sorts of religious and secular ceremonies. The drum beat seems to have in it the very pulse of savage life. As an African traveler has said, early man was born to it, worked to it, worshiped to it, danced to it for days and nights on end, and finally died to it. It somehow brought the spirit world close to him, and through its aid the ordinary, routine acts of everyday living became devout acts of worship.

Drum rhythms possessed an emotional significance to these primitive men that is very difficult for us to realize today. They produced a strange hypnotic and stimulating effect when

Courtesy of The Metropolitan Museum of Art, New York

VARIOUS TYPES OF PRIMITIVE DRUMS

253

continued hour after hour over long periods. So drums came to be thought of as holy instruments, and special guardians were appointed for their protection and maintenance. One of the modern travelers in South Africa tells of coming upon a village which contained a special hut built for the royal drums of the tribe. In this little house, these drums, of various sizes and shapes, were carefully kept and guarded. A row of milk pails stood in front of the stand upon which the drums rested, and daily offerings of milk from a herd of sacred cows were made to the drum spirits. Two women were assigned as guardians for these instruments. They kept them warm by large fires in the drum hut and repaired them by means of skins taken from the sacred cows.

Although we do not attach any special religious or spiritual significance to drums today, in a sense we still worship them! For they are still indispensable for all kinds of music. In the modern symphony orchestra the kettle, side, and snare drums play a most important role in the percussion section; and in popular music the drum still beats out its primitive, savage appeal. It is little wonder that a very famous musician once remarked: *In the beginning, music was rhythm.*

One of the earliest wind instruments to develop was the flute. Primitive man may have discovered its possibilities by blowing his breath across the sharpened edge of a piece of bone or wood. At any rate, the archeologists have found many small flutes made of bird bones in the ruins of the caves used as living quarters by some of our earliest ancestors. These earliest flutes played only one tone (a wonderful example of their sound can be heard on the records made by the Denis-Roosevelt Expedition). Later on, finger holes were introduced so

254

that several tones could be made on one instrument. And the tones were improved by making the flute of wood. Strange to say, the whistle flute, with a mouthpiece much like our modern tin whistle, was probably used before the less-complicated type from which the player produces a tone by blowing his breath across the sharp edge of a hole in the end of the instrument. Sets of these simple flutes were bound together to form

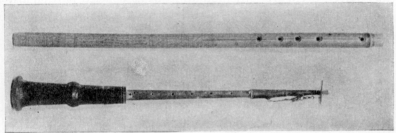

Courtesy of The Metropolitan Museum of Art, New York

PRIMITIVE WOOD WINDS: a flute made of bone and an early reed type of instrument

the Panpipe. (See page 217.) Early civilization connected the idea of the flute's sound with death and rebirth, as well as with love. Even today young American Indians have been known to go to their medicine men and ask them to exercise their powers on a flute, so that the girls they favor may listen to their pleas. The same charm idea connected with the flute seems to exist among all primitive peoples.

Trumpets were probably developed out of a sort of megaphone-like instrument made from hollow tree branches or large canes, into which the player spoke or sang for the purpose of amplifying his voice. (Again note the resemblance to some modern devices used by popular musicians!) Gradually the actual trumpet, in which the air column within the instrument

255

is set in vibration by means of the lips of the player, evolved from this simple megaphone. Capable at first of blaring only one or two tones, these instruments were sometimes made of clay, sometimes of ivory tusks. And their rather terrifying sound was associated with all sorts of magic rites. They were also used as signal horns to communicate war and other signals from hilltop to hilltop. Among primitive peoples, the trumpet was played exclusively by men and was associated particularly with military, funereal, and sunset rites. Even today the coarse sound of the alphorn is heard in parts of Switzerland at sunset at the time of evening prayers. And the wide use of the bugle in modern military life is so well-known as to need no special comment.

A MUSICAL BOW, showing how the
player's mouth is used as a resonator

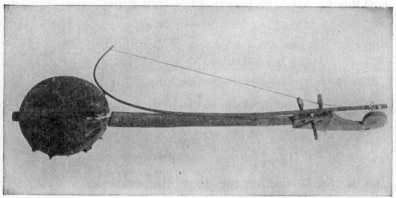

Courtesy of The Metropolitan Museum of Art, New York

A PRIMITIVE STRINGED INSTRUMENT, showing the bow
with which its strings are set in vibration

It is difficult to realize that the primitive ancestors of such
agile and beautifully finished instruments as the violins and violoncellos were such crude music machines as the ground harp
and the musical bow. But such was the case. The ground harp
was made by fastening one end of a single string to the flexible
portion of a wooden rod stuck in the ground and by fastening
the other end to a bark lid stretched over a pit dug in the
ground. This instrument was either struck or plucked, sometimes by several persons at the same time. The musical bow
was shaped something like a hunter's bow, only much larger.
It had some kind of resonating device attached to it, such as a
gourd or clay bowl; or the player's mouth served as a resonator,
as he held the wood against his teeth in the fashion of the modern jews'-harp. These crude devices are a far cry from the
lovely sounds of the modern violin or cello, but they established the principle of producing musical sound by means of
vibrating strings.

Thus we have percussion, wind, and string instruments devised by primitive man, instruments originating in the early stages of human evolution and antedating the formation of states, the establishment of town life, or even the invention of writing. The story of their development into modern orchestral instruments is the story of the development of civilization.

QUESTIONS FOR DISCUSSION

In the text the author says that "the percussion instruments were developed first, which is what we would naturally expect." Why is this true?

An important writer on music says that among savage and uncultured peoples the dance was never thought of as an amusement without any significance. Why did these people dance, and what instruments did they use for accompanying their dances?

What does the following mean?
Primitive man had two very serviceable instruments, his voice and his hands; and the wind instruments which he developed are but prolongations of the voice, while the percussive instruments are simply developments of the idea of marking rhythmic impulses with his hands.

MUSIC TO LISTEN TO

The Laura Boulton records made during the Western African Expedition of the Field Museum of Natural History, Chicago and published by Victor (Album P–10) contain the following fine examples of primitive instruments:

258

EARLY INSTRUMENTS

Drums	Record 89 A and B
Rattles and Drums	88 B
Horn	87 A and 88 A
Musical Bow	87 B
Stringed Lute	86 A

The Belgian Congo records of the Denis-Roosevelt Expedition, published by the Reeves Sound Studios, Inc., New York, contain the following examples of the sound of primitive instruments:

Drums	Record sides nos. 7, 8, 9
Flutes (each one playing only one tone)	Record side no. 5

General Record No. 5014 contains some interesting examples of primitive ritual music played by the Tarascan Indians in the Mexican state of Michoácan on primitive wood-wind instruments and drums.

Camera Study by Arthur Griffin, Boston

SERGEI KOUSSEVITZKY conducting the Boston Symphony
Orchestra. The importance of the conductor is well shown here.

CHAPTER XIV. *THE SOUND OF MODERN INSTRUMENTS*

T H E music lover can get a great deal of real pleasure from his ability to recognize the different tonal qualities of the modern orchestral instruments, not only when they are played singly but also when they sound together in *symphony*. It is not as difficult to acquire this ability as it might at first seem. Let us take the various instruments one by one and learn to recognize their characteristic *timbres*, or tone-colors. Then we can profitably study a few compositions in which these tonal qualities may be heard as essential parts of a whole composition when played by an orchestra.

THE STRINGS

The tone of the stringed instruments is produced by setting into vibration, by drawing a bow across them, strings that are stretched tight over a wooden body, the flat front of which acts as a soundboard, or resonator, in reinforcing the tone. The tension of these different strings is regulated by means of tuning pins inserted in a headpiece on top of the neck. The various pitches are produced by pressing the fingers of the left hand against the front part (or fingerboard) of this neck, thus *stopping* the strings. The bridge is a most essential part of these instruments; it is a wooden crosspiece placed on edge between the soundboard and the lower part of the strings, thus keeping the strings away from the soundboard and at the same time transmitting the vibrations of the strings to the soundboard. This latter, of course, is the most important part of the instrument, for the strings could produce little tone were it not for the vibrating expanse of wood beneath them. Because of the peculiar shape of the soundboard and its careful treatment with varnishes of various sorts, the stringed instruments gain in beauty of tone with the years.

The following diagram clearly illustrates these parts:

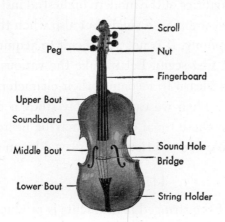

When stringed instruments are played alone, their sound is beautiful enough; and they are often used as solo instruments in concert and chamber music. But when they are played together as the massed string choir of the orchestra, the effect is overpowering in shimmering beauty and warm strength.

262

CONCERTMASTER AND FIRST VIOLIN

FIRST AND SECOND VIOLINS

As used in the orchestra, the first and the second violins are identical instruments; but in their relation to one another they are used as would be the first and second soprano voices in a choir. Developed in the sixteenth century by Italian instrument makers from the *viol*, the violin was first recognized by French dance musicians, because of its agile, brittle tone, as an ideal instrument. It commands a variety of effects possible on no other instrument, this fact making it the most useful individual member of the orchestral family and the backbone of all orchestral writing.

263

VIOLA

The alto instrument of the strings, the viola, is sandwiched between the melody-making violin and the accompanimental string basses. It has a dark, rich, somber tone much like that of a good contralto voice. Someone has amusingly described the viola as an overgrown violin which has had its upper string removed and a correspondingly lower one added in compensation. Since it is only slightly larger than the violin, it is not always easy to distinguish these instruments in the large body of string players of an orchestra. But there should be little chance of confusing their tone qualities.

264

CELLO

CELLO

The cello, usually abbreviated from violoncello, is a baritone violin. It was first developed by the Italians in the middle of the seventeenth century. It is larger, with longer and thicker strings, than the viola. The cello is played by being held between the player's knees rather than under his chin, as is the case with the violin and the viola. Lovely, rich, and mellow, its tone is very romantic in character. Its tone can, as a famous critic once said, be like the voice of a friend bringing comfort and ease in time of trouble. On the other hand, if it is not treated with respect, the cello can sound very rough and quite harsh.

DOUBLE BASS

CONTRABASS OR DOUBLE BASS

The contrabass is a low-toned instrument, sometimes af-
fectionately called *bass viol* or *bull fiddle*. It provides the foun-

266

dation tone for the whole orchestra and so must be of good size, its height being about six feet. It is not a very exciting instrument to play, for it seldom has anything like a melody but is content to provide the single foundation tones upon which the whole orchestral structure is built. Imposing and foundational, this instrument is as necessary to the orchestral whole as it is difficult and awkward to handle.

The modern string group comprises about sixty per cent of the whole orchestra. Usually played with a smooth *legato* tone, the notes being joined together without pause, these instruments are made to produce various contrasting effects: *vibrato*, by a rapid rocking of the finger on the string, thus furnishing an agitated, exciting effect; *pizzicato*, produced by plucking the strings instead of bowing them; *staccato* (literally, *detached*), a series of sharp, accented tones; and *sordino*, a mysterious hushed quality of tone produced by the insertion of a mute clapped onto the bridge of the instrument, thus veiling the tone.

THE WINDS

All of the wind instruments have two essential features: (1) a tube enclosing a column of air and also acting partly as a resonator; (2) some device for setting this air column in vibration, by producing alternating pulsations from the steady breath of the player. This may be, as in the case of the trumpet, the lips of the player; or, as in the case of the clarinet, the quick back-and-forth movement of a single reed. In the oboe and bassoon it is the movement of a double reed; and in the flute and piccolo, the sharp edge of the playing hole, or mouth hole, across which the player blows.

The terms *wood wind* and *brass wind* are not very accurate, since flutes and piccolos and clarinets, usually classified as wood-wind instruments, are often made of metal in order to produce a greater brilliance of tone. But, in general, these terms distinguish two tonal contrasting families. The wood winds have a somewhat liquid, rather soft tonal quality; the brasses, a much more brilliant, powerful tone. The general effect of the wood winds playing ensemble is that of a soft-voiced organ, mellow and reed-vibrant. The brasses when played together form one of the tonal glories of the orchestra, for they can be either rich and golden or rousing and demanding.

Wood Winds

FLUTE

As we have seen, the flute was one of the earliest of all instruments to be developed. Its modern form consists of a long tube (usually of silver) with many keys over the holes in order to control the pitch. It is side-blown and has a very sweet, clear, bright tone. Because of its great agility, composers often give it passages with birdlike trills and runs; but the flute can likewise sound soft and velvety.

PICCOLO

The piccolo is simply a small, high-pitched flute, used for outlining and defining melodies in the orchestra. It is sometimes called the *octave flute*. It is sharp and brilliantly hard in tone, and its shrill sound can, if required, be made to ring out

268

FLUTE

above all the other instruments of the orchestra. The difference in appearance between the flute and the piccolo may be realized by turning to the next page.

269

PICCOLO

OBOE

A double-reed mouthpieced, treble instrument, the oboe has a peculiarly piercing, pungent but pleasing tone. The double

270

OBOE

reed consists of two pieces of wood, their flat-cut sides placed and tied together. The oboe was developed in the late-seventeenth century out of a noisy instrument, the *shawm*. In some form or other, this instrument has been used by all

271

ENGLISH HORN

civilizations of which we have any records, from the Sumerian and Babylonian (c. 2800 B.C.) down to the modern European and American. The present-day instrument is one of the most useful in the whole orchestra.

272

CLARINET   BASS CLARINET

COR ANGLAIS (ENGLISH HORN)

The English horn is an alto oboe, distinguished alike for its lovely, melancholy tone and the fact that it is neither a horn nor any more English than other instruments. It is a fine solo instrument.

CLARINET

A single-reed mouthpieced, treble instrument with a mellow, very sonorous tone, the clarinet is sometimes likened to the dramatic soprano because of the effectiveness and rich color of its tone. The Egyptians used a primitive clarinet made of cane.

273

BASSOON

The bass clarinet is a clarinet with a tone an octave below the usual clarinet.

Originating about the middle of the sixteenth century, the bassoon is really a bass oboe, the tube of which is doubled back

274

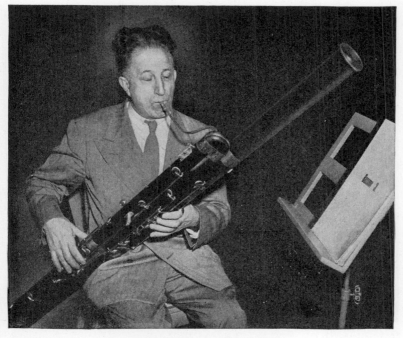

DOUBLE BASSOON

on itself because of its great length. Its tone is deep and low, with a slightly nasal quality which often gives it a touch of humor. The bassoon is a most useful instrument because of its wide range.

DOUBLE BASSOON (CONTRABASSOON)

The double bassoon, or contrabassoon, is a very deep bass oboe, having the same relation to the bassoon as the double bass has to the cello, and it is used in the same way. Its range is about an octave below that of the bassoon. It was Beethoven who first more or less regularly used this instrument in the orchestra.

275

TRUMPET

Brass Winds

TRUMPET

Much of the brilliance of the brass choir is due to the trumpet. It is a treble-pitched instrument of very ancient lineage and, even in the modern orchestral examples, with a powerful, noble tone. This is due to the narrow bore of its tube and the shape of its bell and mouthpiece.

HORN

The horn is often called the *French Horn* because it is supposed to have been in France, during the seventeenth century, according to the ideas of the majority of historians, that this

276

FRENCH HORN

instrument was developed from the hunting horn. It is spiral in shape, like its predecessor, and has a very characteristic tone, smooth in soft passages and thrilling in loud. It is lower in pitch than the trumpet, due to the fact that it has a very long tube (normally over eleven feet), a large bell, and a funnel-shaped instead of a cup-shaped mouthpiece.

277

TROMBONE

TROMBONE

The trombone is easily recognized because of its telescoping slide, a device which makes this instrument easy to play and gives it a peculiarly singing style that is unusual for wind instruments. Tenor and bass sizes are the ones in general use; these have not changed much since the seventeenth century. Its earlier name was the *sackbut,* and it was well-known all over Europe, since it served as the principal instrument for playing ceremonial music at the courts of princes.

TUBA

The tuba is the bass foundational instrument of the brasses. Really a big and rather solemn-toned cornet, this instrument was first constructed in the nineteenth century and, compara-

278

TUBA

tively speaking, has only recently come into general use in orchestras and bands. The circular tuba carried by marching
band players is called a *helicon* or *sousaphone*, the latter term
in honor of the noted American band conductor John Philip
Sousa. In this form it has become a common member of mod-
ern-day dance bands.

THE PERCUSSION

KETTLEDRUMS (TYMPANI)

Kettledrums are big copper basins covered with parchment. They alone of the drums can be tuned to definite pitches. Introduced into Germany from Asia (where they were always used in pairs) around 1500, these instruments were for a long time used with trumpets and were considered symbols of wealth and nobility. When introduced into the orchestra, the means for tuning them were greatly improved.

Along with kettledrums, three kinds of cylinder drums came into the orchestra. They are:

SIDE DRUM (SNARE DRUM)

The side drum is a shallow, two-headed drum with gut or wire strings placed on its lower head, giving it a specific rattling sound when the upper head is struck. It has no definite pitch.

TENOR DRUM

This drum is somewhat deeper in tone than the side drum and it is without snares.

BASS DRUM

The third kind of cylinder drum is the bass drum, a large, rather shallow double-headed drum of indefinite pitch, struck with a thick padded stick. It probably came into Europe from the Turks.

CYMBALS

Cymbals are metal plates which are struck together when special clashing effects are desired. They were used in all East-

TYMPANI

ern music systems from the time of the Assyrians. Even today the best cymbals are imported from China. Modern composers call for a number of different cymbal effects.

BACKGROUNDS FOR LISTENING

TRIANGLE

A steel rod bent into triangular form and struck with an iron rod, the triangle has a high, twinkling sound of no definite pitch. It became a permanent member of the orchestra at the beginning of the nineteenth century, although it was used earlier for special local color effects.

TAMBOURINE

The tambourine is a shallow, one-headed drum, with jingling metallic disks attached to give an Oriental effect when shaken or struck with the hand. It has been used in European music since the thirteenth century.

GONG

A metal instrument of indefinite pitch, the gong is capable of great reverberation. It was borrowed from the East, where it is used to accompany all sorts of songs, dances, religious and secular ceremonies.

GLOCKENSPIEL (BELLS)

Glockenspiels are metal bars of definite pitch, struck with hammers and used in orchestras since the eighteenth century.

TUBULAR CHIMES

Chimes are metal tubes of definite pitch suspended from a frame and struck by hammers. They are louder and not so pleasing in tone as the glockenspiel.

HARP

Really a stringed instrument, the harp is so often used in the orchestra for percussive effects that it is included here. It has a

HARP

wide range. It, too, is a very ancient instrument, for there is reference to it or pictures of it in practically every period of recorded history. In its modern form it is capable of lovely, delicate, and very sweeping, glissando effects.

283

BACKGROUNDS FOR LISTENING

This instrument is really a piano glockenspiel, with tuned steel slabs placed over resonance boxes and struck by hammers actuated by keys. It is very popular in modern orchestration because of its silvery, twinkling effects.

XYLOPHONE

One of the most primitive of all instruments, the xylophone is a series of wooden slabs struck with a stick. The instrument is used only occasionally for percussive effects.

QUESTIONS FOR DISCUSSION

Which of the modern orchestral instruments do you like best, and why? Which do you think is the most difficult to play? Why?

Why do you think it is necessary to include such a large proportion of strings in the modern orchestra?

Why is it necessary to have a conductor for the orchestra to-day?

Who is the concertmaster of the orchestra, and what are his duties?

A book has been written which claims that almost all modern instruments are defective, even the violin. Discuss this charge. (See Chapter XIV in Redfield: Music, a Science and an Art. New York: Alfred A. Knopf.)

MUSIC TO LISTEN TO

The following sections of symphonic compositions illustrate well the tone-color of the various instruments. They have been collected on two records and are published by Columbia (Album Set X250).

VIOLIN: Rimsky-Korsakoff: *Scheherazade*, Fourth Movement

VIOLA: Handel: *Concerto in B Minor for Viola and Orchestra*, First Movement

CELLO: Tchaikovsky: *Symphony No. 4 in F Minor*, Second Movement

BASS: Bach: *Passacaglia and Fugue in C Minor*, arr. by Stokowski

HARP: Ravel: *Introduction and Allegro for Harp, Flute, Clarinet and String Quartet*

COMBINED STRING SECTION: Handel: *Concerto Grosso No. 6 in G Minor*, Second Movement

PICCOLO: Tchaikovsky: *Symphony No. 4 in F Minor*, Scherzo

FLUTE: Ravel: *Daphnis and Chloe*, Suite No. 2

CLARINET: Weber: *Concertino for Clarinet and Orchestra*, Fourth Movement

OBOE: Tchaikovsky: *Symphony No. 4 in F Minor*, Second Movement

ENGLISH HORN: Franck: *Symphony in D Minor*, Second Movement

BASSOON: Tchaikovsky: *Symphony No. 4 in F Minor*, Second Movement

COMBINED WOOD-WIND SECTION: Sibelius: *Finlandia* (Middle Section)

TRUMPET: Haydn: *Concerto for Trumpet and Orchestra*, Third Movement

BACKGROUNDS FOR LISTENING

FRENCH HORN: Weber: *Der Freischuetz*, Overture

TROMBONE: Rimsky-Korsakoff: *Scheherazade*, Fourth Movement

TUBA: Richard Strauss: *Don Quixote*

COMBINED BRASS SECTION: Dukas: *Fanfare* from *La Peri*

TYMPANI: Shostakovich:*Symphony No. 1*, Fourth Movement

Britten: *The Young Person's Guide to the Orchestra*   c   703

We have already referred to this piece in Chapter XII and heard its various treatments of a theme by the different choirs. Play it again from the beginning and you will note that after the different choirs have given us the theme in various guises, we have a series of variations on it by the different instruments as follows (page 18, Miniature Score):

VARIATION A: For the highest of the wood-wind group, the clear, sweet FLUTE and its shrill brother, the PICCOLO, with a background of first and second violins.

VARIATION B: For the gentle, plaintive OBOE, which, as the score assures us, can be forceful enough when the composer wants it to be. This slow variation has an accompaniment of strings playing an unmistakable rhythm.

VARIATION C: For the agile, beautifully smooth and mellow CLARINET. Two of these instruments are used over an accompaniment of strings and (of all things) a tuba!

This picture and those on the next two pages show three groups of the players in the film production of Britten's *Instruments of the Orchestra*.

VARIATION D: Gives the tune to two deep-voiced BASSOONS, again with a marked string accompaniment.

VARIATION E: Here the FIRST and SECOND VIOLINS soar above a polonaise rhythm on the brass.

VARIATION F: The tenor instruments of the modern string family, the VIOLAS, are heard against short repeated chords in the wood winds and brass. Note their peculiar timbre.

VARIATION G: The CELLOS sing with splendid richness and warmth; the clarinets and violins furnish an accompaniment.

287

VARIATION H: The score calls the DOUBLE BASSES the "grand-fathers of the string family, with heavy, grumbling voices." They certainly sound like it here, against a suitable wood-wind background.

VARIATION I: Shows the different effects of which the modern HARP, with its 47 strings and seven foot pedals, is capable. Its tone is heard above a soft string tremolo.

VARIATION J: Features the four HORNS. How rich they sound when played in harmony!

VARIATION K: For two TRUMPETS with a military-like section, accentuated by a strong drum beat.

VARIATION L: Displays the heavy, brassy voices of the TROM-BONES and the still heavier tones of the TUBA.

VARIATION M: Includes parts for the most familiar PERCUS-SION instruments, starting with the TYMPANI, or KETTLEDRUMS, followed by the BASS DRUM and CYMBALS; then the TAMBOURINE and TRIANGLE, the SIDE DRUM and CHINESE BLOCK, the XYLO-PHONE, CASTANETS, and GONG; and, before the final fugue, the WHIP.

Having taken the whole orchestra apart, Britten puts it to-gether again in a fugue, adding instrument after instrument in the same order as before, starting with the piccolo, which has the theme first. At the very end we hear the original Purcell theme thundered out on the brass, while the rest of the or-chestra whirls madly around it. This makes a most exciting finish to an interesting and improving piece.

289

Photograph by E. Williams, Rochester, N.Y

AMERICAN HIGH-SCHOOL STUDENTS LISTENING TO
RECORDS in a class in Music Appreciation

T H E average listener needs a great deal of practice in learning to recognize the manner in which the separate tone-colors (*timbres*) of the instruments combine to form the wonderful *timbre* of the whole orchestra. An important part of the real pleasure that can be obtained from listening to an orchestra concert is that which comes from recognizing the individual tones of the various instruments and realizing how these are united and blended into a glorious and thrilling whole. The ideal way to get this practice is through attending a large number of orchestra concerts and hearing all kinds of music written for this, the greatest of all instruments. But it is also possible to gain excellent results in this respect, as well as to experience some fine musical pleasure, by listening to good radio broadcasts and phonograph recordings of the great orchestras.

Take, for example, an orchestral work written by one of the most important of Russian composers, Rimsky-Korsakoff — the *Capriccio Español*. This is an ideal composition to practice on, for, in addition to the fact that it has been recorded a number of times by good orchestras, its chief value as a musical composition lies in its *orchestral dress* rather than in its quality as music. The composer explained at the time he wrote the music:

My *Cappriccio* is a brilliant composition for the orchestra. The changes of timbres, the happy choice of melodies and rhythms, exactly suiting each kind of instrument, brief virtuoso cadenzas for solo instruments, the sound of the percussion instruments, constitute here the very essence of the composition and not its garb or orchestration. The Spanish themes, of dance character, furnished me with rich material for putting in use many kinds of orchestral effects. All in all, the Capriccio is undoubtedly pure external music, but vividly brilliant for all that.

If we take a look at the score of this composition, we find that it is written in five short sections:

1. A lively Spanish dance tune called an *alborada* (literally, a morning song).
2. A series of *variations* on a theme.
3. The alborada repeated with different orchestration.
4. A *Dramatic Scene* and gypsy song. (We should remember in this connection that the gypsies are a wandering people who came into Europe from Asia in the fourteenth and fifteenth centuries. Those who settled in Spain have always been noted for their musical abilities and their influence on Spanish music. Sidelight)
5. Another Spanish dance, this time a *fandango*, which changes at the end into the alborada of the First Movement.

Now if you listen closely to this composition of Rimsky-Korsakoff's, repeating each section several times if necessary, you will find that these different divisions are distinguished by five special orchestral features:

(1) In the alborada there are two principal tunes or themes:

(If you cannot play these themes on the piano, watch them as someone plays them. Thus you can learn a great deal.)

These are heard at the very beginning on the full orchestra, made up of piccolo, flutes, English horn, oboes, clarinets, bassoons, horns, trumpets, trombones, and tuba, strings, kettle-drums, and a percussive group comprising triangle, tambourine, cymbals, and bass drum. What a magnificent musical apparatus and how well it is suited to the wild, volcanic nature of this Spanish dance! Between the full orchestra outbursts, the themes are heard on a solo clarinet against a pizzicato string background, and toward the end there is a violin cadenza (played by the orchestra's concertmaster), the whole section ending very quietly.

(2) The second section begins with a low throb from the strings, over which four horns play the main theme. Notice the solemn, golden effect of these mellow instruments when they are played in harmony in this way. A few special effects can be listened for as the variations transform the theme in different ways: at the end of the first variation, the English horn (really

293

a reed instrument and not a horn, you remember) with its pungent melancholy quality is answered by the French horn with its full, open tone. This gives us a fine chance to contrast the timbres of these two instruments. In the middle variations (there are five in all), the wood winds form various combinations with the strings, the brass unobtrusively filling in from time to time. In the last variation, the solo flute soars beautifully over the strings to give a lovely, liquid effect. Again the section ends *pianissimo*.

(3) Suddenly the alborada breaks out again on the full orchestra, with harp added. But this time the composer gives to the solo violin the part he assigned to the solo clarinet in the first section. And the cadenza [1] that was originally given to the solo violin is now for the solo clarinet. Thus Rimsky-Korskoff assures a nice change of color without departing too much from his original idea.

(4) The *Scena* (Dramatic Scene) contains five different cadenzas, each of them a magnificent opportunity for displaying a different orchestral color. It begins abruptly with a roll of the snare drum. The first cadenza is in the nature of a fanfare for horns and trumpets in syncopated gypsy rhythm. The drum roll continues *ppp* while the second cadenza is heard first on the solo violin and then repeated by flute and clarinet playing together. The third cadenza is a brilliant flute passage over a kettledrum roll. The fourth is for clarinet over a roll of cymbals. The fifth is a glittering harp passage with a triangle background. How shimmering and glittering are these orchestral colors, laid on here by a master hand!

[1] A cadenza is an ornamental passage, usually at the end of a composition, by means of which a soloist can show his technical virtuosity.

A harp *glissando* [2] introduces the gypsy song, which is attacked by the strings, punctuated with savage chords on the
trombones and tuba, and cymbal strokes. The whole thing is
a mad whirl of color and rhythm: solos for violoncellos, oboe,
and flute follow in quick succession; the whole string section
becomes a huge guitar and accompanies the melody of the
gypsy song, heard *staccato* on the wood-wind instruments. The
pace becomes faster and faster and leads suddenly into

(5) A fandango of the Asturias, the chief theme of which
is heard at the very beginning on the trombones and tuba. Listen to it cut through the glittering accompaniment:

There is a related tune for the wood winds:

All sorts of things happen quickly: a solo violin has a variation of the main theme; the bassoons follow with another effective version of their own; the solo clarinet suddenly comes
in against the fandango accompaniment; and the dance grows
wilder and wilder, until the main theme is heard again on
the trombones and tuba. This whirling fandango suddenly
changes into the alborada of the First Movement, which
quickly grows into a short, rapid *Coda*.[3] The whole work
closes *presto*.

The intense excitement and orchestral glitter of this composition are, as we have said, largely dependent upon its

[2] A *glissando* is a sort of gliding run of tones.
[3] *Coda* is the term applied to any passage added at the end of a composition
or of a section of a composition in order to give a greater sense of finality.

orchestral setting. But how effective this is, especially when it is played by a really first-class orchestra under an imagina-

Courtesy of The Musical Quarterly, New York

JOHANN SEBASTIAN BACH

This is the only portrait of Bach showing him as he looked at the time he wrote the *Passacaglia*. It was painted by Elias J. Haussman and shows Bach at the age of thirty-eight.

tive conductor. An interesting comparison could be made of the different recordings in order to decide which seems to come nearest to what were the composer's intentions when he wrote this music.

296

Next we will study a composition of quite different character. Written for the organ by the great eighteenth-century composer Johann Sebastian Bach, the *Passacaglia in C Minor* has been arranged for the modern orchestra by Leopold Stokowski and played under his direction on several recordings. This music is much more worth-while as music than the Rimsky-Korsakoff piece just studied. Stokowski, whose long career as an orchestral conductor has given him plenty of opportunity for playing all kinds of music, does not hesitate to say that this composition of Bach's is "one of the most divinely inspired works ever conceived." But some of its effectiveness as music is wrapped up, as we will soon see, with its orchestration — with the manner in which it is put on the orchestra. And the more we learn about this, the better we will like it as music.

The *passacaglia* was originally an old stately dance, probably from Spain. It was adapted as a form for instrumental music sometime in the seventeenth century and was much used by composers of that and later times. Its characteristic is a short theme played throughout the whole work (most of the time in the bass) while the other parts furnish embellishments and variations on it. In the case of Bach's *Passacaglia* the theme is very easily recognized and remembered:

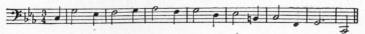

Twenty different versions of this are heard after the theme is first announced at the very beginning of the piece. And since Stokowski has changed the orchestration of these different variations so definitely in his arrangement of the music, this piece is excellent practice in listening to orchestral

297

timbre. Here is the plan in general. Play the music through several times with this page in front of you and you will quickly learn to differentiate between the different tonal groups.

THE ORCHESTRAL MAKE-UP OF
Bach's Passacaglia in C Minor

(Each section is just eight measures in length.)

THEME: Low register of the string basses

VARIATION 1: Theme in bass; variation in upper strings

VARIATION 2: Theme in bass; wood winds (at end, with horn added) in upper register

VARIATION 3: Theme in bass; strings and some wood winds in upper register

VARIATION 4: Theme in bass; strings in upper register

VARIATION 5: Theme in middle register; wood winds

VARIATION 6: Theme in bass; strings in upper register

VARIATION 7: Theme in bass (note descending scale at end); strings (with horn added near end) in upper register

end of first record

VARIATION 8: Theme in bass; strings in upper register

VARIATION 9: Variation in wood winds with strings added at end

VARIATION 10: Theme in bass with brass; strings in upper register

VARIATION 11: Theme in high register on oboe (with horn added at end); accompaniment on strings

298

VARIATION 12: Theme in high strings; accompaniment in bass

VARIATION 13: Theme in middle register of wood winds; variation on wood winds

VARIATION 14: On wood winds

VARIATION 15: Theme on horn; accompaniment on strings

VARIATION 16: Theme in bass; strings in high register

VARIATION 17: Theme in low register of wood winds; accompaniment on wood winds

end of second record

VARIATION 18: Theme in bass punctuated by rests; full strings

VARIATION 19: Theme in bass; strings with high-register wood winds added

VARIATION 20: Theme in bass; full orchestra with brass *fff* at very end

The rest of this important composition is in the form of a *fugue*, the main theme of which (heard a number of times in the course of the music) is taken from that of the *Passacaglia* just heard. As the music goes on and on, notice that there is in it a continuous ebb and flow; yet it builds up to a great climax at the very end. It will be interesting to try to recognize some of the changes in instrumentation as the theme appears throughout this intricate structure of grandeur and mounts to the final climax.

SIDELIGHT

Professor Walter Starkie of the University of Dublin, who made a journey through Hungary and Rumania, living the vagabond life of a gypsy minstrel who had to rely on his fiddle

299

for his bread and butter, tells this story of the origin of the violin in the words of a Hungarian gypsy:

We gypsies from Transylvania know the secrets of the violin and how it came into the world. Every gypsy there believes that the violin had a miraculous origin. Once upon a time there lived in one of the villages of Transylvania a girl whom all the peasants thought bewitched because no man would ask her in marriage in spite of her great beauty and rich dowry. She herself was in love with a farmer, but he would never cast a look her way, though she sighed for him from morn till eve. At last, finding all her efforts fruitless, she prayed to the Devil and he said he would give her a magic instrument which would bring the young man to her feet. "But, first of all," said he, "you must give me your father, your mother, and your four brothers." The girl was bewitched, as I said before, and she gave them all up without a murmur. Then the Devil out of the body of the father made an instrument, and out of the white hair of the mother's head he fashioned the bow, and out of the four brothers he made strings and strung them across the fiddle. "Now off with you," said he, "and play that fiddle into yon youth's ear and he'll follow you to the ends of the earth."

When the girl played, the young man followed her with his eyes set on her as in a trance. And she took his arm and both were wending their way home full of joy when suddenly the Devil appeared in their path and said: "Now it is the time for me to collect my dues: both of you have listened to the Devil's music and you must come off with me to Hell." And off they went. As for the violin, it lay on the ground in the forest until a ragged gypsy happened to pass that way, and he found it. And *he, stranger, is playing it yet through the world, and because it is the Devil's instrument men and women go daft when they hear it, and the gypsy alone knows its secret.*[4]

QUESTIONS FOR DISCUSSION

What difference would you expect between the timbre of an eighteenth-century orchestra and that of the twentieth century? Can you illustrate this by citing musical examples of each?

What factors must we remember when considering even the best phonograph recordings as representative of the effects produced by the orchestra?

MUSIC TO LISTEN TO

In addition to the two examples given in this chapter, the following compositions will give good practice in learning to listen to the orchestra:

Wagner: *Tannhaeuser Overture*
Brahms: Second Movement of *Third Symphony*
Tchaikovsky: First Movement of *Symphonie pathétique*
Weber: *Oberon Overture*

[4] From Walter Starkie: *Raggle-Taggle*. New York: E. P. Dutton & Co., Inc. Copyright, 1933, by Walter Starkie.

RHYTHM IN SCULPTURE
CHILD WITH CAT, 1926, by William Zorach

CHAPTER XVI. *TECHNICAL INFORMATION THAT WILL HELP*

IN SEEKING to understand and appreciate the quality of any phase of human activity, whether it takes the form of games such as football or tennis, or of such creative arts as music and painting, a certain amount of technical information is necessary. By this we mean that there are definite terms and expressions that have a special *meaning* in reference to the activity under consideration. And if we are to follow intelligently the various phases of such an activity, we have to learn the meaning of such specially-used words.

Take, for example, such technical expressions as *first down* or *off side* in football or *let* and *love* in tennis. We can all see that it would be impossible to understand how these games are played, or what is being done at different times by the various players, if we did not know exactly what such terms mean. So, too, in such things as art and music there are certain terms that are used to explain definite aspects of these very important human activities. And if we are to become interested in and really learn to know something about pictures and music, literature, architecture, and sculpture, we have to know what these technical terms mean.

303

BACKGROUNDS FOR LISTENING

It is very difficult to talk about music, for example, unless we have some clear understanding of the means by which its raw materials of sound are organized so that we can understand and enjoy them. These technical elements of the language of music are: (1) rhythm, (2) melody, and (3) harmony. They are present in all the music we hear today; and, while a complete understanding of them and the ways in which they are used would require a great deal of study, the listener can easily gain enough information about them to help his appreciation of music greatly.

RHYTHM

We have already said that of all the means by which physical sound is organized into music, *rhythm* is the most fundamental and most easily perceived. The reasons for this are obvious, if we but look about us in the natural universe. Our word *rhythm* is derived from the Greek word meaning *to flow*. And the modern interpretation of the term is just that — the continued flowing which results from the repetition over and over again of the same or similar things. Think of the significance of rhythm in everyday life! As you know, many of the operations of nature occur rhythmically — in a sequence of alternating tension and relaxation: our waking and sleeping; the succession of days and nights, of summer and winter, of the ebb and flow of the tides, of the beating of the waves upon the shore, of our own as well as the pace of other animals. There is an endless variety of examples of rhythm in nature.

The term rhythm therefore suggests the *lawful periodicity of every phase of our lives*, without which existence would seem chaotic and we would not be able to sense in it the parts that go to make up its whole. Imagine how helpless we would feel without some recognition of the rhythmic sequences that make up our time system — the seconds, minutes, hours, days, months, and years that recur over and over again all through our lives from the cradle to the grave. The recognition of these periodically recurrent signs, as someone has said, makes men feel that life is natural and affords him a certain relief and pleasure and understanding of how he lives.

So all the works of art that have been created by man in the centuries he has lived here on earth conform to a universal truth when they reveal within themselves some kind of rhythmic organization. In such *space arts* as architecture, sculpture, and painting, these rhythmic schemes are obvious to the eye, just as in the *time arts* such as music and poetry they are discernible to the ear. In all art the element of rhythm is especially important because it is the chief means by which the different parts are organized and unified into a whole. And unity, we must always remember, is one of the main requirements of good art.

As a striking example of this, notice the various ways in which the elements of the façade of a building — its windows, doors, masses of space and weight — go to make up a rhythmic design. This design, reiterated in certain ways, is the means which serve to make the building beautiful and understandable to us as we look at it. So, too, the rhythmic arrangements of the details of a painting, the distribution of the elements of a fine piece of sculpture, give us a sense of order and balance which make these arts interesting and enjoyable.

In music the term rhythm implies a particular grouping of successive beats, or pulses, into time patterns that occur

305

systematically over and over again. The points of stress (or tension) which we feel so definitely in the music we hear are called the *accented*, or strong (heavy), beats; opposed to them

RHYTHM IN ARCHITECTURE

Old Queens Building at Rutgers is one of the best-designed of the early American college buildings.

as elements of relaxation are the *unaccented*, or weak (light), beats. And the way in which these two kinds of beats arrange themselves into the time units called *measures* forms the rhythmic, or metrical, pattern of the music we listen to.

If these time patterns occur systematically, the rhythm is said to be regular; if they do not, the rhythm is irregular. Fortunately for the average listener, regular rhythmic patterns

306

group the beats we hear into two great general classes: (1) duple (two-part) time, which arranges the strong and weak beats into groups of two or multiples of two units to the measure; and (2) triple (three-part) time, which groups them into three or multiples of three units to the measure.

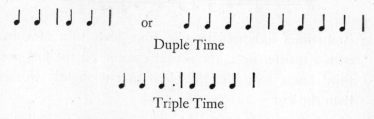

Duple Time

Triple Time

This arrangement is generally indicated in printed music by the numerator of the fraction that is found at the beginning of a music score: 2/4, 3/4, 3/8, or 2/2, for instance. The denominator of this fraction shows the value of the note which is taken as the unit for each measure; that is, a quarter, eighth, or half note. But the listener should learn to recognize the differences between these fundamental rhythmic groups, or time patterns, by listening. Here are some typical examples, arranged in order so that they may be quickly recognized:

DUPLE, OR TWO-PART, MEASURE

The most commonly-used rhythmic patterns in present-day music are these:

2/4: two beats to a measure, each a quarter note

BACKGROUNDS FOR LISTENING

2/2: two beats to a measure, each a half note

Rimsky-Korsakoff
Scheherazade

4/4 (sometimes indicated by C): four beats to a measure, each a quarter note, the accent coming on the first and third beats, with the third-beat accent slightly weaker than the first

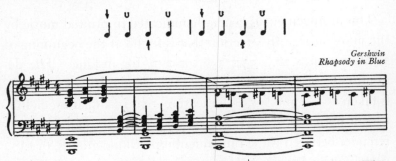

Gershwin
Rhapsody in Blue

Sometimes you see a sign such as this: ₵ in the signature. This sign signifies that there are two beats instead of four in a measure and that the composition is to be played doubly fast for that reason. *Alla breve*, it is called:

Mozart
G Minor Symphony, First Movement

Allegro

TRIPLE, OR THREE-PART, MEASURE

3/4: three beats to a measure, each a quarter note

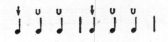

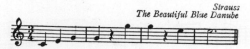

3/2: three beats to a measure, each a half note

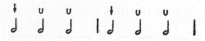

Notice the solemn, dignified effect of this, in contrast to the more flowing, graceful melody above.

3/8: three beats to a measure, each an eighth note

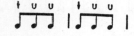

Here again, the effect of this rhythm pattern is quite different from that made by the above melodies.

It is possible, of course, to have 2, 3, or 4 beats in a measure with any length of note as a unit. This note length may be divided in any way — into halves, thirds, etc. This gives us compound meters such as these:

6/8: six beats to a measure, each an eighth note, the accent coming on the first and fourth beats, the fourth being slightly less accented than the first

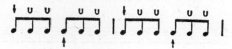

309

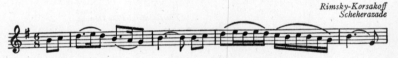

Rimsky-Korsakoff
Scheherazade

9/8: nine beats to a measure, each an eighth note, dividing
into three groups of three eighth notes each

Debussy
Clair de lune

12/8: twelve beats to a measure, each an eighth note, dividing
into four groups of three eighth notes each

Wagner
Siegfried

Composers must have felt the differences between these
rhythm patterns very clearly to have employed so many varying devices for the exact rhythmic effects they wanted. Some
have not hesitated to combine the two- and three-beat patterns
into a five-beat measure. The most famous example of five-beat
measure is the Second Movement of Tchaikovsky's *Symphonie
pathétique*:

and later in the same movement:

TECHNICAL INFORMATION

Regular patterns of meters such as these lay themselves open to being somewhat monotonous from the musical standpoint, and in order to avoid this monotony composers have resorted to all sorts of rhythm tricks. They may substitute an irregular metrical pattern occasionally, such as this from Moussorgsky's *Pictures at an Exhibition:*

More often they resort to syncopation — the shifting of the accented beat from where we expect it to where we do not:

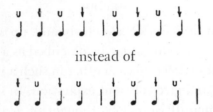

instead of

or  instead of what we naturally expect. This device pulls our attention up, somewhat, and gives the music new interest. Siegfried's Horn Call from Wagner's opera *Die Goetterdaemmerung* is a good example. We get this:

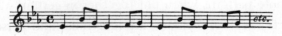

instead of what we might expect:

Like every good thing in life, syncopation can be overdone, and many popular composers, realizing its stimulating effect, have overused it in their music. As an occasional condiment for a musical sauce, it is excellent; when used constantly, it becomes as monotonous as the effects it displaces.

There are other intricacies of rhythmic treatment sometimes used by composers that are quite beyond the scope of such a simple treatment as this. But enough has been given here to enable you to grasp the significance of this fundamental factor of music. Constant and steady practice in recognizing these rhythmic differences cannot but help increase your interest and appreciation.

MELODY

Another musical device closely bound up with rhythmic effects is *melody*. Melody may be described as a particular succession of tones related to each other in such a way as to make musical sense and give coherent expression. In simple terms, a melody is a tune. It cannot be thought of as something separate from rhythm; for whenever we think of the one, we associate the other with it simultaneously. Try to recall even the simplest kind of tune (*Way Down Upon the Swanee River* is a good example) and you will find yourself marking out the rhythm pattern as you do so. Someone has very rightly called these two elements the inseparable Siamese twins of music.

No one knows just what it is that makes a good melody. In spite of many attempts to analyze them and to find out why certain note patterns when put together in certain ways make the effects they do, melodies are individual and personal and

312

uncopyable. Such tunes as these of Mozart and Schubert and Grieg cannot be manufactured by formula:

They remain in our minds as the feature of the music of these composers most easily recognized and longest remembered. Speaking generally, it is music that has plenty of good melody that is popular. And although our ideas as to what constitutes a good tune change as we hear more and more music, melody will always remain for us one of the distinguishing and identifying features in the music we hear.

It is possible, however, to note some of the most individual characteristics of melodies:

(a) They are usually written according to some generally-used scale pattern. Those most common are the *major and minor, chromatic, whole-tone,* and *pentatonic* (five-toned) scales. For the sake of definiteness, a scale may be described as a succession of tones in some arranged order, this order being the result of tradition and historical development. For example, the major scale — the one most used today — is made up of a series of whole and half tones arranged in the following prescribed order:

BACKGROUNDS FOR LISTENING

Tone — Tone — Half tone — Tone — Tone —
Tone — Half tone

If we start at any C on the piano keyboard and play each white key up to the next C, we can get an idea of what this scale sounds like. Melodies based on it are usually broad, rather full, and cheerful-sounding. Here are some typical examples:

and the following, already quoted in this chapter:

TECHNICAL INFORMATION

The minor scale most usually used in our music (there are several different types) comprises these intervals:

Tone — Half tone — Tone — Tone — Half tone
— Tone and a half tone — Half tone

Starting at C on the piano, this order gives us D—E flat —F—G—A flat—B—C. A scale like this gives a different flavor to the melodies which use it, a flavor that is difficult to describe but perfectly possible of recognition. An easy way of sensing the difference between the major and minor scale is by listening to a melody played first in one and then in the other. The old Virginia Reel tune *Pop Goes the Weasel* in major sounds this way:

in minor it becomes:

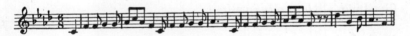

To most ears the minor scales and the melodies based upon them have a more somber and melancholy sound than those in the major, though this distinction is by no means universal, for there are some very lively dance tunes in the minor. Perhaps the terms *veiled* or *subdued* would be better to use in describing the music based on this scale.

The chromatic scale comprises all the notes, both black and white, that lie within the space of an octave on the piano. Thus, we have a series of twelve half tones:

C—C sharp—D—D sharp—E—F—F sharp—G—
G sharp—A—A sharp—B—C

Melodies written in this scale are rather lush and emotional in character in comparison with the more severe and staid major and minor tunes:

Rimsky-Korsakoff
Sadko

The whole-tone scale as occasionally used by Debussy and other comparatively modern composers may be constructed by taking every other key on the piano keyboard, black as well as white. Thus:

It gives a very characteristic color to such melodies as this from Gershwin's *Rhapsody in Blue:*

or this, from Debussy's *String Quartet:*

Much primitive folk music, including jazz, employs the pentatonic scale. This scale is merely a shorter series of tones than those comprising the major and minor scales. It can be represented by such symbols as the black keys on the piano played in succession:

F sharp—G sharp—A sharp—C sharp—D sharp

TECHNICAL INFORMATION

or a series like this:

C—D—E—G—A

If the series is continued, the sixth tone is always an octave higher than the first. Here are two American Indian tunes based on the patterns of the pentatonic scale:

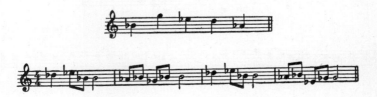

(b) Melodies have the further distinction of being sometimes quite restrained in their flow, sometimes very active and jumpy. In this respect compare this theme from Beethoven's *Seventh Symphony:*

with such a melody as this from Mozart's *Symphony in G Minor:*

(c) Another way in which melodies may be distinguished is by means of their characteristic rhythmic outlines, the rhythm patterns which give them their particular character. Note such examples as:

Schubert
Unfinished Symphony

317

HARMONY

The dictionary defines *harmony as the pleasing concord of simultaneous sounds or strains differing in pitch or quality.* This is not all the musician means by the term, for he has a special technical meaning in mind when he speaks of harmony. To him the term means the simultaneous sounding of tones in groups or clusters called chords and the manner in which these chord groups react to each other. The difference between the effects of melody and harmony upon our musical consciousness can be realized if we compare such a melody as this:

with the following, in which it is supplied with a chordal or harmonic background:

318

While the melody alone has, of course, musical contour and meaning, it is not until we hear the chords beneath it that we realize its full beauty and significance. Another splendid example is the well-known tune of Handel's:

which, when supplied with its appropriate harmonies, becomes so much more majestic and impressive in its effects:

The harmony used by composers has become richer and more colorful through the years. In the earlier days, composers employed harmonic devices that were largely consonant: chords that were static and finished in effect, needing nothing to complete their meaning. Gradually music became more and more dissonant, as chords were thought of as means for restless and disturbing effects as well as the more restful and calm consonant musical ideas. These *dissonant* chords required others to follow them and complete their meaning. The process of furnishing a consonant close to a dissonant chord is called a *resolution*:

319

Consonant Dissonant Consonant
Chord   Chord   Chord
resolves to resolves to

The music of composers as late as the eighteenth century consists principally of consonances, with dissonances added occasionally to give interest and zest to the music, much as a dash of pepper or other condiment is used to make food more interesting. Today the tendency is the other way — more dissonances than consonances are employed, giving the music a restless, rather strained effect.

Harmony to our ears is almost as essential a part of the music we hear as are melody and rhythm. Although we of necessity have treated these three factors separately, as a matter of fact they are bound together inextricably in present-day music. The composer does not think of them as separate entities when he writes. He conceives his musical ideas in terms of melody, rhythm, and harmony combined for their full effect. So we, too, in listening must learn to realize how much of the music we hear is conditioned by the weaving together of these three important and elemental factors.

MUSIC TO LISTEN TO

Melody is a natural part of vocal music and so can be illustrated by some of the world's great songs. Listen to these:

Handel: *Ombra mai fu* (from the opera *Serse*)

HMV   DB 1901

One of the finest melodies in existence from an early Italian opera, with magnificent supporting harmonies.

320

TECHNICAL INFORMATION

Schubert: *The Erlking*   v   15825

A wonderful song, written when the composer was still in his 'teens. Look up its story.

Schubert: *Ave Maria*   v   11–9836

The words of this song are from Scott's *Lady of the Lake.* They are sung by Ellen, a Highland maid.

Wagner: *Elsa's Dream* (from the opera *Lohengrin*)
                                              c   12321   d

This famous opera aria tells of the dream of one of the principal characters in *Lohengrin,* in which a brave knight in shining armor comes to help her.

Rimsky-Korsakoff: *Song of the Indian Guest* (from the opera *Sadko*)   v   1570

Quoted in the text on page 316 as a fine example of a chromatic melody.

Wagner: *Immolation Scene* (from the opera
    Die Goetterdaemmerung)   v   m 978

This is the final scene from Wagner's great set of four operas based upon the old Norse saga of the *Ring of the Nibelung.* These operas tell the story of Siegfried. After his death in this last of the four, Bruennhilde, his wife, tells the tale of his betrayal and of her desire to share in the eternal honor of her hero. She has his body placed on a huge funeral pyre, lights this herself and, mounting her horse, rides into the flames. All this is wonderfully told in the orchestral score, which is full of melodies and harmonies, dissonant chords constantly resolving into consonant, taken from the *Ring* operas.

THE PARTHENON, beautiful form in Greek architecture

CHAPTER XVII

FORM IN GENERAL AND PARTICULAR

ANOTHER important technical term that is used in discussing music and its meaning is *form*. We do not have to listen very long to people talking about the various arts before we come upon some such expression as this: "The form of this piece of music is not as good as it should be," or "His form is satisfactory enough, but he doesn't have much to say." What do critics mean when they talk this way? Simply this: A work of art has certain qualities that put it apart by itself, certain edges that mark it off from its surroundings. For instance, a picture occupies so and so many square inches of space, a symphony three quarters of an hour of time, etc. Within these limits each art work has a shape or form of its own, some plan of being by which the elements which go to make it up are organized so that it becomes different from everything else. Its different parts are definitely related to each other and to the whole in such a way as to give it particular meaning and significance. An American poet has put it this way:

323

Form is the build of any organism,
Living or dead, of a whole tree or a leaf,
A whole poem or a word.

It is easier to illustrate what this means than it is to try to explain it. Centuries ago, one of our prehistoric ancestors wanted, for some reason or another, to show his fellows what

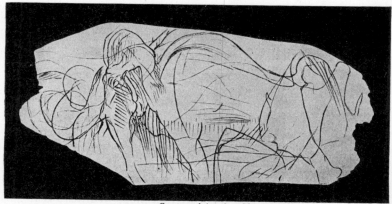

Courtesy of American Museum of Natural History, New York

AN EARLY DRAWING OF A MAMMOTH, on an ivory tusk

a mammoth looked like. The only material he seemed to have had at hand for his purpose was the tusk of one of these huge animals, and on it this prehistoric artist scratched in the ivory a lifelike drawing of an elephant-like animal. But — and this is the point — he had to adapt and arrange his lines and change the proportions of his drawing so that they would fall within the limits set by the shape and size of the ivory tusk. The result, we say, has form: the appearance of the animal was suited to certain conditions. The meaning of the drawing to us today is due to the way its parts were related to each other and fitted together so as to form the whole effect.

Take another example from our own art of music. One of the finest simple tunes ever written is this one which came out of the county of Londonderry in Ireland years ago. We do not even know who its composer was, but we realize readily enough that he knew how to manipulate his materials so as to give his music particular point and meaning. In other words, the tune has good form:

Let's look at this tune briefly. The germ out of which it grows is its first phrase, which we have labeled A, a wonderful melody with a decided Irish twist to it. Now see what happens. After being heard once, it is repeated at a higher pitch with a different ending, thus making it even more telling. Then it comes a third time at the original tonal level, and it is repeated a fourth time with still another ending that gives a full and satisfying close.

Then comes the contrasting melody, B. It makes an attempt to rise but sinks back further than the point from which it set out. It tries again but is able to soar no higher than before; and when it falls back, it reaches a point that suggests it will take off again immediately. And at the third attempt, this phrase B rises grandly to the climax of the whole song, a climax which gives the tune its essential character and sweep. After this mounting surge, we are ready for the peaceful concluding A again, a conclusion that suggests a majestic descent to earth after a heaven-soaring flight.

What gives this music meaning, what makes it what it is, different from anything else ever written, is its peculiar way of being put together, its build, its form. Meaning and form are here bound together, the one dependent upon the other, born at the same time in the artist's mind, just as have been the veins and arteries and the blood they contain in his body.

One more example, this time from the art of poetry. No better way could be found of demonstrating the manner in which the *pattern* of expression chosen by a poet directs the *feeling* that he would communicate to us than the familiar illustration of this little poem by the English poet William Wordsworth, written about 1800, after the death of one he loved:

> She dwelt among the untrodden ways
> Beside the springs of Dove,
> A maid whom there were none to praise
> And very few to love.

> A violet by a mossy stone
> Half hidden from the eye!
> Fair as a star, when only one
> Is shining in the sky.

She lived unknown, and few could know
 When Lucy ceased to be;
But she is in her grave, and, oh,
 The difference to me!

Now if we examine this carefully, we see that its lines are made up of a certain formal pattern of light and heavy beats — four in one line and three in the next, alternately. Reading it aloud, as all poetry should be read, will make this clear enough:

She dwelt a-mong the un-trod-den ways
Be-side the springs of Dove,
Etc.

In addition, the last word of every other line rhymes — ways, praise, Dove, love, etc. These constructional features are carried strictly throughout the three short verses.

So far, the poem is interesting enough as the form goes. But we will get no idea of how the poet's shaping of his material helps him convey his meaning to us until we look at this little masterpiece from another angle. The first eight lines, quietly descriptive in character, are really all about one thing — Lucy's loneliness. Each of them is a little more intense than the last, the climax being reached through the lovely figure of one lone star shining in the sky. Then comes a sudden release from the mounting tension, for the theme is treated in a matter-of-fact way with no hint of what is coming:

She lived unknown, and few could know
 When Lucy ceased to be;

Then comes the tragedy, the emotional revelation from the mind of the poet:

> But she is in her grave, and, oh,
> The difference to me!

Thus the whole meaning of the poem, the great sorrow which the poet strives to communicate to us, depends upon the form given to his expression by the writer. If this seems farfetched to you, read this literal translation which might be made of the poem. It contains all the ideas, but in it form and meaning perish together:

> She lived along one of the lonely roads
> That run by the sources of the Dove.
> She was a girl whom no one praised,
> And few people loved her.
>
> She was like a violet growing by a stone
> That is difficult to be seen.
> She was fair as a star
> Shining alone in the sky.
>
> She lived such a lonely life
> That few knew when she died;
> But now she is in her grave,
> What a great difference it makes to me!

There is constant need for good form, or design, in all art. The art of music, because of its peculiar transitory nature — the fact that it has gone almost as soon as it comes — seems to need it even more than the others. Every good artist needs

328

A PRECURSOR OF SWING from the art of 11,000 years ago

What appear to be ballet skirts on these dancers are merely spots where the rock of the cave on which they were painted has crumbled and fallen off. This mural was found on the ceiling of a shallow cave near the Libyan Desert in Africa. Notice how well this primitive artist filled the space that was available to him; in other words, what good form he showed.

to know how to arrange the different parts of his composition so as to give them a unity that will produce as good effects as possible upon the consciousness of the beholder or listener. This is especially true of the composer. He must have some definite scheme of organization in mind as he writes a composition. If he does not, his music will simply consume time and say little, be nothing but a hodgepodge of sounds and rhythms.

329

There are, of course, different ways of achieving an ideal of good organization in music. Some composers have been individualistic enough to formulate their own schemes and to write music that is as original and personal in its formal pattern as it is in its emotional expression. This can be said to be particularly true of the modern composers.

But most of those who have written music have made liberal use of certain ready-shaped formal formulas that have come down to them from the practices of the past. In the case of such great men as Bach, Beethoven, Schubert, and Brahms, this has had a stimulating rather than restraining effect upon musical creation. These men, and many other composers, used the formal schemes that had been developed by their predecessors; and they used them in such a way as to give us some of our finest compositions. So it is wise for the listener to become well-acquainted with the most-used of these formulas, or forms. In so doing he can definitely increase his sensitivity to what the composer is trying to say to him musically; and he will not feel lost as he tries to learn to listen to great music.

It is not difficult to learn to follow these general schemes of organization used by so many of the good composers. Without attempting to give in detail all the schemes that have been employed in the instrumental music written up to this time, this chapter should provide enough information to enable the general listener to orient himself in the music he is apt to hear in concert or on the radio.

First of all, we must consider the two general classes into which instrumental music naturally divides itself: Program Music and Absolute Music. The first type is music that tells a story, music which is associated in the mind of the composer with some poetic or extra-musical idea. It is music, as one writer has put it, in which the composer "confesses" what he had in mind as he wrote his composition. On the other hand, there is Absolute Music, which does not need anything in the way of help from explanations or suggestions outside itself. In listening to this kind of music we do not need to have any ideas as to what prompted its composer to create it. This is music for music's sake, and our enjoyment of it will come largely from musical causes. We do not need to seek any particular extra-musical ideas in it and so can interpret it as we please. Contrary to what many people think, most of the fine music that we have inherited from the past is absolute in type. Later on we will have an opportunity to consider some representative examples of both these types of music.

In Program Music, ready-shaped formal formulas do not come into question. The development of the music simply follows the needs of the program. This is not to say, of course, that Program Music has no need for form or design. Rather, its pattern is forced upon it through the details of the program which the composer has adopted for his musical story. He takes a suitable poetic or philosophical or narrative idea and, using a few themes as musical material, lets his music run along and describe and develop as seems best. This is clear enough in such program works as Smetana's *The Moldau* and Prokofieff's *Peter and the Wolf*, to be studied in some detail later.

Our real concern with formal patterns is in connection with Absolute Music, for in it there is nothing in the way of an underlying poetic program to carry the listener along structurally. Fortunately for him, composers have not employed a great number of conventional formulas in Absolute Music, and a little study should enable him to familiarize himself with them. He should first consider as a whole the general plan of the piece to which he is listening. Is it long and extended, or just a short, "small" instrumental piece? If the latter is the case, it will probably have some title descriptive of its general character: March, Waltz, Étude, Nocturne, Prelude, Polonaise, or the like. Certain composers have specialized in these comparatively short pieces and have given us some fine examples of what it is possible to say musically within a short time-span.

A longer composition may be made by putting some of these shorter pieces of contrasting character together in what is called a *suite*. Literally, a suite is a composition made up of a series of units which center around some musical idea and which together form a unified whole. Just as we have suites of rooms or furniture in everyday life, so in music we have suites of pieces, each piece complete in itself but all of them intended to be played together in sequence and giving their best effect when so used.

Then there is a whole group of compositions, including some of the greatest music ever written, that may be considered together under one head. These are works of an extended type, and they take anywhere from half an hour to over an hour to play. They are made up of a number of divisions, or *movements* (frequently three, generally four, and sometimes five). Each of these movements, while keeping its own identity, is an essential part of the whole and cannot be removed from the whole without losing its character. This type of composition has been in process of development for the last two

332

hundred years, and the different members of the group have received various names, according to the use for which they were designed:

1. A *sonata* (literally a composition that is sounded, or played, in distinction to one that is sung) is a work of this type, written for one or two solo instruments.
2. A *trio* is a composition of this type for three instruments.
3. A *quartet* is a sonata for four instruments, the most general combination being two violins, a viola, and a cello.
4. A *quintet* is a sonata for five instruments.
5. A *sextet* is a sonata for six instruments. (And so on, septet, octet, nonet, etc.)
6. A *symphony* is really a sonata for orchestra.
7. A *concerto* is a sonata for solo instrument (or instruments) *and* orchestra.

For the sake of convenience, we may identify this sort of extended musical composition as one of the *sonata-group compositions*. The reasons for such a name are obvious. Tradition has dictated that each movement or section of this kind of composition shall be written according to a different formal pattern. What these are we shall see.

We have, then, the following instrumental forms, considered in relation to the piece of music as a whole:

Short Pieces

March: a strongly rhythmical piece designed and fitted to accompany marching; therefore, usually written for military band.

Waltz: while originally designed for dancing, this kind of piece is often heard in concert. It then consists of a number of short waltz themes strung together, with an introduction and concluding *coda*.

Étude: literally a study designed for technical practice, the term is often applied to an artistic concert piece of special difficulty.

Nocturne: a "night piece," dreamy, rather subdued in character. Many fine nocturnes were written by Chopin.

Prelude: in the strict sense, an introductory section, but often used for short piano and organ pieces.

Extended Pieces

The Suite: an instrumental composition free as to the character and number of its movements, built around some central musical (or program) idea.

The Sonata-Group Compositions:

    Sonata

    Trio

    Quartet, Quintet, Sextet, etc.

    Symphony

    Concerto

The listener's next step in the recognition of formal patterns in music is to learn to recognize the most common formulas according to which the separate, shorter divisions of a work are written. The sections of the sonata-group compositions are made up of musical material which hangs together naturally and which is developed out of musical ideas called *themes* — basic structural units which contain figures of characteristic melodic, rhythmic, and harmonic outlines. These themes are capable of being enlarged upon in a number of interesting ways and have been so treated by composers ever since the time of Haydn.

334

FORM

The simplest of these sectional forms may be called a *one-part*, or *unitary*, *form*. This comprises a musical section based upon and characterized by a single musical idea. Composers are not very partial to this kind of form, for it gives little chance for contrast, upon which musical interest so much depends. Early experiments in writing instrumental music showed that there were two things that could be done with a musical idea or theme to stretch it into an extended composition: repeat it, or vary it. And since anything in the way of literal repetition is bound to be dull, the early composers adopted the idea of repeating a theme a number of times, each time a little differently. This modification of the one-part form is called *Theme and Variations*, and it can be represented literally by the formula $A—A_1—A_2—A_3$, etc. It has been used by many composers from the earliest days of instrumental music down to the present.

Another way of organizing an extended piece out of a single musical idea is the *rondo*. In this form the principal theme appears a number of times, but with contrasting sections sandwiched in between. Thus we can represent the rondo with this formula: $A—B—A—C—A$. There are different kinds of rondos, but they are all alike in this sense.

A sectional form that has often been used, especially by the earlier instrumental composers, is the *binary*, or *two-part*, *form*. This is compounded out of and characterized by two parts, each centering around one idea. The familiar tune *America* illustrates the binary idea: the first section (comprising the first 6 measures) contrasts strongly with the second section (the remaining 8 measures). Many of the waltzes which Schubert and Brahms wrote for the piano are in two-part form.

335

But the most-used of all the sectional forms is the *three-part*, or *ternary, form*, made up of three sections arranged in the order A—B—A. This kind of repetition after contrast seems to be a natural sort of formal expression, for we find it used in all sorts of musical compositions:

1. In simple songs and popular tunes, such as the English folk song *Drink to Me Only With Thine Eyes* and the American *Turkey in the Straw*. Many of the popular tunes of the day use this form, whether or not the composers are aware of the fact.

2. In short instrumental pieces, such as the prelude, nocturne, étude, impromptu, etc. In the popular minuet, the B section is called a *trio*.

3. For the slow movements of the sonata-group compositions. The slow movement is usually the second movement of a sonata, symphony, etc.; and when it takes the form of a lengthened-out song it goes by the name of *song form*.

4. In the first (sometimes the last) movements of the sonata-group compositions. This is its most complex and at the same time most usual use. Here it goes by the rather confusing name of *sonata form*. It was first worked out in the form in which we know it today by Haydn and his immediate predecessors of the eighteenth century. It has been popular with composers ever since, for it seems to provide an almost ideal vehicle for providing musical variety, contrast, and unity at the same time.

In the sonata form two strongly contrasting theme-groups are presented, in each of which one theme is definitely predominant. One of these groups is powerful, aggressive, masculine in character; the other is relaxed, lyric, feminine. And the

336

contrast between these two groups furnishes the dramatic interest in the first great section of the movement, which we will call the A section. In the second, or B, part of the sonata form, instead of giving us some new material, the composer *develops* the themes presented in A. Rapidly changing suggestions and new combinations of the themes appear, in various keys and with changed rhythmic effects. The musical ideas are pulled apart and reassembled in new ways. There are no fixed rules or patterns, but this development section always challenges the composer's technical resources and imaginative powers. Beethoven met these challenges magnificently in his nine symphonies and his many quartets. Then, after all the bustle and excitement, the first section (A) returns with the same themes repeated in order to give a sense of unified finality.

It is helpful to outline or diagram the plan of this sonata form, if we keep in mind the fact that in art no diagram can be exact. What we are discussing would cease to be art if it could be diagramed exactly. And we must also remember that deviations were generally made by various composers who held true to the tried and useful *general* scheme:

An Introduction (sometimes but by no means always)

A: The section presenting the contrasting theme-groups, called the Statement or Exposition

    1. First theme-group dominated by one main theme, which is often repeated and then connected by means of *bridge passages* to

    2. The contrasting theme-group (again dominated by a main theme), leading with definite finality to the end of the section.

B: The Development section in which the themes of A are developed in different ways

Not all the themes are so treated, but attention seems mainly centered on the main theme of A_1. This section is marked by constant new and interesting changes of melodies, rhythms, and keys.

C: The section in which the theme-groups are again presented for our attention, called the Restatement or Recapitulation

    1. The first theme-group is restated and connected, this time in the same key with

    2. The contrasting theme-group restated, after which the section comes to a close.

Usually a Coda, or additional terminal section, providing a final climax to the whole movement.

Nowhere can this sonata-form idea be better illustrated than in the First Movement of Beethoven's popular *Fifth Symphony*. If you listen to this carefully with the diagram before you, you will find that the whole movement divides itself into four almost exactly equal parts: the Statement, Development, Restatement, and Coda sections. There is no Introduction.

338

In the Statement, the first theme-group is built around this theme:

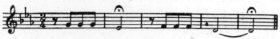

The second theme-group is dominated by this lovely, lyric theme:

and finishes with this:

The Development, or B section, is short and very powerful, based largely on the first main theme. In the Restatement (C) we hear all the themes again as we heard them in A; but at the end, as if Beethoven could not have enough of his strong, rhythmic first theme, we have a Coda of rather unusual length for this concluding section, all based upon

What a magnificent, closely knit, and tremendously effective movement this makes! Here, as in no other place in music, the form and content are so closely linked that one is unthinkable without the other. Another excellent example of this sonata form is found in the First Movement of Prokofieff's charming *Classical Symphony*, discussed at some length on page 358.

There remains one final step in the listener's formal recognition process. This is to see how these sectional forms are generally used to make up the larger sonata-symphony-quartet-concerto type of composition. Here again composing tradition plays a large part in determining the choice made by writers from Haydn to Shostakovich. The usually accepted practice has been this:

The First Movement of these works (of a vigorous, quick, *allegro* character) is written in sonata form.

The Second Movement (usually *andante* or *adagio*) is, in contrast, slow and lyric in character. It may be in sonata form, a theme and variations, or in the ternary type of song form.

The Third Movement is almost always dancelike in character, providing welcome relief for the listener after all the seriousness of the first two movements. With Haydn and Mozart it was a minuet and trio (that is, a kind of ternary form). Beethoven substituted the *scherzo*, in which the tempo of the minuet was speeded up and the general mood lightened. Later composers have usually followed Beethoven in this.

The Fourth Movement is again rapid and complex, something like the First in character but with more of an air of finality, leading to a triumphant or an irresistible close. It is usually in rondo or sonata form.

There are a few forms which are often used by composers that do not fit exactly into these schemes of classification. We can at least mention some of them here. One of the most important of these is the *overture*, literally an opening piece. Very often this is borrowed from the opera, in which it serves to set the mood of the work as a whole, or of the individual acts.

340

Many opera overtures make excellent concert pieces — that of Wagner's *Tannhaeuser* or *Tristan und Isolde* or *Parsifal*, for instance. Composers have often applied this term to independent concert pieces, written in sonata form in the style of operatic overtures. Thus we have Tchaikovsky's *Romeo and Juliet Overture*, this composer's first important work, and Brahms's *Academic Festival Overture*.

Another of these unclassifiable forms is the *fantasia*, a kind of piece in which any formal demand is subordinated to imaginative treatment; or, as the dictionary puts it, a composition characterized by freedom of fancy, unrestricted by set forms. Classic examples are the great fantasias which Bach wrote as introductory movements to some of his organ fugues and the three great fantasias which Mozart wrote for the piano. While they do not follow any ordained or set form, it can hardly be said that these beautiful pieces lack form! The *fugue* is a contrapuntal form largely used in the seventeenth and early eighteenth centuries.

All this discussion of formal principles and practices probably seems confusing to the listener who is trying to gain musical experience. As we have said in another place, by this time he may be ready to turn his back on the whole matter and ask, *After all, what is the use? Can I honestly expect to enjoy music any more by trying to follow these architectural plans and understand all these technical terms, many of them so confused and inexact in meaning?*

The only answer we can give is that even a slight acquaintance with the way music is put together helps to remove this sense of bewilderment and futility from which so many suffer when listening to great music. In its place there will come,

341

gradually but none the less surely, the pleasure of observing the composer's designs and of realizing how they are or are not being fulfilled. This sense of design and plan in music becomes an almost intuitive part of the listener's equipment and, when added to the sensuous pleasure to be obtained from listening, helps his experience and cultivates his taste. *Form is by no manner of means all there is in music. It is not even the most important aspect of it.* But the more one understands it, the surer he is of his musical judgment.

We will have more to say about these various aspects of form as we go along.

MUSIC TO LISTEN TO

In order to summarize the material of this chapter, this list has been prepared to give illustrations of all the points discussed.

PROGRAM MUSIC

Smetana: *The Moldau* (see pages 330–331)
Prokofieff: *Peter and the Wolf* (see page 350)

ABSOLUTE MUSIC

Form in Connection with the Composition as a Whole
(Conjoint Forms)

Short Pieces

March
Sousa: *The Stars and Stripes Forever*

Waltz
Strauss: *Tales from the Vienna Woods*

FORM

Étude
Chopin: *Étude in C Minor, Op. 10, No. 12*

Nocturne
Chopin: *Nocturne in F-Sharp Major, Op. 15, No. 2*

Prelude
Rachmaninoff: *Prelude in C-Sharp Minor, Op. 3, No. 2*

Polonaise
Chopin: *Polonaise in A Major, Op. 40, No. 1*

Extended Pieces

Suite

Bach: *Suite No. 2 in B Minor*	V	M 1123
Tchaikovsky: *Nutcracker Suite*	C	MM–627
Piston: *The Incredible Flutist*		
(Ballet Suite)	V	M 621

Symphony

Beethoven: *Symphony No. 5 in C Minor*	C	MM–498
Prokofieff: *Classical Symphony*	C	MX–166

Concerto

Grieg: *A-Minor Concerto for Piano*		
and Orchestra	C	M–313

Chamber Music

Schubert: *Trio for Piano and Strings,*		
Op. 99	V	M 923
Beethoven: *Quartet in G Major,*		
Op. 18, No. 2	C	M–66
Schubert: *Quintet in C Major, Op. 163*	C	M–497
Brahms: *Sextet in G, Op. 36*	V	M 371

343

BACKGROUNDS FOR LISTENING

Form in Connection with the Separate Divisions of a Composition

(Sectional Forms)

One-part (Unitary) Form
Bach: *Prelude in C Major, No. 1, Well-tempered Clavichord*

Theme and Variations
Haydn: *Surprise Symphony*, Second Movement
Elgar: *Enigma Variations*

Rondo
Dohnányi: *Suite for Orchestra*, Op. 19, Last Movement
Mozart: *Concerto in D Minor*, Last Movement

Two-part (Binary) Form
Schubert: *Twelve Laendler*, Op. 171

Three-part (Ternary) Form
In short instrumental compositions
Dvořák: *Humoresque*
Chopin: *Nocturne in F-Sharp Major*, Op. 15, No. 2
Mozart: *Minuet* from G-Minor Symphony, Third Movement

In slow movements (song form)
Mendelssohn: *Spring Song*, Op. 62, No. 6

In sonata-form movements
Beethoven: *Symphony No. 5 in C Minor*, First Movement
Prokofieff: *Classical Symphony*, First Movement
Mozart: *Symphony in G Minor*, Fourth Movement

Unclassified Forms
Overture
Mozart: *The Marriage of Figaro Overture*

344

FORM

Brahms: *Academic Festival Overture*
Tchaikovsky: *Romeo and Juliet Overture*

Fantasia
Mozart: *Fantasia in C Minor for Piano*
Chopin: *Fantaisie-Impromptu*, Op. 66

Fugue
Bach: *Organ Fugue in G Minor* (The Little)

OTHER ASPECTS OF FORM

1. Form in Poetry

Can you see what the form of Milton's famous sonnet quoted below is?

On His Blindness

(Written about three years after he had
become blind at the age of 44)

When I consider how my light is spent,
  Ere half my days in this dark world and wide,
  And that one talent which is death to hide,
  Lodged with me useless, though my soul more bent
To serve therewith my Maker, and present
  My true account, lest He returning chide;
  "Doth God exact day-labor, light denied?"
  I fondly ask. But Patience, to prevent
That murmur, soon replies, "God doth not need
  Either man's work or his own gifts. Who best
  Bears his mild yoke, they serve Him best. His state
Is kingly: thousands at His bidding speed,
  And post o'er land and ocean without rest;
  They also serve who only stand and wait."

345

2. Form in Renaissance Painting

Can you apply the description of form given in the text to Fra Angelico's picture on the facing page: *Death and Assumption of the Virgin?*

3. Form in Architecture

For examples of good form in architecture, see pages 27, 168, 225, and 322.

4. Form in Living

Good form is much the same thing in sport and in art. Both the high jumper and the ballet dancer co-ordinate their muscular actions in such a way as to produce the best possible effect. In other words, their form is the same!

Int. News Photo.   *Courtesy of Ballet Theatre*

FORM IN SPORT AND ART

FORM IN RENAISSANCE PAINTING

Like his contemporaries, Fra Angelico (1387–
1455) painted religious subjects. But see how, in
telling the story of the death and reception into
heaven of the Virgin, the painter makes use of
form to increase the beauty of his picture.

347

A SCENE FROM THE BALLET APPALACHIAN SPRING,
for which Copland wrote the music

CHAPTER XVIII

MUSIC WRITTEN FOR OR-CHESTRA

T

HERE are two great classes into which the music written for the orchestra can naturally be divided, as you read in Chapter XVII. Such a classification, of course, is not the only one that could be made, but it is a convenient one and one that helps us understand the nature of orchestral style. Let us review it briefly.

On the one hand is Program Music — music that tells a story which, in the mind of the composer, is associated with some poetic idea or extra-musical suggestion. *Extra-musical* is a term used to indicate that the origin or source of the musical inspiration of the composer is external, that some definite experience or situation or object supplied the stimulus to create the picture in terms of music. It is music, as one writer has well said, in which the composer "confesses" what he had in mind as he wrote.

On the other hand there is Absolute Music, which stands on its own feet as music, without any help from explanations or suggestions outside itself. In hearing this kind of music we are given no idea of what prompted the composer to write it, nor do we need to know. For this is music for music's sake, and our enjoyment of it comes from musical reasons. We do not need to seek any particular extra-musical ideas in it, and

Courtesy of Decca Records

so we can interpret it as we please. Contrary to what many people, think, a great deal of fine music is absolute in type.

In this chapter we will consider some representative examples of both these kinds of orchestral expression.

Serge Prokofieff: *Peter and the Wolf*   D A—130

Here is program music *par excellence*, for it not only suggests extra-musical ideas by the nature of its music, but it fairly hurls them at us in the form of a folk tale recited as the music progresses. Designed as a simple story for young listeners, this clever music can teach music lovers of all ages a great deal about the way program music is put together. In the first place, there is a very definite association of orchestral ideas with program ideas. In the story, Prokofieff tells us at the very beginning that he had in mind the fact that listeners "will be able to distinguish the sonorities of the several instruments." So, during the performance a bird is represented by the flute; a duck by the oboe; a cat by the clarinet; the fussy old grandfather, appropriately enough, by the bassoon; Peter, the hero, by a jolly tune on the strings; and the hunters' shooting by the drums. These associations are skillfully made and help a great deal in our enjoyment of this piece.

In the case of some of these associations the instruments do sound like the thing being described. For instance, many birds' songs do have a lyric, flutelike quality; and we have all heard the reedy quack, quack of a duck happily sailing away on the pond. Most certainly, drums can be made to imitate the shooting of guns. But the association of a clarinet with the sly cat that tries to gain its own ends through the distraction of the attention of others, or of the jaunty hero with a tune played by the string quartet, is purely arbitrary. The important thing to realize is that some association has been made by the composer, and the effectiveness of the musical story depends to a great degree upon our recognition of such associations.

The linking of orchestral color with program ideas is not the only association made in this kind of music, however. If we listen closely, we will quickly realize that in this piece a definite theme goes with each character of the orchestral fairy tale. For example, the bird's theme is:

351

the duck's:

and Peter's tune:

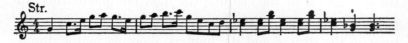

So in all good program music, definite themes are chosen and then developed to suit the needs of the program. Wonderful examples of this may be heard in *Till Eulenspiegel's Merry Pranks* by Richard Strauss and *Les Préludes* by Liszt. (If you wish to investigate the themes of these pieces, you can find them in *Discovering Music* by McKinney and Anderson.) In absolute music, while the themes are abstract and have no connection with extra-musical ideas, they are developed in an even more elaborate and logical way.

A third characteristic of program music, easily recognized here, is that the music does a great deal more than just tell a story. It suggests, implies, stirs the imagination in a way that words alone can never do. On the other hand, because of its very nature, it cannot describe or particularize exactly; its meaning must always be different for each person who listens to it, and this meaning must depend upon his background, his powers of perception, and his imagination. For this reason program music is an ideal art, for it makes the listener a direct participant. How much more effective this musical fairy tale is than an animated cartoon would be on the same subject! In listening to the music's comment upon and elaboration and enrichment of the text, we have to picture in our mind's eye the different events as they transpire and imagine just how the characters looked and acted. In the movies, we would have all this done for us; we would simply be onlookers, and so the final effect could not be as stimulating or enjoyable.

Let us take a few examples. The music's description of the quarrel between the duck and the bird over the respective merits of swimming without flying and flying without swimming; the grumpy nagging of the old grandfather, who thinks only about himself and his past; the stupid complacency of the duck; the eager sympathy of Peter; the greedy cruelty of the wolf — all these are wonderfully characterized by the music. The story is no longer merely for children but one that is fresh and interesting for imaginative people of any age, be it seven, seventeen, or seventy.

Franz Josef Haydn: *Surprise Symphony,*
    Second Movement   c   m–363

In direct contrast to this delightful program piece just studied is the *Andante,* or the Second Movement, of Haydn's *Surprise Symphony.* This characteristic eighteenth-century music has a stately, conventional quality; it has no thought of telling a story or communicating any other than purely musical ideas. Therefore we say that it is an outstanding example of absolute music. The second of four sections, or movements, that go to make up the whole symphony, it is slow and sustained in nature, in contrast to the rather brisk moods of the other movements. It consists of a theme, so simple and

353

straightforward that it reminds us of a folk dance, and four variants or variations of it.

As we have seen, the *Theme and Variations* is one of the earliest of the forms that were developed by writers of instrumental music in order to show their ingenuity and ability and to express their musical ideas clearly. It goes away back to the sixteenth century and has really changed very little since that time. One writer has amusingly described it as a sort of musical dinner consisting entirely of one kind of fish served in many different courses and with many different kinds of sauces and cooking.

There is good reason for the continued popularity of this particular form, for it provides ample opportunity for the display of orchestral color and change of mood. The listener, after he has learned the theme so that he can never forget it, naturally gets a great deal of pleasure out of following the various changes which it undergoes at the hand of the composer. Sometimes it is easily recognized; at other times it seems almost buried under a mass of musical construction. Its pattern might be thought of in this way, if we let the symbol A represent the theme: $A—A_1—A_2—A_3—A_4$ and so on. In other words, the whole composition is based upon different versions of A.

In this Second Movement of the *Surprise Symphony* it is easy to hear that the main theme consists of two parts, and that the composer varies each one in its respective order:

Tacked on at the end is a charming and very characteristically Haydn coda. These are the interesting ways in which the composer varies his two-part theme:

Variation

I. He lets us hear it with an embellishment of ornamental passages, like colored threads that are woven into a tapestry for ornamental effect.

II. He gives it to us in a subdued, melancholy mood, with some scale passages that vary the second part.

III. The third variation is characterized by a repetition of the notes contained in the first part of the theme, producing a soft, rather choppy effect with wood winds and strings.

IV. There is a loud proclamation of the theme by the whole orchestra, with accompanying, syncopated chords and running passages for strings.

In the coda, suggestions of the theme are heard, the whole ending very quietly with three soft chords.

(In the recordings of this movement, the theme and first two variations take up the first record side, the second two variations and coda the second record side.)

This music with its quiet aristocratic bearing is typical of the period that produced it, a period during which the monarchs and their aristocratic princes, living on feudal-like estates with complete authority over their subjects, were the great patrons of art and music. Haydn was for a long time employed by a Prince Esterhazy as orchestral leader and composer, in charge of all the music produced in his castles in and around Vienna. In providing these fashionable audiences with their musical

355

entertainment, Haydn worked out many of the principles of modern orchestral writing.

Sir Edward Elgar: *Enigma Variations*   V   M 475

Now let us go back to the program style and listen to a piece in this same form — theme and variations. Much later in origin than the Haydn music just heard (more than a hundred years separate the two pieces), the *Enigma Variations* by the Englishman Elgar comprise a set of fourteen musical portraits of his friends. As the composer wrote after finishing his music in 1899:

I have just sketched a set of variations on an original theme, which have amused me because I've labeled them with the nicknames of my particular friends. This is to say, I've written the variations each one to represent the mood of the "party." I've tried to imagine the party writing the variation him (or her) self, if they were foolish enough to compose. I warn you [and we listeners should heed this warning, for these Elgar variations are certainly very free in comparison with the Haydn variations] *that the apparent connection between the variations and the theme is often of the slightest texture.*

Here is the *Enigma* theme in its essential characteristics, not too easy for one to remember. Listen to it a number of times and try to fix it in your musical mind so that you can see what happens to it:

356

MUSIC FOR ORCHESTRA

Variation

I. Tender and gentle: a portrait of Lady Elgar, the composer's wife.

II. Quick and fluttering: a picture of an amateur pianist friend who always practiced runs and exercises at the keyboard before starting to play serious music.

III. Something like a mazurka in style: an amateur actor who could easily turn his deep voice into a high falsetto when playing an old man's part.

IV. Strong and violent: an English country squire of high spirits and great energy.

V. Dreamy and contemplative: dedicated to the son of the well-known English poet Matthew Arnold.

VI. A portrait of Isabel Fitton, a talented viola player. So the variation is "led by a solo viola and shared by all the nicest conversationalists in the orchestra."

VII. Against a drum background, stubborn and argumentative: a friend with whom Elgar loved to argue.

VIII. "A lovely, gracious lady, whose manner evoked for the composer the courtesy of the bygone Victorian age."

IX. The most beautiful of all, dedicated to one of the composer's closest friends, a great lover of music. Elgar tells us that it is "the record of a long summer evening's walk, when my friend grew nobly eloquent (as only he could) on the grandeur of Beethoven and especially of his slow movements."

X. A feminine friend, charming, fluttering, with a slight hesitation of speech.

XI. A friend and his dog, with whom Elgar loved to walk.

One critic has said of it: "If I were a policeman, I think I should ask Mr. G.R.S. of this variation to produce his dog license. The behavior of those basses, paddling with the theme after a stick thrown into the pond by the violins, and the subsequent barking of the brass, can hardly be mere coincidence."

XII. Picture of a serious-minded, cello-playing friend.

XIII. The most Romantic of all the variations, a thought of a friend then on the high seas enroute to Australia. "The soft tremor of the drums suggests the throb of the engines of a liner, while the quiet undulations of the violas suggest the peaceful motion of the waters."

XIV. A self-portrait of the composer in the form of a spirited march. We can forgive the somewhat bombastic nature of this music when we realize that in it the composer after long years of unrecognized struggle finally feels that he has arrived, musically speaking.

This fine piece, a Romantic expression of the end of the nineteenth century, had immediate and deserved success at the time of its first performance. It remains one of the few works of its composer played with any frequency today. Elgar and three of the "Variation" friends are shown on page 359.

Serge Prokofieff: *Classical Symphony*   c   MX–166

As a further example of absolute music, let us examine briefly a short symphony written in 1917 by the composer of *Peter and the Wolf*. Prokofieff calls this a Classical symphony, for he based it on a study of and a love for the music of the eighteenth century, although it is full of the color, technique,

and mocking wit of the present. Very short as symphonies go (it takes only about twenty minutes to play), it is made up of four movements or sections, each of them contrasting with the others in style and structure, and each leading toward a definite musical conclusion at the end of the whole work.

The First Movement is brisk and lively, based on two strongly contrasting themes:

The Second Movement is a typical song-form, or ternary, type. It is much slower and more lyrical and comprises three sections, the first of which is made out of a high melody:

The second, middle section is based on a more excited tune in the bass:

after which the first section returns, this time with a few more embellishments.

The Third Movement is in the form of a dance — an animated and yet graceful gavotte.

The Fourth Movement is very much like Mozart's finales, brisk and limpid. It has these main themes:

360

There is something brittle and rather hard about this music, no telling of a story, no lingering over lovely passages or even expressing of deep emotion. Its clever charm and bright humor are quite typical of its time and its composer. Prokofieff is still writing music in Russia, and his latest compositions show much more depth of feeling and sincerity of expression. He, like everyone else of his generation, has been strongly affected and deeply moved by the terrible tragedies of the war.

Aaron Copland: *El Salón Mexico*   v   m 546
              Appalachian Spring   v   m 1046

When the Brooklyn-born (in 1900) and Paris-educated composer Aaron Copland visited our sister republic to the south in 1932, he visited the famous dance hall in Mexico City called *Salón Mexico*. Like thousands of visitors before and after him, this *hot spot* for tourists fascinated the American composer. He said:

It wasn't the music that I heard there or the dances that at-tracted me as much as the spirit of the place. In some inexplica-ble way, while milling about in those crowded halls one really felt a live contact with the Mexican people. Other tourists will

*pull out their snapshots to show you what a country looks like,
but a composer wants you to know what a country sounds like.
I remember quite well the moment I conceived the idea of composing a piece about Mexico and naming it El Salón Mexico.*

This music, written years after Copland's visit, is the result.
Appropriately enough, he has taken a number of Mexican folk
tunes and, as he says, *strung them together like beads on a
string.* In so doing he has written a truly American piece, in
the broadest sense of the term. While the program and the
themes are from Latin America, the treatment is twentieth-
century U. S. A. — dissonant, even raucous in spots, with loud
and often somewhat jazzy instrumentation and hard, metallic
rhythms. But the music does exactly what it sets out to do: its
purpose, as Copland tells us, is not merely to quote Mexican
folk tunes literally but to heighten them without in any way
falsifying their natural character and simplicity. Here is Mexico seen through the eyes of a present-day rather sophisticated
American, and it is a musical view that has been very popular
with thousands of listeners all over this and other countries.

It is interesting to see how Copland has changed since the
writing of his first important work for the orchestra, *Music for
the Theatre*, in 1925. In this composition he was, in the words
of one of his admirers, symbolic of the New World, for the
music "places us, immensely, alertly, in the stream of metallic,
modern American things." It frankly uses jazz as a means of expression and delights in dissonance. Twenty years later he wrote
music for a ballet called *Appalachian Spring*, which is so different as to seem, almost, as if it had been written by a different composer. For this later music is Romantic, full of feel-

362

ing, and inspired by a lovely, very simple theme — that of the celebration of the coming of spring by a pioneer newly-wed couple in their farmhouse in the Pennsylvania hills in the early

*Courtesy of Samuel Goldwyn Productions, Inc.
and R. C. A., Victor Division*

AARON COPLAND GOES OVER A SOUND TRACK

Copland has written the musical scores for a number of important films, including *Our Town*, *The City*, and *Of Mice and Men*.

part of the last century. "A man and a woman build their new house with joy and love and prayer; during the spring celebration they are visited by a group of revivalists who remind them of the strange and awesome aspects of human life. At the end the couple are left with a quiet and strong joy in their new house." Such is the simple program.

BACKGROUNDS FOR LISTENING

After Copland had finished this music for a ballet and it had been performed by Martha Graham, he then arranged parts of the composition for performance by a symphony orchestra. This was first played in the fall of 1945 and had a great success wherever it was heard. Here are the sections of this orchestral suite as given by the composer:

1. Very slowly — Introduction of the characters, one by one, in a suffused light.
2. Fast — Sudden burst of unison strings starts the action. A sentiment both elated and religious gives the keynote to this scene.
3. Moderate — Duo for the Bride and her Intended — scene of tenderness and passion.
4. Quite fast — The Revivalist and his flock. Folksy feelings — suggestions of square dances and country fiddlers.
5. Still faster — Solo dance of the Bride — Presentiment of motherhood. Extremes of joy and fear and wonder.
6. Very slowly (as at first) — Transition scene to music reminiscent of the Introduction.
7. Calm and flowing — Scenes of daily activity for the Bride and her Farmer-husband. There are five variations on a Shaker theme. The theme sung by a solo clarinet . . . is called Simple Gifts.
8. Coda — The Bride takes her place among her neighbors. At the end the couple are left in their new house. Muted strings intone a hushed, prayer-like passage. The close is reminiscent of the opening music.

One of the New York critics said this of the work after its performance in 1945: "It is completely simple, homely, dedi-

364

cated, and a lovelier work you would have to go far to find."
Can you perhaps suggest why Copland's style has changed in
this way?

Samuel Barber: *Essay for Orchestra*, Op. 12   v   18062

Unfortunately the word essay has taken on a wrong meaning in the minds of many of those engaged in the important
task of learning how to master their native language. To them
it means something difficult and technical, a task assigned by
a teacher for the improvement of their ability to think logically and express their thoughts clearly. As a matter of real
fact, this term should be used in quite a different way, for it
describes one of the most important forms of creative writing
in the English language. The essay is a work short enough to
be read at one sitting and yet wise, philosophical, and witty
enough to contain the author's brilliant comments upon and
impressions of the world in which he lives (Sidelight 1).

There have been many serious and philosophical essays written and published in the attempt to examine such things as
the nature of knowlege and how it may be used to guide our
understanding. Locke's *Essay Concerning Human Understanding*, published in the seventeenth century, is one of these.
Another is Pope's *Essay on Man*, published in 1732, a work
which tries to show that the scheme of the world as we know
it and see it all about us is the best that could be devised and
that our failure to realize this fact is due to our very limited
vision and understanding. This is a viewpoint that certainly
should be helpful to us today! There have been other essays
which have been biographical, such as the series written by
Macaulay and by Lamb. If anyone would learn how interesting

365

and amusing and brilliant an English essay can be, he should read such works of Lamb as *A Dissertation Upon Roast Pig* and *A Chapter on Ears* (Sidelight 2).

We may, then, define the essay as a short, compact work in good style and representative of clear thinking, with excellent and logical development of the author's material from his personal point of view. It is in this sense that the American composer Samuel Barber (born in Pennsylvania in 1910) has entitled his seven-minute-long orchestral piece an *Essay for Orchestra.* For it tells no story nor represents any extra-musical subject. It is conservative in style, in distinction to so much music written at the same time (1937). It is brilliantly and expertly put together, with fine workmanship and sure technique. And yet it is full of poetic feeling and shows great imagination. It is without doubt one of the best American examples of absolute music yet written.

Here is the main theme used for the development of this piece:

Notice how in the brooding first section, marked *Andante sostenuto,* this melodic and rhythmic pattern is used over and over again; and how the second part of the piece, marked *Allegro molto,* makes use of a skittish sort of *pizzicato* theme for strings and wood winds, working this up to a vigorous climax and strongly changed mood. At the end, the noble sustained mood of the opening section is regained, the whole work ending with a beautiful passage for three muted trumpets, played very quietly. A fine piece of music, Mr. Barber!

SIDELIGHTS

1. Here is an excerpt from a Classic essay written in 1710 by Sir Richard Steele. It is a description of one of the famous eighteenth-century clubs, where kindred spirits gathered to discuss affairs of the day.

The Club at "The Trumpet"

Habeo senectuti magnam gratiam, quae mihi sermonis aviditatem auxit, potionis et cibi sustulit. — Tull. de Sen. (I am much beholden to old age, which has increased my eagerness for conversation, in proportion as it has lessened my appetites of hunger and thirst.)

Sheer Lane, February 10

After having applied my mind with more than ordinary attention to my studies, it is my usual custom to relax and unbend it in the conversation of such as are rather easy than shining companions. This I find particularly necessary for me before I retire to rest, in order to draw my slumbers upon me by degrees, and fall asleep insensibly.

This is the particular use I make of a set of heavy honest men, with whom I have passed many hours, with much indolence, though not with great pleasure. Their conversation is a kind of preparative for sleep: it takes the mind down from its abstractions, leads it into the familiar traces of thought, and lulls it into that state of tranquillity which is the condition of a

367

thinking man when he is but half awake. After this, my reader will not be surprised to hear the account which I am about to give of a club of my own contemporaries, among whom I pass two or three hours every evening. This I look upon as taking my first nap before I go to bed. The truth of it is, I should think myself unjust to posterity as well as to the society at "The Trumpet," of which I am a member, did not I in some part of my writings give an account of the persons among whom I have passed almost a sixth part of my time for these last forty years. Our club consisted originally of fifteen; but partly by the severity of the law in arbitrary times, and partly by the natural effects of old age, we are at present reduced to a third part of that number: in which, however, we have this consolation, that the best company is said to consist of five persons. I must confess, besides the aforementioned benefit which I meet with in the conversation of this select society, I am not the less pleased with the company in that I find myself the greatest wit among them and am heard as their oracle in all points of learning and difficulty.

*   *   *

The greatest wit of our company next to myself is a bencher of the neighbouring inn, who in his youth frequented the ordinaries about Charing Cross and pretends to have been intimate with Jack Ogle. He has about ten distichs of Hudibras [1] *without book, and never leaves the club till he has applied them all. If any modern wit be mentioned, or any town frolic spoken of, he shakes his head at the dullness of the present age and tells us a story of Jack Ogle.*

[1] A long poetic satire, written by Samuel Butler, against the Puritans. It was published in three parts between 1663 and 1668.

368

For my own part, I am esteemed among them because they see I am something respected by others, though at the same time I understand by their behaviour that I am considered by them as a man of a great deal of learning, but no knowledge of the world; insomuch that the Major sometimes, in the height of his military pride, calls me the philosopher: and Sir Jeoffrey, no longer ago than last night, upon a dispute what day of the month it was then in Holland, pulled his pipe out of his mouth and cried, "What does the scholar say to it?"

Our club meets precisely at six o'clock in the evening; but I did not come last night until half an hour after seven, by which means I escaped the battle of Naseby, which the Major usually begins at about three-quarters after six; I found also that my good friend the bencher had already spent three of his distichs, and only waiting an opportunity to hear a sermon spoken of that he might introduce the couplet where "a stick" rhymes to "ecclesiastic." At my entrance into the room, they were naming a red petticoat and a cloak, by which I found that the bencher had been diverting them with a story of Jack Ogle.

I had no sooner taken my seat but Sir Jeoffrey, to show his good-will towards me, gave me a pipe of his own tobacco and stirred up the fire. I looked upon it as a point of morality, to be obliged by those who endeavour to oblige me; and therefore, in requital for his kindness, and to set the conversation a-going, I took the best occasion I could to put him upon telling us the story of old Gantlett, which he always does with very particular concern. He traced up his descent on both sides for several generations, describing his diet and manner of life, with his several battles, and particularly that in which he fell.

369

This Gantlett was a game-cock, upon whose head the knight in his youth had won five hundred pounds and lost two thousand. This naturally set the Major upon the account of Edgehill fight, and ended in a duel of Jack Ogle's.

Old Reptile was extremely attentive to all that was said, though it was the same he had heard every night for these twenty years, and, upon all occasions, winked upon his nephew to mind what passed.

This may suffice to give the world a taste of our innocent conversation, which we spun out until about ten of the clock, when my maid came with a lantern to light me home. I could not but reflect with myself, as I was going out, upon the talkative humour of old men, and the little figure which that part of life makes in one who cannot employ this natural propensity in discourses which would make him venerable. I must own, it makes me very melancholy in company, when I hear a young man begin a story; and have often observed that one of a quarter of an hour long in a man of five-and-twenty gathers circumstances every time he tells it, until it grows into a long Canterbury tale of two hours by that time he is threescore.

The only way of avoiding such a trifling and frivolous old age is to lay up in our way to it such stores of knowledge and observation as may make us useful and agreeable in our declining years. The mind of man in a long life will become a magazine of wisdom or folly, and will consequently discharge itself in something impertinent or improving. For which reason, as there is nothing more ridiculous than an old trifling story-teller, so there is nothing more venerable than one who has turned his experience to the entertainment and advantage of mankind.

370

2. Here is an excerpt from a Romantic essay written in 1820 by Charles Lamb. It is about Christ's Hospital, a celebrated English charity school for boys:

Christ's Hospital Five-and-Thirty Years Ago

I was a poor friendless boy. My parents, and those who should care for me, were far away. Those few acquaintances of theirs, which they could reckon upon being kind to me in the great city, after a little forced notice, which they had the grace to take of me on my first arrival in town, soon grew tired of my holiday visits. They seemed to them to recur too often, though I thought them few enough; and, one after another, they all failed me, and I felt myself alone among six hundred playmates.

O the cruelty of separating a young lad from his early homestead! The yearnings which I used to have towards it in those unfledged years! How, in my dreams, would my native town (far in the west) come back, with its church, and trees, and faces! How I would wake weeping, and in the anguish of my heart exclaim upon sweet Calne in Wiltshire!

To this late hour of my life, I trace impressions left by the recollection of those friendless holidays. The long warm days of summer never return but they bring with them a gloom from the haunting memory of those *whole-day-leaves*, when, by some strange arrangement, we were turned out for the live-long day upon our own hands, whether we had friends to go to, or none. I remember those bathing excursions to the New River, which L. recalls with such relish, better, I think, than he can — for he was a home-seeking lad and did not much care for such water-pastimes: — How merrily we would sally forth into the

371

fields and strip under the first warmth of the sun and wanton like young dace in the streams; getting us appetites for noon, which those of us that were penniless (our scanty morning crust long since exhausted) had not the means of allaying — while the cattle, and the birds, and the fishes, were at feed about us, and we had nothing to satisfy our cravings — the very beauty of the day, and the exercise of the pastime, and the sense of liberty, setting a keener edge upon them! — How faint and languid finally we would return, towards nightfall, to our desired morsel, half-rejoicing, half-reluctant, that the hours of our uneasy liberty had expired!

It was worse in the days of winter, to go prowling about the streets objectless — shivering at cold windows of print-shops, to extract a little amusement; or haply, as a last resort, in the hope of a little novelty, to pay a fifty-times repeated visit (where our individual faces should be as well known to the warden as those of his own charges) to the Lions in the Tower — to whose levée by courtesy immemorial, we had a prescriptive title to admission.

QUESTIONS FOR DISCUSSION

The author suggests that music is an ideal art because it makes the listener a direct participant in it. What do you think is the attitude of the present time toward direct participation in music, painting, games, sports, etc.?

Prokofieff has said that he strives for simplicity and melody in his music:

Of course, I have used dissonance in my time, but there has been too much dissonance. Bach used dissonance as a good salt for his music. Others applied pepper, seasoned the dishes more and more highly, till all healthy appetites were sick and music was nothing but pepper. I think society has had enough of that. We want a simpler and more melodic style of music, a simpler, less complicated emotional state, and dissonance once again relegated to its proper place as one element in music, contingent principally upon the meeting of melodic lines.

Do you think that the music by Prokofieff which you have heard embodies these principles?

Can you describe in your own words the difference between the Classic and Romantic styles as illustrated by the music in this chapter?

Turn the page and notice the difference between the kinds of orchestra used in the eighteenth century, the nineteenth century, and the twentieth. These diagrams will help you understand why Haydn's and Elgar's music sound so differently.

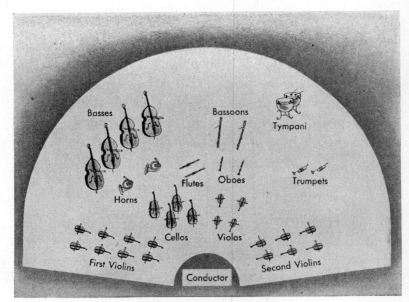

HAYDN'S ORCHESTRA

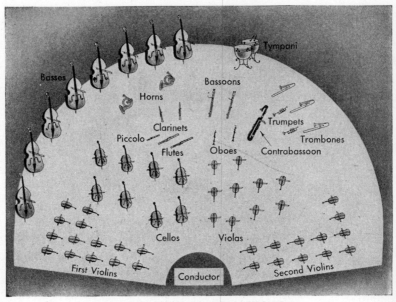

BEETHOVEN'S ORCHESTRA

374

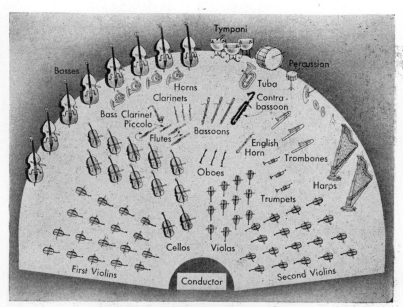

WAGNER'S ORCHESTRA

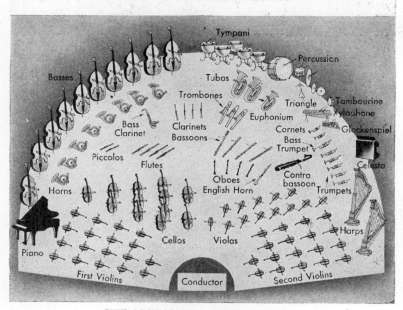

STRAVINSKY'S ORCHESTRA

Courtesy of A. Friedberg

A WELL-KNOWN STRING QUARTET

The background is a reproduction of an actual quartet score.

WE SHOULD not think, because so much of the music we know and like these days is orchestral music, that this kind of composition is all there is to good music. As we have intimated in an earlier chapter, the interest in orchestral music is a comparatively recent fad with music lovers. Composers have devoted a great deal of attention and spent tremendous energy in writing for other instruments, and the true music lover will want to know something of this wonderful music and will not be content simply to learn about the works written for his favorite instrument — the orchestra.

Take the piano, for example. The most popular of all solo instruments because it is, comparatively speaking, easy to play, the piano as we know it today is quite a modern musical mechanism. It was invented in the early part of the eighteenth century by Cristofori, an Italian instrument maker who wanted to improve upon the tone of the keyboard-stringed instruments then in use — the clavichord and the harpsichord. Rapidly improved by German, English, and American piano makers, this instrument has proved an inspiration for composers of all kinds for over two centuries; consequently the repertoire of music written for it is exceedingly rich and varied.

A BEAUTIFUL EIGHTEENTH-CENTURY
HARPSICHORD

Moreover, it can on occasion play music that was originally written for such other instruments as the violin, orchestra, and organ. Since it is one of the few instruments capable of furnishing both solo part and harmonic accompaniment, it functions in a way that the violin, clarinet, and trombone never can. And since it is as well suited to the demands of the virtuoso as to those of the modest amateur, it is no wonder that its use has become world-wide.

Without attempting to go into detail regarding the music written for the piano, we can give an excellent idea of its peculiar style by suggesting three compositions for the listener from the pen of composers who knew this instrument well and loved it especially:

378

Mozart: *Fantasia in D Minor*

Written in characteristic Classic style, this music shows how expressive and warm piano tone can be, at the same time how lyric and agile the instrument is.

Moussorgsky: *Pictures at an Exhibition*

This series of tonal impressions was written by the most famous of all Russian composers as a token of appreciation for the work of one of his friends who was a painter and architect. After the artist's death in 1847 an exhibition of his paintings was held in St. Petersburg (Leningrad), and Moussorgsky describes it in his long program piece for piano, later arranged for orchestra by other composers. Hartmann was not much of a painter, and we would probably know little of his work today if it had not been immortalized in this music by his friend. The various *canvases* are connected by a theme

which suggests the composer's wandering about through the exhibition, enjoying the different pictures. *My own face peeps out through all these intermezzos,* he said. The best sections of this well-known work are these:

III. *The Old Castle,* in which a long tuneful melody suggests the picture of an Old-World castle before which a troubadour stands singing.

379

IV. *The Tuileries Gardens in Paris,* famous playground for children and their nurses.

V. *Bydlo,* in which a crude Polish oxcart is musically depicted, lumbering slowly across our field of vision and finally disappearing from sight.

VII. *Picture of Two Polish Jews,* one rich, the other poor. Done with high humor but without malice.

X. *The Hut on Fowl's Legs,* a strange title suggestive of one of Hartmann's drawings representing a medieval Russian witch's home.

XI. *The Great Gate at Kiev,* representing Hartmann's architectural design for a monumental gateway to this old Slav city. The music, like the city itself, is full of the atmosphere and flavor of Old Russia.

Note throughout this descriptive piece how well the piano's percussive tone is adapted to the descriptive demands of the music. It might be interesting to compare this original piano version with such an orchestral transcription of this music as that made by Ravel. Such a comparison brings out the peculiar, individual timbre of the piano in contrast to the varied hues of the orchestra.

Debussy: *The Sunken Cathedral (La Cathédrale Engloutie)*

This piece shows the piano to be the impressionistic instrument *par excellence.* Composers using this suggestive style of writing employed the piano with great skill and effect. In this prelude (one of a set of 10) Debussy sketches for us an old Breton legend of a submerged city on the coast of France, its life going on beneath the waves, with the sound of its cathe-

380

From the Collection of Alfred V. Frankenstein

THE GREAT GATE AT KIEV

This is one of the paintings by Hartmann that inspired Moussorgsky's *Pictures at an Exhibition*.

dral bells plainly heard through the water. Here again we can compare a piano and an orchestral version of the same music, for this lovely piece has been transcribed for the orchestra by various arrangers. If you listen to Stokowski's version, you will find that it is more realistic but much less imaginative than the Debussy original.

Another type of instrumental music very popular in its day (the eighteenth century) is chamber (room) music, a type of composition designed for playing in the salons and drawing rooms of the European nobility and aristocracy, for the entertainment and pleasure of the noble guests rather than with any idea of pleasing audiences in a concert hall. Because of its intimate style and personal flavor, this music has a certain character that is entirely lost in works written for large instrumental combinations. The instruments speak clearly and distinctly, sometimes blending together, sometimes answering each other in effective and brilliant dialogue. Composers, moreover, are apt to make use of counterpoint in writing this kind of music, a device which makes use of various simultaneously sounding musical lines, rather than grouping notes together in the chord clusters we find in harmony. These actively weaving lines give impetus and movement to the music; and since they can be clearly heard in music written for small instrumental combinations, they are ideal for chamber music.

Some of the greatest composers — particularly Beethoven, Schubert, and Brahms — have written effective chamber music. Here are a few typical single movements from some famous quartets and quintets. They have been chosen for purposes of illustration not only because of their unusual musical interest but also because they show various formal patterns discussed in an earlier chapter .

Mozart: *Eine Kleine Nachtmusik*, First Movement

This is lively music originally written as a serenade for string orchestra (composed of a few violins, violas, cello, and bass). These serenades were a popular feature of eighteenth-century social life, when some prince or noble would give a garden party at which a tiny little orchestra would furnish a pleasant musical background for social conversation. Not too serious, but possessing charm and elegance, this Mozart music has

382

kept its popularity as a modern concert number. In sonata form (easily enough followed), this movement uses these two contrasting themes:

Mozart: *Eine Kleine Nachtmusik,* Second Movement

Here is a typical chamber-music slow movement in song form. The first part of this *Romanza,* as Mozart calls it, is in major and is based on the following theme:

The second, contrasting part is in minor, somewhat quicker in effect, using this musical idea:

How beautiful and calm the first part seems as it returns after this change!

Schubert: *Quintet for Strings and Piano in* A, Op. 114, Third Movement

In this composition the composer uses a rather unusual instrumental combination: violin, viola, cello, double bass, and piano. But he puts them together in such a manner as to let no single instrument overbalance the others. This gay, charming dance-like scherzo (Third Movement) proves this well. Its first section is an animated conversation between piano and violin. Its second section lets a four-note theme be distinctly heard. And then the first section is heard again. In the Trio, or large contrasting part of the movement, we likewise hear two themes, the first given out by violin and viola, the second by the piano. A repetition of the scherzo section brings the movement as a whole to a delightful close. We have in reality this (follow as you listen): [1]

A   Scherzo

[: 1st theme group, piano and violin conversation:]

[2nd theme group, four-note theme prominent]
[1st theme group repeated   :]

B   Trio

[: 1st theme   Repeated, detached notes :]

[2nd theme   Slower and more sustained]
[1st theme   Repeated   :]

A   Scherzo

1st theme
2nd theme
1st theme

Schubert: *Quintet in* A, Fourth Movement

This is the movement that gives this composition its popular nickname, for in this Fourth Movement we hear a series of

[1] [: :] means Repeat.

variations based on the theme of an earlier song by Schubert —
Die Forelle (The Trout). This jolly theme is first heard on
the violin:

The variations follow the following instrumentation. Listen
carefully and you can practice listening for timbre differences
and the recognition of contrapuntal lines:

I. Theme given out by the piano; the other instruments sup-
   ply an accompaniment.
II. Theme heard on viola and cello, with the violin weaving
   an elaborate and flowery counterpoint above and below.
III. Theme on the double bass, assisted by the cello. This time
   the piano has a running accompaniment.
IV. Theme again heard on double bass in minor, later on in
   major.
V. Theme on cello, with different form and harmonies.
VI. Theme alternates between violin and viola, with the piano
   giving an accompaniment suggestive of the leaping trout.

Another instrument that was more popular in the eighteenth century than it is now is the organ. One of the earliest
keyboard instruments to be developed, the organ is in principle nothing but a huge Panpipe, or syrinx — an early shep-
herd's instrument consisting of tubes of varying lengths bound
together in such a way that they could be blown upon by the
player's breath. In the modern organ the air is supplied mechanically (usually by an electric blower), and its admittance
to the pipes controlled by means of keys, one of them for each

THE ORGAN IN A FAMOUS AMERICAN
SCHOOL, Phillips Academy, Andover, Massa-
chusetts

pitch produced. The tone of the organ is broad and dignified,
capable of wide variance from very soft to tremendously loud
and powerful.

No better organ music has ever been written than that composed by J. S. Bach (1685–1750), who was by profession a

386

church musician and a virtuoso organist known all over central Europe at the time. Many of his organ compositions took the form of the fugue. The fugue is another contrapuntal device by means of which a single theme keeps imitating itself throughout the composition. It is heard singly in one part or voice, and then in another and another, gradually building itself into a complex, powerful composition that "packs a real wallop" at the end. Nothing could better illustrate the vital, strong, constantly moving quality of contrapuntal music than does this form of the fugue.

J. S. Bach: *Fugue in G Minor* (*The Little*)

In this particular fugue, Bach has taken a lively theme (even though it is in minor) that can easily be recognized and remembered, no matter how complex the contrapuntal parts around it:

Listen to the whole work carefully and you will easily recognize the various *entrances* of this sturdy tune, each of them separated by short musical sections of quite different character, called *episodes*. The whole composition builds itself into an imposing architectural form, with the climax coming at the very end. Bach wrote dozens of good, well-constructed fugues but none more effective and imposing than this.

It will be interesting and informing to compare the orchestral version of Bach's *Passacaglia and Fugue*, which you studied in an earlier chapter, with the original organ version to be found in the same record album as the *"Little"* *G-Minor Fugue.*

In what way does the piano differ from its predecessors, the harpsichord and the clavichord? What effect did this change have upon the music written for keyboard-stringed instruments?

Why do so many people find chamber music difficult to listen to? Do you agree with them?

Do you know of any changes made in the production of organ tone today? Have these changed the kind of music written for the instrument?

MUSIC TO LISTEN TO

Mozart: *Fantasia in D Minor* [2]   v m 483

Moussorgsky: *Pictures at an Exhibition*
    Piano version recorded by Moiseivitsch   HMV
    Orchestral version recorded by Boston
        Symphony Orchestra   v m 102

Debussy: *The Sunken Cathedral*
    Piano version recorded by Rubinstein   v 36289
        or recorded by Gieseking   c 17077 D
    Orchestral version recorded by
        Philadelphia Orchestra   v m 116

Mozart: *Eine Kleine Nachtmusik*   v m 428
                                v DM 1163

[2] The symbols in the list of records may be interpreted as follows:
   v Victor   HMV His Majesty's Voice (English Victor)   c Columbia

OTHER INSTRUMENTAL MUSIC

Schubert: *Quintet for Strings and Piano*   V   M 312

Bach: *Fugue in G Minor*

  Organ version recorded by E. Power
    Biggs   V   M 1048
  Orchestral version recorded by
    All-American Orchestra   C   11992

In addition to these pieces of music actually described in this chapter, the following examples will be of value to the listener:

Piano

Beethoven: *Sonata in C-Sharp Minor*, Op. 27,
    No. 2 (*Moonlight Sonata*)   V   M 1115
Chopin: *Fantaisie Impromptu*, Op. 66   V   M 1110
    Polonaise in A-Flat, Op. 53   V   11–9065

Chamber Music

Mozart: *Quintet* (K. 516)   C   M 526
Smetana: *Quartet No. 1* (*From My Life*)   C   M 405

This is one of the few examples of program chamber music.

Organ

Reubke: *Sonata on the 94th Psalm*   V   M 961

This is the greatest of all Romantic pieces for the organ, showing the full resources of the instrument.

A GROUP OF AMERICAN STUDENTS, making recordings
of their songs

CHAPTER XX. *IN CONCLUSION AND RETROSPECT*

I N T H E first ten chapters of this course, we considered the general backgrounds of music as an art and saw how this art developed in the United States and the other countries of the American continents.

The second group of ten chapters has been devoted to giving information that will help a listener increase his knowledge of music, sharpen his ear for what the music has to say to him, and improve his taste so that he can learn to decide just what is, or is not, good music in so far as he is concerned.

People differ a great deal in their ideas about the value of information. That we are living in an age which puts a high premium on facts is shown well enough by the popularity of the *information programs* that are given in such numbers on the radio. These are devoted entirely to what a prominent American writer has called the *fatal futility* of facts. The process of accumulating facts has little value in itself other than that of training the mind to remember things. It is what we do with these facts that is really important, and this is something the listener must always remember.

For example, the author of these chapters has gathered together in them a considerable number of facts regarding the history and theory of music. These have been arranged so that you can refer to them time and time again, somewhat in the way in which you go to a dictionary or an encyclopedia. You can study the chapters thoroughly and learn a lot about the way our European system of music came to be what it is, about the technical resources of the instruments that are used to produce music, and about the manner in which music is put together according to what we call good form. But unless you use this information to increase your ability to hear what is in the music, or to appreciate better that which you do hear and thus increase your pleasure in living and your understanding of the world, these facts themselves will be of little use.

There is not much point in talking or writing about music unless you are able to hear it, too; for music is an art of the ear rather than merely of the mind. This is where phonograph records can be of great help. The author has included in these chapters a great many examples of recordings in order to illustrate exactly what he was talking about. It is not expected that you will be able to hear all of these records. But the lists have been made as complete as possible in order to fit the resources of various record libraries. Naturally, the more you hear, the better will be your understanding and appreciation.

Here, in general, is what you should get out of a study of the various chapters in this section:

Chapter Eleven: An understanding of the debt which we Americans of the present day owe to Europe as the source of so much of our culture; and of how European music, which in turn was borrowed from Asia, came to develop in the way it has. The list of music at the end of this chapter gives an excellent summary of the styles of the different important periods in European music.

Chapter Twelve: An understanding of the nature of the symphony orchestra as the most important and popular musical instrument of our time.

Chapter Thirteen: A knowledge of how our modern instruments that go to make up the symphony orchestra began: as primitive, crude means to heighten the music which early man could make with his own voice and the rhythms he could pound out with his own hands.

Chapter Fourteen shows the listener how he can increase his pleasure in music through learning to recognize the different tone qualities of the modern orchestral instruments and gives help for acquiring this ability. Real listening is necessary here.

In Chapter Fifteen the listener is given further practice in learning to recognize the timbres of the different instruments. Two very enjoyable compositions are analyzed from this viewpoint: Rimsky-Korsakoff's *Capriccio Espagñol* and Bach's *Passacaglia*, and detailed help is given in showing exactly what goes on in them instrumentally.

Chapter Sixteen gives detailed information about the three technical elements of the language of music — rhythm, melody, and harmony. There is a great array of facts here, mostly given for reference. But the listener should finish the chapter with a definite idea of what rhythm does in the music he listens to; with an ability to recognize (by hearing them) the difference between the two fundamental rhythmic groups generally employed in European music; with an ability to recognize some of the characteristics which go to make up good melody; with a listening acquaintance with at least half a dozen of these melodies; with an understanding of what harmony contributes to music and the differences between consonant and dissonant harmonies.

Chapter Seventeen contains a great many facts about form — what it is, and how certain forms have become customary with European composers. These should be used for reference only. But a general idea of the way music is put together and an acquaintance with some representative examples of forms used by composers, both in short and extended pieces of music, should be gained from the study of these facts. The list at the end of the chapter would require weeks of listening effort, literally, but it can be used as a guide for listening experience over a period of many years.

Chapter Eighteen: Seven orchestral pieces of widely differing character are briefly discussed here. From these the listener can choose those that best suit his taste or are most readily available to him. Included in the group are several important pieces by American composers. Also suggested is the difference between the orchestras used by Classic, Romantic, and Modern composers.

Chapter Nineteen: Not all great music, by any means, has been written for the orchestra. In the last chapter of this section, the author illustrates briefly music that has been written for some of the most important ensemble and solo instruments outside the orchestra. Three piano compositions are listed, and two of them can be compared directly with orchestral transcriptions. Four movements of chamber music are illustrated, the four movements that usually go to make up a work written in this style: the first, or *Allegro*; the second, or slow, movement; the third, or dance-like, movement; and the fourth, concluding, movement. And a final, brief illustration of organ music ends the chapter.

This general section can be used for a short term's study or it can be spread out over a whole year's recitation schedule, according to the amount of time available and the quantity of music used in illustration.

INDEX

ITALICS INDICATE A CREATIVE WORK OF SOME KIND — A PIECE OF MUSIC, A PAINTING, SCULPTURE, OR LITERATURE.

Aboio, 147
Absolute music, 330–332, 342–345, 349–350
African music, 85–89, 98–99, 102, 136–137, 140, 143, 150, 248, 250, 253–254, 258–259
Alphorn, 256
American characteristics, 5, 21–32, 189–190
American music, backgrounds of, 34; commercial, 14–16, 60–63, 79; film, 58–59, 66–68, 79; folk, 48–55, 74–78, 80–81; Indian, 41–44, 63, 71, 132–135, 149–150, 162–165; Negro, 44–48, 63–66, 71–74, 85–103, 105–109, 136–138, 140, 143, 150; radio, 59, 68–69, 79; theater, 55–59, 78–79
Anderson, Marian, quoted, 63–65
Angelico, Fra, *Death and Assumption of the Virgin*, 346, 347
Armstrong, Louis, 103; quoted, 97
Art, 8, 167–172
Asia, 126, 128, 216–221, 223, 235, 240–241
Aztecs, 41, 130–135, 195

Bach, Johann Sebastian, 386–387; *Air* from *Orchestral Suite No. 3 in D Major*, 18; *Brandenburg Concerto No. 4*, 234; *Jesu, Joy of Man's Desiring*, 19; *Little Organ Fugue in G Minor*, 345, 387, 389; *Passacaglia*, 285, 297–299, 387; portrait, 296; *Prelude in C Major*, 344; *Suite No. 2 in B Minor*, 343
Ballads, American, 74–78
Ballet, 348, 364
Bambuco, 148
Barber, Samuel, 186; *Essay for Orchestra*, Op. 12, 365–367
Bass clarinet, 273, 274
Bass viol, 266–267, 285, 288, 298–299
Bassoon, 274–275, 285, 287, 293, 295
Batuque, 147
Baxter, Dave, 122
Bay Psalm Book, 181, 196
Beethoven, Ludwig van, *Moonlight Sonata*, 389; orchestra of, 374; *Quartet in G Major*, Op. 18, No. 2, 343; *Symphony No. 1*, 247; *Symphony No. 3*, 234; *Symphony No. 5*, 19, 247, 338–339, 343, 344; *Symphony No. 7*, 317; *Symphony No. 9*, 247
Béguine, 145

397

INDEX

400

INDEX

INDEX